101 Careers in Healthcare Management

Leonard H. Friedman, PhD, MPH, FACHE, is professor of Health Policy and Management and director of the Executive Master of Health Administration degree program at the George Washington University. Prior to arriving at the George Washington University in 2008, he was a faculty member at Oregon State University, beginning in 1992. Dr. Friedman's scholarly work has concentrated on the mechanisms of organizational change and strategic decision making in health service organizations. Dr. Friedman's research has explored building the resilience of healthcare organizations to respond to environmental jolts, using systems approaches to reduce medical errors, and, most recently, helping understand the roots of organizational excellence in healthcare. His teaching responsibilities have included graduate and undergraduate classes in healthcare management, organization theory and behavior in healthcare, healthcare law and regulation, strategic management, and leadership in healthcare organizations. His work has been published in a variety of healthcare management journals. He is the coeditor of *Essentials of Management and Leadership in Public Health* and is the coeditor of *Advances in Health Services Management*. Dr. Friedman has been the chair of the Healthcare Management Division of the Academy of Management and the Association of University Programs in Health Administration. Dr. Friedman is a fellow of the American College of Healthcare Executives.

Anthony R. Kovner, PhD, MPA, is professor emeritus of Public and Health Management at New York University (NYU) Wagner Graduate School of Public Service. Dr. Kovner has written nine books, including coediting *Healthcare Delivery in the United States* (11th edition, Springer, 2015), and *Evidence-Based Management in Healthcare: Principles, Cases and Perspectives* (AUPHA, 2017). He has written 43 peer-reviewed articles on healthcare management, and has published 40 case studies. In 1999, Dr. Kovner was awarded the Filerman Prize for Educational Leadership from the Association of University Programs in Health Administration. He was director of the graduate program in health policy and management at NYU Wagner for over 20 years. Dr. Kovner has had extensive management experience in healthcare as a senior manager in two hospitals, a nursing home, a group practice, and a neighborhood health center. He has served as a consultant to the New York-Presbyterian Hospital and Healthcare System, the Robert Wood Johnson Foundation, the W. K. Kellogg Foundation, Montefiore Medical Center, and the American Academy of Orthopaedic Surgeons, among others. He was a board member of Lutheran Medical Center in Brooklyn, New York, for 25 years. He is a founding member of the Advisory Council for the Center for Evidence-Based Management, headquartered in the Netherlands.

Careers in Healthcare Management

101

Second Edition

LEONARD H. FRIEDMAN, PhD, MPH, FACHE

ANTHONY R. KOVNER, PhD, MPA

SPRINGER PUBLISHING COMPANY

Springer Publishing Company, LLC
11 West 42nd Street
New York, NY 10036
www.springerpub.com

Acquisitions Editor: David D'Addona
Compositor: Exeter Premedia Services Private Ltd.

ISBN: 978-0-8261-6662-3
Ebook ISBN: 978-0-8261-6663-0

17 18 19 20 21 / 5 4 3 2 1

The author and the publisher of this Work have made every effort to use sources believed to
be reliable to provide information that is accurate and compatible with the standards generally
accepted at the time of publication. The author and publisher shall not be liable for any special,
consequential, or exemplary damages resulting, in whole or in part, from the readers' use of,
or reliance on, the information contained in this book. The publisher has no responsibility for
the persistence or accuracy of URLs for external or third-party Internet websites referred to
in this publication and does not guarantee that any content on such websites is, or will remain,
accurate or appropriate.

Library of Congress Cataloging-in-Publication Data
Names: Friedman, Leonard H., author. | Kovner, Anthony R., author.
Title: 101 careers in healthcare management / Leonard H. Friedman, Anthony R.
    Kovner.
Other titles: One hundred one careers in healthcare management | One hundred
    and one careers in healthcare management | 101 careers in health care
    management
Description: Second edition. | New York: Springer Publishing Company, LLC, [2018] |
    Includes index.
Identifiers: LCCN 2017027312 | ISBN 9780826166623 | ISBN 9780826166630 (e-book)
Subjects: | MESH: Career Choice | Health Services Administration | United
    States
Classification: LCC RA971 | NLM W 21 | DDC 362.1068—dc23
LC record available at https://lccn.loc.gov/2017027312

Printed in the United States of America by Gasch Printing.

To All Our Students: Past, Present, and Future

CONTENTS

Contents

Contents

FOREWORD

Some things change and some things stay the same. When I first considered the field of health administration as a career in the 1980s, I knew for sure that I wanted to help people and that I was fascinated by hospitals. Everyone I talked to suggested that I become a hospital chief executive officer (CEO). At that time, careers in healthcare management focused on hiring and firing, budgeting, planning, and executing within a fairly narrow field—the hospital. Hospital executives worked in academic medical centers, big community hospitals, small rural hospitals, and government-owned facilities. One hallmark of the profession, however, was a focus on helping patients get better and creating an environment where the best healthcare could be delivered by doctors, nurses, and other caregivers. A large part of the hospital executive's day-to-day life involved building and managing relations with physicians and the board of directors, and, to a lesser extent, the management of people. There were pressing needs to create great services and attract patients.

Today, the field of healthcare management is much more expansive. Healthcare is delivered in hospitals, but also in clinics and outpatient surgical centers, wellness centers, nursing homes, and also through telemedicine, and mobile and other technologies. Healthcare executives now emphasize skills in understanding community needs, and working to improve the health of the population—something that may mean they never enter a hospital at all. The day-to-day life of today's healthcare executive involves population health assessment, predictive analytics, information technology, and quality improvement. Healthcare executives in hospitals, community health centers, insurance companies, and software companies must find ways to work together—to collaborate, as well as compete—to design and offer services. Leaders have begun to recognize the importance of human capital as well, and work to develop, motivate, and inspire all the people who get this work done—beyond physicians and nurses, to those who clean rooms, use sophisticated technologies, and go to patient homes either in person or through technologies such as telemedicine and mobile or e-health.

And yet, helping people and caring remain central to the profession. Healthcare executives create environments where individuals can provide excellent care. And the profession offers a deep sense of meaning to those who are privileged to work in the field.

Since my first experiences in healthcare administration, the field of practice has expanded, and so has the field of health administration education. I have been fortunate to serve on the board of the Association of University Programs in Health Administration for several years. This has given me a front row seat to the exciting and innovative changes that have resulted in a wide variety of ways to pursue a career in health administration.

I wish someone had offered a book like this when I was beginning to explore a career in healthcare. It took me decades to understand the many options that exist outside of the view of a single aspiring healthcare leader (or within my own network). I have shared the previous edition with students, and seen them find opportunities they did not know existed. This volume provides a wonderful perspective on what's "out there" across different settings and different jobs.

Reading the views of the executives presented here will give aspiring leaders insights into what is possible. If you identify even one job or work opportunity that you did not know about before, you will see the value in the money and time spent. And, in addition to hearing from healthcare professionals, you will also learn from individuals leading educational programs in the field.

I know that every student or manager who reads this book will see vast possibilities to make a difference, to help people, and to lead in an ever-changing healthcare field. You will also see in the narratives that, even as where you may work and what you may do evolves, the core of the profession remains: helping people, improving health, and creating excellence.

This book is a terrific travel guide for your career. Best wishes on the journey!

Christy Harris Lemak, FACHE
Professor and Chair
Health Services Administration
University of Alabama at Birmingham

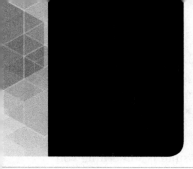

PREFACE

In 2013, the first edition of *101 Careers in Healthcare Management* was published. The objective of the book was to share with readers our thoughts about why healthcare management matters, how students could enter into this critical field of practice, and throw light on the breadth of opportunities available in a wide range of health sector organizations. In the 4 years since the release of the first edition, healthcare remains the largest fraction of the U.S. economy that has absorbed significant jolts.

First and foremost, the Patient Protection and Affordable Care Act (ACA) was implemented across the country, and provided comprehensive health insurance to an additional 22 million persons. At the time that this preface is being written, the president and the majority parties of both houses of Congress are calling for the ACA to be "repealed and replaced." The effect of this action to consumers and providers of health services is not clear. But regardless of the political decisions made, healthcare organizations and healthcare leaders will need to keep in mind our role in caring for patients who put their health and well-being in our hands.

Beyond the ACA, healthcare organizations continue to confront profound challenges including workforce shortages, movement away from volume toward value, protection of vulnerable patient data stored on electronic medical record systems, continuing growth of mergers and acquisitions, shift of physicians into ever larger group practices (many of which are owned by hospitals), decrease in reimbursement, and need to replace or upgrade an aging infrastructure. Taken as a whole, healthcare organizations are facing a series of environmental stressors that require managers and administrators to fundamentally think and operate in ways that will test the abilities of everyone—from the most senior executives to the front-line employees.

OVERALL GOAL OF *101 CAREERS IN HEALTHCARE MANAGEMENT*

Given all of these internal and external environmental challenges and opportunities, it is important to understand that highly effective healthcare management is absolutely essential if the organizations that make up the health sector are to operate at their optimum levels. Our goal is to give readers the information needed to understand the discipline of healthcare management and explore the many types of careers available to those with a bachelor's or master's level degree. One of the important parts of the book is the voice of the practitioner. We have included interviews of people who represent the diversity of healthcare management, ranging

from those who hold the title of Chief Executive Officer to practitioners just starting their careers. Our goal is to give the reader a sense of what is possible and
the ways in which individuals considering healthcare management can position
themselves to get the job they wish to obtain. It is important to understand two
critical points:

1. For those of you thinking that a job in the C-suite is something you
   would like to obtain, keep in mind that it takes years of progressively
   responsible experience to get to the point where you can put the
   word "chief" in front of your title. Moving into these roles will likely
   require you to change jobs, relocate more than once, take risks, and
   quickly learn from your mistakes. In many high-tech fields, smart,
   energetic, and visionary entrepreneurs can form a company from
   virtually nothing and earn fame and fortune seemingly overnight.
   Healthcare management is fundamentally different. While there
   is a tremendous need for persons with a spirit of entrepreneurship
   and the willingness to push boundaries, the majority of healthcare
   management is focused on creating and sustaining systems that
   allow care to be delivered to patients in a consistently safe and
   effective manner.
2. Not everyone wants to be the boss. As Buckingham and Coffman
   note in their book, *First, Break All the Rules*, it is most critical that
   you uncover the job that is the right fit for your talent and passion.
   There is an assumption that everyone wants to climb the ladder of
   success and move up the corporate hierarchy. There is a certain
   level of seduction with a fancy title, nice office, personal executive
   assistant, and (of course) increasing levels of compensation. All of
   these things are wonderful, but if you are not happy and fulfilled
   with the work itself, nothing else matters.

Healthcare management is not a career that jumps out at most students. When
the words *healthcare* and *career* are used together, most students think of clinical
occupations. Furthermore, as portrayed in the media, healthcare management is
not exactly shown in the most favorable light. Typically, healthcare executives are
portrayed as heartless bureaucrats whose only job is to get in the way of heroic
physicians and nurses doing everything possible to care for sick or dying patients.
The fact is that nothing can be farther from the truth. As you read through the job
descriptions and the interviews with our practitioners, keep in mind how persons
employed in healthcare management work directly and indirectly for the benefit
of the patient.

DISTINGUISHING FEATURES

Persons who read the first edition of *101 Careers in Healthcare Management*
will recognize that the fundamental structure of the book is unchanged. What

is different this time is that all 101 job descriptions have been updated, including new salary information. We have sought out practitioners from around the country who are representative of the tremendous diversity in this discipline. Readers should note that the practitioner interviews in this book are those who agreed to our request to include their words. Stated another way, this is a convenience sample of managers rather than a truly representative sample. Those reading this book should either see themselves in the portraits of our practitioners or imagine themselves in the roles that are highlighted. The final distinguishing feature of this edition is the recognition of the rapidly changing political and policy landscape in which healthcare organizations find themselves. This book is not intended to be a "how to" on influencing policy or politics. Rather, our focus is on how healthcare leaders can be most effective in rapidly changing and uncertain environments. One way of achieving this goal is a discussion around the essential competencies that all healthcare leaders are going to require for a highly dynamic future.

INTENDED AUDIENCE

There is a primary audience and a secondary audience for the second edition of *101 Careers in Healthcare Management*. Our primary audience is students in high school, community college, and bachelor's degree programs around the country. We wish to spotlight the many opportunities available in healthcare management for as many potential students as possible. In addition to students, it is important that this book gets into the hands of guidance and career counselors in high schools and colleges. We heard anecdotally that the first edition of *101 Careers in Healthcare Management* was made a required text for the students in an undergraduate healthcare management program.

The secondary audience for this book is persons already working in the health sector and are interested in healthcare management opportunities in their organization or elsewhere. Very often, working adults get stuck doing the same thing day after day and lose sight of the many options available to staff with their education and experience.

CONTENTS

The second edition of *101 Careers in Healthcare Management* is designed to serve as a comprehensive examination of our discipline in a straightforward and pragmatic manner. The layout of the book is as follows:

- The context for healthcare management and a brief history of the field
- Obtaining the education required for a career in healthcare management
- Strategies for finding jobs in healthcare management
- An in-depth discussion on preparation and professionalism
- Job descriptions and practitioner interviews grouped around the various parts of the health sector, including
  - Acute care hospitals

- o Commercial health insurance
- o Consulting firms
- o Durable medical equipment
- o Executive search firms
- o Federal, state, and local government healthcare organizations
- o Health information technology and health informatics
- o Health sector association management
- o Healthcare regulatory agencies
- o International health
- o Long-term care organizations
- o Mental health organizations
- o Pharmaceuticals and biotechnology
- o Physician practice management
- o Public health organizations
- Competencies required of healthcare leaders for an uncertain and unknowable future

The intent of this book is not to provide a comprehensive listing of every possible job available in the field for persons with an interest in healthcare management. Rather, we hope that you will be given enough information to whet your appetite and begin your own search process on the many opportunities that are part of this dynamic and crucial field of practice.

Leonard H. Friedman
Anthony R. Kovner

ACKNOWLEDGMENTS

It is somewhat difficult to believe, but September 2017 marks the start of my 25th year as a full-time faculty member in higher education. The journey began in 1992 at Oregon State University, and since 2008 has continued at the George Washington University (GW). To be completely forthcoming, this is the longest time I've ever done one thing in my life. Having earned my PhD just prior to my 39th birthday, I am pretty late in the game. Stated another way, maybe I finally found what I wanted to do when I grew up.

There are so many people who have made an important difference to me all along this journey. Dr. Michael V. Kline saw the potential in me that I did not recognize when he offered me admission to the Masters in Public Health program at California State University, Northridge. Mike also taught me how to effectively listen to others. One of my long-term mentors is Quint Studer, founder of the StuderGroup. In 2014, Quint personally inducted me into the StuderGroup Fire Starter Hall of Fame. This honor was one of the true highlights of my professional career. Every day, I look at my faculty role as providing purpose, performing worthwhile work, and making a difference.

My faculty colleagues at GW have been and continue to be an inspiration to me with their dedication, passion, and commitment to exemplary healthcare management education. Thanks go to Doug Anderson, Bob Burke, Lorens Helmchen, Leah Masselink, Wayne Psek, and Joy Volarich. In 2014, we launched a brand-new executive Masters in Health Administration (MHA) program here at GW. While many faculty were critical in realizing that effort, including those mentioned in this paragraph, I had the honor and privilege to work closely with Ricky Allen, Jack Friedman, Sam Hanna, Don Lewis, Fred van Eenennaam, and Andy Wiss. Thanks to them and so many others for making our executive MHA a source of pride and pleasure. Finally, thank you to all the faculty, students, staff, and alumni of our program at GW. This program has been operating continuously since 1959. I hope that my years as the director are remembered as helping to drive our collective work forward.

Special thanks go to Mira King and Sara Tavakoli for their investment of time, energy, and effort to help pull the many elements of this book together. I could not have done this without them.

Thank you to Sheri Sussman, David D'Addona, and everyone at Springer Publishing. It was a joy working with Sheri on the first edition of *101 Careers in Healthcare Management*, and it is because of her encouragement and persistence that this second edition came to be.

As he eases into retirement, I want to express my unbounded appreciation to my friend and coauthor, Tony Kovner. I first met Tony in 1995 at the Association of University Programs in Health Administration (AUPHA) annual meeting, and have enjoyed his company these many years later. He remains a man of honor, high standards, and commitment to excellence in healthcare management education.

Finally, thank you to family. My wife, Lydia, is someone whose love, support, and encouragement serve to make me whole. Thank you to my stepsons, Spencer, Teddy, and Will. You are remarkable young men. To my daughters, Lynn and Allison, know that your dad loves you completely. Finally, my two grandsons, Baelin and Julian, bring a level of joy that I did not believe possible. All of you make my life complete.

Leonard H. Friedman

I am concluding 60 years in healthcare management and healthcare management education (45 years), but who's counting? I can yet recall sitting in a class in hospital management at Cornell in 1961, listening to a retired hospital administrator, and wondering what I would do when I grew up (I was 25 years old at the time).

During my 38 years of tenure at New York University (NYU) Wagner School of Public Service, many colleagues and friends have shared my enthusiasm for teaching and advising graduate students and alumni in healthcare management. They include John Billings, Steve Finkler, Jim Knickman, Roger Kropf, John Donnellan, Victor Rodwin, Charlotte Wagenberg, and Willie Manzano. Alumni who have learned and shared with me include Sofia Agortsas, Claudia Caine, Toby Bressler, David Kaplan, Peter Karow, Sherine Khalil, John Sendach, Sumir Sahgal, and Jacob Victory. Administration at NYU Wagner has provided full support to the health policy and management program, and I specifically thank Dean Sherry Glied and Associate Dean Ellen Lovitz.

My main acknowledgment for this second edition is to my coauthor, Len Friedman, who has done most of the work, particularly in organizing the interviews and resumes of alumni. Len has worked ceaselessly to improve healthcare management education for 25 years. Thanks to his wife, Lydia Middleton, who served for many years with distinction as the leader of the health management education professional organization, AUPHA. Thanks as well to those who have shaped my thinking and my practice concerning healthcare management education for over 40 years—John Griffith, Ken White, Gary Filerman, Christy Lemak, Steve Mick, and Steve Loebs.

I wish to thank three unforgettable mentors who have advanced my career and molded my character—my father, Sidney J. Kovner, for his honesty, love, and intelligence; my PhD adviser, Conrad Seipp, for his kindness to me and commitment to equity in healthcare; and my department chair at Wharton/University of Pennsylvania, Robert Eilers, for his personal example as a mentor, scholar, teacher, husband, and father.

My family is more distinguished than I am—wife Chris Kovner, professor of nursing, and daughters Sarah, historian, and Anna, economist (PhDs all). They have shared their love with me, and Chris has put up with my compulsive work habits all these years. We are expecting happy lives for our beloved grandchildren, Zachary, Ava, Lily, and Stella. Their fathers, Seth Meisel and Matthew Connelly, deserve some thanks too. Thanks as well to Victor Kovner, Michael Rosenthal, and Jack Karp, dear friends, who have been steadfast in their friendship and career support.

Anthony R. Kovner

PROLOGUE

Summer 1967—For most readers, this is a time in history that many of us who were there at the time found generally forgettable aside from the release of The Beatles' album, "Sgt. Pepper's Lonely Hearts Club Band." In my case, this summer was a turning point, though I was not aware of the significance at the time. That summer, I was 14 years old and looking for something to do to keep me occupied before school started again in the fall. In our local newspaper, I saw a brief announcement that Mt. Sinai Hospital (prior to becoming the Cedars-Sinai Medical Center) was looking for volunteers to work at the hospital. As an aspiring physician (I saw myself becoming a pediatrician), this sounded like a good way to spend several hours per week transporting patients and doing the sorts of things that hospital volunteers back then typically did. I could not have been more wrong.

The volunteer assignment at Mt. Sinai was to work on a team dedicated to producing the disposable parts and supplies for the patients who were in Mt. Sinai's new home dialysis program. Rather than purchase these disposable supplies from commercial vendors, the hospital decided to buy the parts in bulk, teach a group of teenagers to assemble the parts, sterilize them in house, and make them available to the patients in the program. Working under the supervision of the parent of one of the patients, this group of several dozen teens produced home dialysis supplies for 3 years. While such an audacious undertaking would never be allowed today (imagine what the risk managers would say), my colleagues and I spent collectively tens of thousands of hours working to save money for the hospital and helping to make home dialysis available to patients who needed this critical clinical service.

That summer of 1967 was the start of my personal journey in healthcare. I knew that this is where I belonged. Beginning in 1972, I paid for my undergraduate education working full time as a dialysis technician in two inpatient and one outpatient dialysis centers, hoping that my work in clinical medicine would help convince approximately three dozen medical schools to admit me to their MD program despite my lackluster grades. Unfortunately, this turned out not to be the case. Despite the dozens of rejection letters, my goal of wanting to make a difference in healthcare had not dimmed. The question was how to accomplish this goal if I could not be a physician.

Rather than take the reader through a detailed chronology of events, suffice it to say that after leaving dialysis, I spent 5 years teaching science and math in grades 6 through 12, directed a federally funded healthcare program, and spent 7 years in higher education administration. A turning point in that journey took place when I was running the federal healthcare program without the benefit of any education in management or administration. I was fortunate to discover a year-long graduate certificate program offered through the University of California, Los Angeles (UCLA) School of Public Health examining the core principles of healthcare management. That was my "Eureka, I have found it!" moment. That certificate gave me the opportunity to learn from some of the best faculty at UCLA, and develop an understanding of why management and administration in healthcare made such a profound difference in delivering high-quality healthcare.

Building off what I discovered at UCLA, it made sense to continue my education, but the specific direction was unclear. Fortunately, my professional work in higher education administration was at the University of Southern California, where the School of Public Administration (now the Sol Price School of Public Policy) offered a PhD degree that could be taken primarily in a weekend-intensive format, thereby allowing me to continue working full time at the university. In addition to required areas in organization theory and organization behavior, I had the good fortune to focus on healthcare administration and the applied behavioral sciences. Earning the PhD gave me the opportunity to apply what I learned and bring the discipline of healthcare management to students at Oregon State University, where I served on the faculty from 1992 to 2008, and now at the George Washington University.

An important reason for sharing this story with you is to make clear why I am so very passionate about what I do, and why this field is of such importance to me. While I have never had the opportunity to hold a management or leadership role in a traditional healthcare organization, knowing that I have played a role in educating countless numbers of students at a bachelor's, master's, and doctoral level who graduate and then enter the field of healthcare management is satisfying beyond measure. Throughout the years in higher education, I have reflected on the principle of the healthcare flywheel that is central to the work of the StuderGroup. Purpose, worthwhile work, and making a difference are as applicable in higher education as they are in healthcare. I would be remiss not to note with equal measures of pride and humility that I am the only full-time educator inducted into the StuderGroup Fire Starter Hall of Fame. Educating students for a future of consequence is at the heart of what I try to do every day.

As you read the various chapters and read the stories of the practitioners, try to imagine yourself in a role best aligned with your skills, talent, and passion. It is my sincere hope that your own desire to make a difference in healthcare will be ignited by this book. The work done by the persons highlighted here is important beyond measure. I invite you to join us on this journey to discover a small fraction of the opportunities that await you in healthcare management.

Leonard H. Friedman

Summer 1963—This dateline marked a turning point in my life, though I was not aware of the significance at the time to my career. I was 27 years old, newly married, and finishing up my graduate degree at Cornell's Master of Public Administration (MPA) program in public administration with a specialization in healthcare management. My father had just died at age 59 years. I had gone to graduate school eventually to take over the family business (he and my uncle owned three small for-profit hospitals in New York City). Now, without consulting me, my uncle engaged in selling the business to real estate developers to convert the hospitals into apartment buildings.

In 1963, a professor at Cornell named Rodney White, who was a Canadian sociologist, advised me to pursue a PhD in preference to the Doctor in Public Health degree, which at that time he found to be inferior since universities hired only tenure-track professors with PhD degrees. White was high on a specific opportunity at the University of Pittsburgh with Cecil Sheps, MD, who was head of the healthcare program at the School of Public Health. I met with Dr. Sheps, who informed me that I could study for a PhD at U.S. government expense in a public traineeship program at the University of Pittsburgh and that he would also help find me a part-time job. But the School of Public Health did not award a PhD degree. A PhD was possible only in the Department of Sociology in the School of Arts and Sciences, or in the School of Public and International Affairs.

I liked being a student at Cornell, was curious to learn how hospitals and other organizations worked, and thought that I would still like to run a hospital someday. At the time, I was not impressed with the retired manager who taught hospital management at Cornell. Certainly he was biased against and knew little about for-profit hospitals.

I really didn't know what I wanted to do, or who would hire me, or what I would make a living doing 50 hours or more each week. My decision making was biased by (a) my father's example—I wished to emulate him, although he had viewed hospital management as a way to make money, rather than as a calling to help others; and (b) I liked studying and learning, which was what I had been doing these past 2 years. My wife got a job as a secretary in a small medical group for two internists, so with the traineeship we had enough money on which to live. Sociology was too theory driven and too far from applied management, which was what I was interested in. At the School of Public and International Affairs at the University of Pittsburgh, I chose to specialize (there were limited choices) in economic and social development, and collaborated on my dissertation with a renowned sociologist, Charles Perrow, whose recent work concerned how organizations were structured appropriately and inappropriately as related to the work itself. Technology in organizational work had often changed yet many of the leading firms lagged behind in reorganizing their structure, resulting in dysfunctional performance. With Perrow's support and supervision, I decided to apply his schema to the organization of eight hospital nursing units in four different Pittsburgh hospitals. Sure enough, I found that where the technology was relatively simple, such as in the routine labor and delivery unit, staffing was inefficient, and where the work was complex, as in neurosurgery, the nurses in the unit lacked specialized training and skills. This is not the place to discuss the limitations in my methodology, although I yet stand by my conclusions.

After 3 years of PhD work, I went to work for Dr. Sheps, who had become general director of the Beth Israel Medical Center in New York City. He "stockpiled" me as an assistant administrator in the Beth Israel Hospital and within 6 months appointed me as administrator of the Gouverneur Health Services Program (the top two managers had resigned in a power dispute with him). Beth Israel ran Gouverneur under contract with the City of New York with the help of a large grant from the Office of Economic Opportunity. This was the first of my several management jobs for the next 12 years—group practice director in the Department of Medicine, then first program director of the Wharton program in Health Care Management at the University of Pennsylvania (this was an academic job but my work was mostly managerial), senior health consultant for the United Autoworkers in Detroit, Michigan (where I assisted with negotiating benefits and writing speeches and position papers), and finally chief executive officer (CEO) of Newcomb Hospital, a 235-bed hospital in Vineland, New Jersey. During these 12 years, I was fired twice and resigned from a third position. During the same period, my first wife left me and I met and subsequently married Chris Tassone (Kovner). (Chris and I have two lovely and accomplished children and four grandchildren. Chris is a professor of nursing, also at New York University, and an expert on the nursing workforce.)

I was recruited to NYU in 1979 as director of the Program in Health Care Management and Policy. I have worked at NYU for the past 38 years. The NYU position was my first job in which I did work that I had actually done before. At NYU, I also later managed to get fired from my position as director of the health program (which didn't affect my tenure) in exchange for a 25% increase in salary. The stories of these firings and resignations is a subject for another book, Part One of which, *Health Care Management in Mind*, was published by Springer Publishing in 2000.

I am as passionate as Len Friedman about why healthcare management is so important to me. While at NYU, I have directed four large demonstration programs for several large foundations ranging from rural healthcare to interdisciplinary professional education to hospital community benefit. I have consulted and served on the boards of several large health systems, spent the past 10 years of my professional life learning and writing about and teaching evidence-based management, ran a large accredited healthcare management program at NYU, and developed with New York-Presbyterian and NYU a large demonstration healthcare management program for nurse leaders. As Len says, worthwhile work and making a difference have been the secret of my happiness at work. I was asked what I wanted my legacy to be (in the context of raising money for an endowed chair, which I didn't think was worth the cost) and I said "my legacy is what I have learned and shared with my students, hundreds of them, some of whose career success has resulted from learning with me from our mistakes."

What strikes me in reading over these two prologues, Len's and mine, is the time we didn't use to the full measure of our capacity and youthful energy: Len producing for 3 years disposable parts and supplies for home dialysis patients, and my working for 10 years, before I went to Cornell, in a variety of jobs that didn't add much value—serving in the reserve officers corps of the air defense (machine guns permanently damaged my hearing), managing for my father a small nursing home (an RN was effectively in charge, before, during, and after my management stint), and selling stocks and bonds (mostly to my father) as a registered representative on Wall Street.

Oh, if I had then a guide like *101 Careers in Healthcare*, and access to the networks and opportunities cited here!

Anthony R. Kovner

PART I

OVERVIEW OF HEALTHCARE MANAGEMENT

CHAPTER 1
INTRODUCTION TO HEALTHCARE MANAGEMENT

The purpose of this book is to help the reader make career choices based on the best available evidence. We want to share with you the knowledge and information required to either enter the field of healthcare management or, for those already working in healthcare, move into increasingly responsible and complex roles. Additionally, we wish to give the reader a sense of the breadth and depth of career opportunities available in the field of healthcare management. Because of the inherent limitations of this book, we will not be able to provide the reader with specific, personal advice and guidance. For that, we recommend that persons needing this information contact the program director of their local certified undergraduate or accredited graduate program. Before diving into the specifics of the education and process for finding a job in healthcare, we should take a few minutes to define what we mean when we say *healthcare management*, and share some perspectives about the breadth and depth of opportunities in the field.

As of the writing of the second edition of *101 Careers in Healthcare Management*, healthcare remains the largest segment of the economy of the United States. According to the Center for Medicare & Medicaid Services (CMS), $3.2 trillion was spent on health services in 2015 (CMS, n.d.). This figure represents just under 17.8% of the total gross domestic product (GDP) or $9,990 per capita. Our level of spending on health services is the highest of any nation. Where does this money go? Again, according to CMS, in 2015 we spent $1.02 trillion on hospital services; $640 billion on physician and other clinical services; $96 billion on other professional services including physical therapy, optometry, chiropractic and other similar services; $128 billion on dental services; $320 billion on prescription drugs; $64 billion on durable medical equipment; $157 billion on long-term care; $89 billion on home health services; $163 billion for other health, residential, and personal care services; and $59 billion for other nondurable medical products. The remainder includes expense categories such as governmental administration for programs like Medicare and Medicaid, net cost of commercial health insurance, public health activities, and investment in research (CMS, n.d.).

Three trillion two hundred billion dollars is an enormous sum and it begs the question—who gets all this money? Most of the money spent on health services funnels into various types of organizations—all of which require professionally trained and experienced managers and administrators. While there are a number of physicians and other clinical practitioners who remain in solo or small group practices (and this number continues to shrink annually), the vast majority of health services and supporting structures are housed in small, medium, and large

TABLE 1.1 NUMBER OF HEALTH SECTOR ORGANIZATIONS IN 2015

Type of Organization	Number
Community hospitals	5,627
Physician practices/clinics	730,366 physicians in group practices
Long-term care	45,600 nursing homes and assisted living
Health insurance companies	857
Pharmaceutical manufacturers	263
Healthcare consulting firms	Thousands of large and small firms
Healthcare-related associations	Thousands of associations of all sizes
Medical equipment manufacturers	735

organizations. Table 1.1 gives the reader a sense of the number of different health service organizations in operation in 2015.

These numbers do not account for all the federal, state, and local governmental health service organizations, associations, retail pharmacies, and individuals working as independent contractors. Taken in the aggregate, healthcare is a very big business with multiple lines of service and support. As a result of all these different parts to the healthcare industry, the reader will frequently hear the term "health sector" used, which is just another way of expressing the sum total of the various firms and organizations that either directly or indirectly touch on the delivery of health services to the individual patient.

WHAT IS HEALTHCARE MANAGEMENT?

So, what exactly is healthcare management, and what is it that healthcare managers do? For the purposes of this book, let us stipulate that healthcare management is the practice and application of business management principles within the context of health sector organizations. Note that here, healthcare management does not propose to manage the health of individuals or communities. We are not referring to clinicians who treat and manage illness and disease. Rather, our focus is on the management of the various forms of organizations that are part of the health system. It is important to note that the practice of healthcare management will differ depending on which part of the health sector we happen to be examining. While the core principles of management are the same, there are critical differences in the way in which management is practiced depending on the mission, design, and operation of the organization.

By way of illustration, let us compare and contrast the essential management challenges faced by a not-for-profit hospital and a small, mid-size commercial health insurance company. We will assume that the two organizations generate the same amount of revenue each year—the hospital through the provision of patient services, and the insurance company through the sales of insurance to individuals and employer groups. Both of these organizations face similar challenges in making enough money to cover all short- and long-term expenses; attracting and retaining high-quality employees; competing with similar organizations in their market; assuring that technology is up to date; and staying current with federal, state, and local governmental regulations. While similar in many respects, there are a number of critical differences that make managing hospitals and health insurance companies particularly complex. The hospital operates as a not-for-profit firm (the most common structure among hospitals in the United States), and while they are exempt from paying most taxes, they must provide a level of community benefit equal to the amount of money not paid in taxes. The hospital gets reimbursed for services by multiple payers, who typically pay a different rate for the same service. In many cases, the primary knowledge workers in hospitals (physicians) are not employed by the hospital and are, therefore, not under the direct control of the hospital management. Finally, for hospitals that operate emergency departments (EDs), federal legislation requires that the hospital evaluate and stabilize every patient who enters the ED regardless of their ability to pay. The health insurance company most likely operates as a for-profit firm that pays all applicable taxes. All of the key knowledge workers (sales staff, underwriters, claims, customer service representatives, et al.) are directly employed by the organization. If someone wants health insurance, they must pay the monthly premium and if not, the insurance is canceled. The point to this single example is to illustrate that while hospitals and health insurance firms both occupy important parts of the health sector, the administrative and managerial demands on both of these organizations have important differences.

WHAT IS THE ROLE OF THE HEALTHCARE MANAGER?

Healthcare managers are responsible for carrying out the administrative and managerial functions of their respective organizations. On a macro level, we can think of managers occupying entry level, middle, and senior/executive management positions. There is an immense amount of literature on what managers do, but for the purposes of this book, we turn to the work of Dr. Henry Mintzberg for a brief examination of managerial roles. This is not the only structural analysis available, but in our assessment, this set of role definitions works well for health sector organizations. According to Mintzberg, all managers fulfill three main roles with multiple subroles under each one (Mintzberg, 1989). These roles and subroles are as follows:

Interpersonal Roles	Informational Roles	Decisional Roles
Figurehead	Monitor	Entrepreneur
Leader	Disseminator	Disturbance handler
Liaison	Spokesperson	Resource allocator
		Negotiator

Each of the roles involve the following activities (Mind Tools, 2017).

Interpersonal

The managerial roles in this category involve **providing** information and ideas.

    Figurehead
    Leader
    Liaison

Informational

The managerial roles in this category involve **processing** information.

    Monitor
    Disseminator
    Spokesperson

Decisional

The managerial roles in this category involve **using** information.

    Entrepreneur
    Disturbance handler
    Resource allocator
    Negotiator

In the final analysis, managing is about getting the work of the organization done through the efforts of other people. Highly effective health sector managers understand that in order to do their job properly, two conditions must be met. The first is a thorough knowledge and understanding of the industry and the work involved. For example, a person charged with managing the implementation of a health information technology (IT) system must be well versed both in the technical aspects of IT and the nuances of healthcare. The second condition (and perhaps the most important) is the ability to activate each of the roles indicated by Mintzberg with all of the stakeholders in the organization in order to achieve the desired results—in this case, a successful IT implementation that satisfies the needs of the end users. Stated another way, successful healthcare managers understand and embrace the principle that when distilled to its essence, healthcare is inherently a people business. The only way that entry-level, middle-, or executive-level managers accomplish their work is through outstanding relationships with persons throughout their organizations and others including patients, family members, payers, suppliers, regulators, governmental officials, the media, and uncounted others.

There is a large and growing demand for health sector managers and administrators. The Bureau of Labor Statistics stated that there were 333,000 persons employed in the field as medical and health service managers in 2014, and that the job outlook for the period 2014 to 2024 was faster than average (U.S. Department of Labor, 2015). The median annual pay for medical and health service managers in 2016 was $96,540. Taken in the aggregate, there is a high level of demand for skilled and dedicated persons who wish to make a tangible difference in making high-quality healthcare accessible to persons across the country.

Given the results of the presidential election in November 2016, there is a great deal of uncertainty regarding the viability of the Patient Protection and Affordable Care Act (ACA) and what this will mean to health sector organizations. While many questions remain at this time, there is no doubt that people will continue to seek out health services, and it is up to healthcare managers to operate their organizations in a manner that provides safe and effective care.

The upcoming chapters focus on a brief history of healthcare management, the education required for a career in healthcare management, how to find the right job in the field, and the critical competencies in preparation and professionalism. We conclude this book with some thoughts about the competencies that healthcare leaders will need for an uncertain future. We invite you to join us on this exciting journey of discovery.

REFERENCES

Bureau of Labor Statistics, U.S. Department of Labor. (2015). Medical and Health Services Managers. In *Occupational Outlook Handbook*, 2016–17 Edition. Retrieved from https://www.bls.gov/ooh/management/medical-and-health-services-managers.htm

Center for Medicare & Medicaid Services. (n.d.). Historical. Retrieved from https://www.cms.gov/Research-Statistics-Data-and-Systems/Statistics-Trends-and-Reports/NationalHealthExpendData/NationalHealthAccountsHistorical.html

Mind Tools. (2017). Mintzberg's management roles. Retrieved from https://www.mindtools.com/pages/article/management-roles.htm

Mintzberg, H. (1989). *Mintzberg on management*. New York, NY: The Free Press.

CHAPTER 2
A BRIEF HISTORY OF HEALTHCARE MANAGEMENT

Chapter 1 gave you a good sense of what healthcare management is and what it is that healthcare managers do. Before examining education for the profession and recommending strategies to find a job in the field, it is worth taking a bit of time to look back at the history of healthcare management as a career.

The early days of healthcare management coincided with the growth of hospitals, and transformation of medical practice into a science-based activity. Up until the later 19th century, hospitals were typically institutions where cure was infrequent and death was commonplace. For example, the first voluntary hospital in the United States was established in 1751 at the Pennsylvania Hospital to care for the sick and poor. A condition of admission to the Pennsylvania Hospital was the requirement of patients to scrub floors and serve food to others. Patients who had adequate personal resources were cared for at home by private physicians and rarely, if ever, set foot in a hospital. Hospitals were typically "managed" by physicians (often whose clinical skills had diminished), nurses, or the clergy.

By the late 19th century, several important scientific discoveries and advances in medical practice began to transform hospitals into the organizations we see today. Antiseptic technique and developments in anesthesia simultaneously reduced the incidence of infection and allowed surgery to be performed without inducing needless pain and suffering. Coupled with this was the professionalization of nursing that began in 1873, with the opening of three schools of nursing in New York, New Haven, and Boston (Starr, 1984). Along with these and other developments was the release in 1910 of the Flexner Report. This report was important in that it called for the uniform training of physicians and reduced the number of proprietary medical schools (Starr, 1984). The net effect of implementing the Flexner Report was to reduce the number of physicians in practice, but assure patients and state licensing boards that all physicians had a similar depth and scope of educational preparation.

As clinical care improved, hospitals began to shift away from providing almost exclusively charity care toward a model where patients were asked to pay for their care, resulting in hospitals starting to be run as a business. This change required a group of workers not previously seen—administrators and managers arranged in a bureaucratic structure. Day-to-day control of the hospital shifted from physicians and members of boards of trustees to professional managers. Concurrent with the growth of professional management was the significant increase in the number and size of hospitals. In the period between 1875 and 1925, the number of hospitals in the United States grew from just over 170 to about 7,000, and the number of hospital beds increased from 35,000 to 860,000 (Rosner, 1989). In 1933, the American College of Hospital Administrators (ACHA) was founded to represent the professional interests of this growing number of hospital administrators. In 1985, ACHA was rebranded as the American College of Healthcare Executives (ACHE), in part to reflect the fact that there were many persons practicing healthcare management outside of the hospital setting.

Over the past two decades, we have witnessed an important shift in the profession and practice of healthcare management. While the profession has its roots in hospital administration and hospitals continue to employ large numbers of clinical and nonclinical staff in administrative and managerial roles, hospitals are not the only venue at which healthcare managers practice. As noted in Chapter 1, we use the term "health sector management" to draw attention to the variety of organizations that are either directly or indirectly involved with providing care to patients—the focal point of our healthcare system. For our purposes, let us categorize the health sector into units as shown in Table 2.1.

Excluded from this categorization are practitioners who work in solo practice or small groups. This includes most dentists and therapists (physical and occupational). Also excluded are individual consultants or any other health sector professional who works outside of a "traditional" organizational setting.

It should be noted that within each of the organizations mentioned, there are multiple types and variations. For example, long-term care includes, but is not limited to, organizations such as nursing homes, assisted living, adult day care, home health care, and hospice. Public health includes organizational forms such as county health departments, the U.S. Public Health Service, Centers for Disease Control and Prevention, Indian Health Service, and many others.

The point to this discussion is that healthcare management has undergone a profound transformation since Benjamin Franklin founded the Pennsylvania

TABLE 2.1 HEALTH SECTOR ORGANIZATIONS

Delivery Organizations	Direct Support Organizations	Indirect Support Organizations
Hospitals	Health insurance	Regulatory agencies
Physician group practices	Health information technology	Universities and other educational programs
Long-term care	Consulting firms	Executive search firms
Federally qualified health centers	Pharmaceutical manufacturing and sales	Research and development
Public health	Durable medical equipment	Healthcare associations
Mental (behavioral) health	Biotechnology firms	
Military health and the Veterans Administration (VA)		
Correctional health		

Hospital in 1751. The diversity and complexity of organizations connected at some level to the delivery of care to the patient require highly professional and competent management. The subsequent chapters detail what is required in terms of educational preparation and the personal attributes crucial for success in this field.

REFERENCES

Rosner, D. (1989). Doing well or doing good: The ambivalent focus of hospital administration. In D. Long & J. Golden (Eds.), *The American general hospital: Communities and social contexts* (pp. 157–169). Ithaca, NY: Cornell University Press.

Starr, P. (1984). *Social transformation of American medicine*. New York, NY: Basic Books.

CHAPTER 3
EDUCATION IN HEALTHCARE MANAGEMENT

To introduce this chapter, we would like to invite you to participate in a thought experiment. Imagine, if you will, that you have always wanted to be a physician. Let us ignore for a moment the need to have passed the federal and state licensure exams as a condition to practice medicine. You read all the books you can find, watch every television show featuring doctors (real and fictional), and go so far as to track down every possible medical source on the Internet including videos of clinical procedures. Once this is accomplished, do you think you are ready to start caring for patients? No? What is missing? That is right—reading about practicing medicine and watching videos is no substitute for the years of classroom education and practical experience needed to be an effective physician. One of the most tiresome sentiments we hear is that anyone can be a manager. No special training or experience is needed. In fact, all managers really have to do is get out of the way of those who do the "real" work in the organization. Our assertion is that this perspective about management needing little or no formal education and experience is naive at best, and potentially dangerous at worst.

In the previous chapters, we discussed the necessity for highly effective healthcare management, and noted that the practice of healthcare management has undergone several significant changes over the past 55 years. Perhaps the most important of those has been the growing professionalization of the field. The need for increased professionalization of management has been driven by a number of factors including changes in reimbursement from primarily out-of-pocket payment for services to largely third-party payment; the development of scientific medicine and standardization of medical education (Starr, 1984); the increasing complexity and sophistication of medical diagnosis and treatment; the rapid growth of medical and information technology; federal and state regulations; and the ever-increasing numbers of elderly adults who require treatment for illness and disease. In the early days of healthcare management, hospitals were run by nuns (in the case of faith-based facilities) or physicians, and physician practices had virtually no management other than perhaps a bookkeeper, or at best an office manager.

As healthcare management has grown in scope and sophistication, the need for formal education in the profession has also evolved. While a number of persons holding healthcare management positions have clinical training and were moved into management roles, the trend has been for those wishing to work in management to have specific training in the field. Beginning with the first graduate program in health administration at the University of Chicago in 1934, the field of healthcare management education has blossomed. At the present time, for students who wish to either enter the field or for those already in healthcare who want to develop their skills, there are four primary educational opportunities: bachelor's, master's, doctoral, and executive education.

BACHELOR'S DEGREES IN HEALTHCARE MANAGEMENT

In the listing of job descriptions, we can see that many healthcare management jobs require a bachelor's degree as the entry-level credential. While midlevel and senior leadership positions typically require a master's degree, the Bachelor of Arts (BA)/Bachelor of Science (BS) in healthcare management is a very useful degree to hold for those seeking entry-level positions in this field. In our experience, most students earning a BA/BS in healthcare management ultimately decide to return to school to work on their master's degree.

Many colleges and universities offer a BA/BS degree in healthcare management or administration. In addition, several schools of business provide a BS in business administration, with a focus on healthcare management. While there are more than 200 schools that provide a BA/BS in healthcare management or some variation thereof, students should look for a program that is fully certified by the Association of University Programs in Health Administration (AUPHA). AUPHA provides a link to every certified undergraduate program in North America. All certified undergraduate programs require that students receive academic preparation in a liberal arts foundation (computation, communication, critical thinking, and social and cultural context), 23 content areas specific to healthcare management, and an experiential/applied-learning component containing a minimum of 120 hours in an internship. For students interested in undergraduate study in healthcare management, it is helpful if they possess strong verbal and written communication skills, good computational ability, and demonstrated leadership experience.

MASTER'S DEGREES IN HEALTHCARE MANAGEMENT

Unlike many other graduate professional fields that have but one well-known and widely accepted degree, healthcare management does not fit this norm and is a potential area of confusion for prospective students. There are two important considerations that students need to keep in mind: the name of the degree and the home of the graduate program.

Perhaps the best known and most common master's degree in healthcare management is the Master of Health Administration (MHA). In addition, the Master of Science (MS), Master of Business Administration (MBA), Master of Public Health (MPH), Master of Public Administration (MPA), Master of Health Services Administration (MHSA), and Master of Science in Health Administration (MSHA) can all provide students with the highly focused academic preparation needed to assume midlevel and senior management roles in healthcare management organizations.

In addition to the specific degree, prospective students need to pay attention to the location of the healthcare management program. As one might expect, a healthcare-focused MBA will be in a school of business and will have a very strong emphasis on business principles. Similarly, a healthcare management MPH degree will be housed in a school of public health and those students should expect to hear about population health, epidemiology, biostatistics, and environmental health and safety. In reviewing the breadth of the field, healthcare management programs are also located in schools of public administration, nursing, medicine, allied health, and many others. The important thing to remember is that the location of the program is always linked to the focus of the educational preparation of the student.

As is the case in undergraduate healthcare management education, there are more than 200 schools offering master's degrees in the discipline. A large number of those programs are members of AUPHA but, in this case, graduate programs are accredited by the Commission on Accreditation of Healthcare Management Education (CAHME). Information about currently accredited graduate healthcare management programs is available on CAHME's and AUPHA's web pages. The 2017 criteria for CAHME accreditation require all programs to have a curriculum that is aligned with the program's mission and types of jobs that graduates typically enter. In addition, each accredited program is required to develop student competencies in the following: healthcare system and healthcare management, communications and interpersonal effectiveness, critical thinking, analysis and problem solving, management and leadership, and professionalism and ethics. Students should expect to spend a minimum of 2 years' full-time study in their master's degree program. There are a handful of programs that require students to complete a year-long administrative residency at the conclusion of the 2 years of courses.

Many students wonder why they should seek out an accredited graduate program. For us, the answer lies in the role that accreditation plays for the student and the field of practice. Enrollment in a CAHME-accredited graduate program assures the student that the program meets a minimum set of standards in terms of faculty, university support, curriculum, student and alumni support, and evaluation. There are a handful of well-known business schools and public health programs that have chosen not to stand for CAHME accreditation. For those other programs that are not CAHME accredited, our advice to prospective students is *caveat emptor*—let the buyer beware.

MHA OR MBA?

One of the most commonly asked questions is whether a student should seek a straight MBA degree or an MHA (or equivalent) degree. The simple answer depends on what sort of career path the student plans to pursue. The MBA is a generic business degree (granted, there are varying degrees of rigor and prestige depending on the school and the alumni) that can be applied into almost any business environment. Students who already have a BA/BS in healthcare management would be wise to consider an MBA as they already have a good background in healthcare. In general, students who are committed to a career in the health sector should seriously consider an MHA or equivalent. Healthcare organizations are fundamentally different than virtually any other business, and persons who wish to be effective in a management role need to have a fine-grained understanding of the healthcare context that is possible only in MHA-type programs.

DOCTORAL DEGREES IN HEALTHCARE MANAGEMENT

For most professional roles in healthcare management, a doctoral degree is not necessary. However, for those who wish to enter an academic or research career, a doctoral degree is necessary. There are comparatively few schools that offer focused doctoral preparation in healthcare management, but those can also be found through the AUPHA web page. Most university faculty members who teach in healthcare management have doctoral degrees in fields other than healthcare management, but their academic work applies their theoretical and research specializations to the context of the health sector.

COMBINED DEGREE PROGRAMS

There are a number of universities that offer healthcare management degrees combined with other academic degrees. The most common additional degrees are in business, law, medicine, and public administration. We recommend that students interested in combined degrees talk with the program directors of the respective degrees to check on length of time required to complete the degrees, and whether classes taken for one degree can be used to satisfy the requirements of the other.

EXECUTIVE HEALTHCARE MANAGEMENT PROGRAMS

A growing trend is toward executive education in healthcare management. In many organizations, persons who have skill and education in a particular discipline, such as medicine, nursing, medical technology, pharmacy, social work, and others, and who are exceptionally competent in their work are frequently promoted to management roles. The issue here is that management represents a set of skills and competencies over and above what they currently possess. The other consideration is that for persons already working full time in a healthcare-related profession, they typically cannot dedicate 2 years of full-time study to earn their degree in management. It is for this group of adult learners who are already working in the field for whom executive educational programs have been developed. Most executive students have a minimum of 3 years' experience in the field, and classes are taught in some combination of face-to-face and online delivery formats. In order to be CAHME accredited, executive master's programs require a minimum of 120 face-to-face or online synchronous hours. While most executive programs are designed for master's level education, there are a few executive doctoral programs available. The latter are structured for senior executives who wish to earn a doctoral degree while still maintaining their work responsibilities. AUPHA maintains a comprehensive listing of executive master's or doctoral healthcare management programs.

ONLINE HEALTHCARE MANAGEMENT PROGRAMS

Another growth area is pure online degree programs. In contrast to executive programs that require several years of professional experience and have a face-to-face course delivery component, most online programs can be taken by students with no field experience, and are taught exclusively in an online format. Both bachelor's and master's online degrees are available from a variety of schools. There are a small but growing number of AUPHA-certified undergraduate and CAHME-accredited online programs available for prospective students. It should be noted that there is significant debate in the field about whether healthcare management can be taught in a pure online format. We strongly recommend to students considering a fully online program to do your homework before enrolling. Ask about the quality of the instructors. Find out what fraction of the students graduate from the program, and how many graduates are working in the health sector. What sorts of student support systems are in place? Does the program offer support for students seeking field experiences? Ask to talk with current students and alumni regarding their impressions and experience with the program.

PAYING FOR YOUR EDUCATION

Undergraduate or graduate education can be an expensive endeavor regardless of where you choose to go to school. One way to think of this is that you are making an investment in yourself and your future. Taking out loans through the school's financial aid office is a common method of paying for school. Some students decide to work full or part time in order to finance their education. Some programs require that students go to school full time and do not permit outside work arrangements. Others permit part-time employment, but recommend that work be limited to no more than 20 hours or so a week. Other programs are structured to accommodate the needs of working adults. In some cases, where the student is married or is in some other committed relationship, the couple will live off the income of the working partner while the other is in school. The best advice here is to chat with the program director and ask about working and going to school.

Another opportunity to help finance an undergraduate or graduate education is through scholarships or grants that are made available through the department, college, or university. Again, ask the program director about eligibility for these scholarships. Many graduate programs have available research assistantships that help offset the cost of tuition. There are also outside scholarships exclusively available to healthcare management students. In this case, we recommend researching scholarships offered by the various professional associations including the American College of Healthcare Executives (ACHE), Medical Group Management Association (MGMA), Healthcare Financial Management Association (HFMA), Healthcare Information and Management Systems Society (HIMSS), and many others.

REFERENCE

Starr, P. (1984). *Social transformation of American medicine*. New York, NY: Basic Books.

CHAPTER 4
FINDING JOBS IN HEALTHCARE MANAGEMENT

There are several ways for you to find a job in healthcare management. Some of those methods will be traditional, and others will be a bit more creative. However, regardless of the path that you choose, there are three important things to keep in mind. First, outstanding educational preparation is a necessary, but not sufficient, condition. Virtually every employer is also looking for experience in the field. That experience can come from full- or part-time employment in a healthcare organization, volunteer work in a hospital or clinic, or clinical training. Employers are also looking for leadership experience in almost any setting. Holding an officer position in a fraternity or sorority, playing intercollegiate sports, active participation in a community organization, or significant volunteer experience can make an important difference for persons seeking their first job in the field. Students who come in with an undergraduate or graduate degree (along with a strong grade point average [GPA]) coupled with work experience and holding leadership roles will have a much better chance of finding a job than someone with an equally strong education but without any previous leadership roles.

The second important point to consider is that healthcare management is, at heart, a relationship-based business. Persons who are successful in this field know that human relationships are absolutely vital in order to achieve the goals of providing safe, effective, and efficient healthcare. Given the importance of relationships to career success, we frequently use the phrase, "Network or no work." It is essential that you go out and meet people in the industry, be able to talk about yourself, your talents, and why you want to enter this business, and, in a word, "sell" yourself. While many jobs in healthcare management are advertised in traditional formats, many entry-level positions come about because of networking, talking with human resource managers, and connecting with the faculty at your school who frequently are the first to know about job opportunities.

We have a third, and frequently not always obvious, consideration when searching for either your first job in healthcare management, or one that takes you to the executive suite. It is embodied in the ancient wisdom, "Know thyself." Why is it important to know who you are before you seek a position in our field? The reason is that in most cases, health sector organizations want people whose personal values closely align with those of the organization. Stated another way, you need to fit within the culture of the organization rather than make the culture adjust to you. In order to help determine the goodness of fit, you need to be highly aware of your personal values and the things that matter most to you. If you know those attributes, you can then determine how well you fit within the values and culture of the organization.

One final thought before we enumerate the ways to find jobs in this field is to keep your ego in check. Your first job, whether with an undergraduate or graduate degree, will almost certainly not be in middle management or higher. We have seen too many students return to us and ask why they failed at securing a job. More often than not, the student set unreasonable demands, had unrealistic expectations, or otherwise came across as arrogant and unwilling to be a team player. Higher level jobs with increasing levels of responsibility will come to those who prove themselves willing to pitch in, get their hands dirty, follow through on what they have promised, and admit what they do not know.

TRADITIONAL PATHWAYS

In today's human resource environment, most entry-level jobs are made available through the web portal of the organization, and require submission of a cover letter and resume. These are just the first steps in a long process that culminates in being offered a job in healthcare management.

Prior to starting a search for a job, two documents are essential—the resume and cover letter. There are a large number of different templates you can use for both, but regardless of whether you use a precrafted template or just go ahead and write your own, keep in mind a few simple rules:

1. You have one opportunity to make a good first impression. Both, the cover letter and resume must be absolutely perfect in terms of construction and composition; that means no spelling and grammar errors anywhere in the documents. Avoid the temptation to use fancy and overly ornate type fonts; 10- to 12-point standard fonts like Times New Roman, Arial, Calibri, or Tahoma are generally good.
2. Your resume should never be more than two pages long unless you have extensive professional experience. Make sure that if you have previous professional experience that you document your accomplishments in concise and honest metrics. Your resume needs to be crafted to meet the specific needs of the organization to which you are applying.
3. Your cover letter needs to be personalized for the organization. Too often, we have seen students send out a "one size fits all" cover letter that is overly generic and not fine-tuned for the specific organization. Worse yet, some students cut and paste the language from previous cover letters without even changing the name and address of the person to whom the cover letter is intended. You need to adjust your cover letter to speak to the requirements found in the position description of the job for which you are applying. Also, take the time to learn as much about the organization as you can from their web page and write about the alignment of the organization's values with your own. Include specific examples of your own leadership accomplishments and link them to the job for which you are applying.

We also recommend that you work through several drafts of your cover letter and resume seeking to make each draft better than the last. Be sure to ask persons who are comfortable giving you critical feedback to carefully read and critique your cover letter and resume. Once the resume is done and you have the main parts of your cover letter thought out, you can then begin the hard work of looking for a job in healthcare management.

There are some very fortunate persons who are hired into a full-time position directly out of school without having to go through a search process. We recommend familiarizing yourself with the breadth of career opportunities available in healthcare management. Some good web sites for this purpose include the following:

- ExploreHealthCareers is a good starting point with many excellent resources: explorehealthcareers.org/en/Field/13/Health_AdministrationManagement
- U.S. Department of Labor Bureau of Labor Statistics contains up-to-date information on employment, job outlook, wages, and links to other relevant web sites: www.bls.gov/ooh/management/medical-and-health-services -managers.htm

The search for jobs in healthcare management should be started using the web links from specific healthcare organizations' human resource pages and a number of the larger healthcare associations. The associations and the scope of their jobs include the following:

- American College of Healthcare Executives (www.ache.org)
  ACHE has a current membership of over 38,000 persons in hospitals, health systems, and other healthcare organizations. As a member of the ACHE, you can search job opportunities and post your resume.
- Medical Group Management Associations (www.mgma.com)
  MGMA has a membership of over 33,000 persons whose role is focused on managing physician practices. MGMA makes available a comprehensive career center for both job seekers and employers.
- Health Information and Management System Society (www.himss.org)
  HIMSS represents 38,000 members whose work is in the area of health information technology. Their web page has a link to their very complete career services pages.
- Healthcare Financial Management Association (www.hfma.org)
  HFMA is the leading professional association for over 40,000 healthcare financial management professionals. Their job bank allows members to review job listings and post their resumes.
- American College of Health Care Administrators (www.achca.org)
  ACHCA is the leading professional association for leaders in the long-term care field. Their web page includes a link to a comprehensive career page listing both job opportunities and permits job seekers to post their resumes.
- American Public Health Association (www.apha.org)
  APHA provides a career development center that offers job listings and career tips specifically for persons interested in federal, state, and local public health organizations.

The prior listing is a sample of some of the larger, dedicated healthcare management professional associations that include career services as part of their member benefits. In addition to the professional associations, most large healthcare organizations have human resource (HR) departments, and if the HR department is large enough, they will post their job vacancies on their web page.

In addition to the professional associations mentioned, there are many other associations targeted at meeting the needs of special populations of healthcare managers and leaders. All of the associations listed provide professional networking opportunities and typically welcome student members:

■ National Association of Health Services Executives (Following excerpt from www.nahse.org/about-nahse.html used with permission)
NAHSE's purpose is to ensure greater participation of minority groups in the health field. Its basic objective is to develop and maintain a strong viable national body to more effectively have input in the national healthcare delivery system. It has provided a vehicle for Blacks to effectively participate in the design, direction, and delivery of quality healthcare to all people.
■ National Forum for Latino Healthcare Executives (www.nflhe.org)
■ Institute for Diversity in Health Management (www.diversityconnection .org/diversityconnection/homepage/index.jsp)

Additional opportunities for graduates of healthcare administration programs are in the active duty military and the U.S. Public Health Service (USPHS) Commissioned Corps. The Medical Service Corps operates branches within the U.S. Army, Navy, and Air Force. Members of the Medical Service Corps hold important managerial roles in military hospitals in the United States and around the world at U.S. military installations. Persons thinking about the Medical Service Corps must possess a bachelor's or master's degree in healthcare management and are commissioned as an officer in the Army, Navy, or Air Force with the requisite service obligation.

The USPHS Commissioned Corps provides managerial and leadership opportunities for persons possessing a master's degree from a CAHME-accredited program. Members of the USPHS Commissioned Corps wear uniforms and have military-type rank. They have opportunities to serve in governmental agencies in the United States and overseas.

NONTRADITIONAL PATHWAYS

Earlier in this chapter, we introduced the concept of network or no work. Owing to the importance of relationships in healthcare management, frequently job opportunities are first known to people who know other people who know other people. The question then is how do you get to be in this information and knowledge loop? We have a number of very practical suggestions. First and foremost, you need to take an active role in one or more professional associations. These associations are listed earlier in this chapter. Very frequently, they offer reduced membership dues for students or persons early in their careers. Find the association that is best aligned with your personal career goals and aspirations. Most of these associations have local or state officers. Arrange a meeting with these people to introduce yourself and seek their input to how you should structure a job search. Every one of these associations has an annual meeting with thousands and sometimes tens of thousands of persons attending. Go to the annual meeting and, if possible, to local/ regional meetings to meet persons in the field and introduce yourself to those in the field. While these meetings involve an investment of time and money, it is crucial to attend and meet the persons who can bring in new management talent.

Another related suggestion is to arrange for informational interviews with healthcare leaders in your local community. We suggest that you not open the conversation by asking if they have any jobs in their organization. Start by finding out about them, how they got into this business, and what suggestions they have for persons who want to obtain a job in healthcare management. You might ask if they know of neighboring organizations that are looking to fill administrative vacancies.

Do not ignore the important role that alumni from your undergraduate or graduate schools can play in helping you land a job in healthcare management. Talk with the program directors to get information about alumni who are working in the field. Program alumni can help with resume reviews and mock interviews, and can introduce you to persons in their network. Remember that alumni will not knock on your door—you must take the initiative to seek them out and enlist their help.

Finally, you might think about taking a full- or part-time job in the organization at what might to you seem to be something far below your education and aspirations. The reasons for this are twofold. First, most organizations advertise job vacancies first to their current employees and give hiring preference to those already working there. Second (and perhaps more important) is that you give yourself ready access to managers throughout the organization and have the opportunity to prove yourself and your willingness to accept responsibility and consistently do a good job. You also get the opportunity to know and experience the culture of the organization first hand. You might be surprised at how often very competent frontline workers are quickly moved into managerial or supervisory roles.

The question you should be asking is: How do you differentiate yourself from everyone else applying for the same job? The answer to this question resides in the domain of professionalism and preparation. We discuss these areas in detail in the next chapter.

CHAPTER 5
PREPARATION AND PROFESSIONALISM

Now that we have talked about the education required for a job in healthcare management and some strategies associated with seeking out that job, let us spend some time providing several thoughts and ideas around preparation and professionalism that are required for management jobs in the health sector. Our approach to this topic is to provide you with a list and discussion on the 12 most critical attributes that healthcare leaders must possess regardless of the portion of the health sector in which you are seeking employment. These elements of preparation and professionalism are the accumulation of our many decades of experience dealing with thousands of students. It is not possible to evaluate which of these recommendations is more valuable than another, but all must be part of your persona when searching for a job, or while at work. While our focus is on early careerists, rather than middle or senior managers, these "rules of the road" are applicable to everyone in healthcare management. There is no specific order to these ideas, and all of them must be kept in mind as you move forward in your career in healthcare management.

1. **Attitude**

   One of the things we continuously emphasize to our students is that you need to think and behave like a high performer. Stated another way, attitude is everything. Think for a moment about how the outward attitude of others affects you. Whom would you rather be around at school or at work? Person A comes across to others as positive, energetic, enthusiastic, generally upbeat, and possesses a "can-do" approach to tasks. In contrast, Person B comes across to others as grumpy, frowning, negative with respect to the organization and people, and waits for others to step up when faced with a task or assignment. While these are a bit of a caricature, we are sure that you have met variations of both types of people at school, work, or in social settings.

   While no one expects you to always be happy and cheerful (you are allowed to have bad days), the outward face that you display to the world is, for most persons, the clearest signal of who you are and how you relate to others. Your ability to understand your emotions (sometimes referred to as "emotional intelligence," or EQ) and then adjust them as needed is a vital attribute of highly effective leaders.

2. **Continuous Learning**

   Assuming that most of you began your formal education when you were 5 years old and walked into your kindergarten class for the first time, you have spent the vast majority of your life in school. Classes, readings, homework, various assignments, large and small, and tests/quizzes have been the rhythm of your life. Now that you have dedicated years working toward either your bachelor's or master's degree in healthcare management, you are so ready for graduation to release you from schooling so that you can get on with your life.

While graduation is an important and necessary benchmark, we have a duty to inform you that your real education is about to start once you begin your first full-time job in the health sector. Much of the theory that you learned while in school will still be good, but the examples and applications will likely be out of date or completely obsolete within 5 years. To stay current in the field regardless of the part of the health sector in which you work will require you to participate in at least one professional association that is aligned with your area of interest. Read everything you can about the strong and weak environmental signals that impact your work. Stay current with what is happening in your community, the nation, and the world, even if it has no obvious connection to healthcare. Continuing formal and informal education is essential for every healthcare leader.

3. **Credibility**

For our purposes, credibility is the attribute where people believe what you say and do not question your word or your intentions. As young children, we are taught to tell the truth and admit when we have made mistakes. Too often, as we grow up and move through the various developmental stages of life, we forget these important lessons. We learn that it is okay to make up excuses, shirk responsibility, or (worse yet) throw others "under the bus" if it means saving ourselves when we make mistakes and do not want to own up to our errors. While this might seem like an acceptable short-term strategy, keep in mind that at work, you and your behaviors are constantly under examination. Accept responsibility when mistakes are made. While there may be some immediate loss of face, others will appreciate your willingness to own up to your errors.

Another reason that credibility is important is captured in the phrase, "underpromise and overdeliver." Too often, in professional settings, we agree to take on a job or project that is due by a certain date. Frequently, other obligations arise, and promises made get pushed aside or forgotten. Others are counting on you to do your part on a project or activity, and excuses as to why you were unable to fulfill your commitment are simply unacceptable. Once you have agreed to take on the assignment, you are obligated to deliver your part(s) fully and on time. Effort is meaningless—the only thing that counts is results. Your personal credibility is a function of keeping your word and making good on those things that you promise to do.

4. **Engagement**

The great American actor, director, and writer, Woody Allen, is quoted as saying, "Eighty percent of success is showing up." For us, the remaining 20% of success happens when you fully engage with whatever you are doing. While we may quibble with whether this 80:20 ratio is accurate, there is no doubt that engagement is essential for persons in any organization to be successful. For example, we know that college undergraduates who become involved with faculty research, student-led clubs and organizations, or athletic programs graduate in a shorter time and with higher levels of satisfaction than students who just show up and take classes.

What does engagement mean in the healthcare workplace? First and foremost, showing up is much more than just physically being in your office or attending a meeting. Think about what it means to be "in the moment" when you are in class, working in a group, or being part of a meeting. All your attention is on what is happening at that moment. It means that you are not checking your e-mail, posting messages to social media, or daydreaming about how nice a day it is outside. Being in the moment allows you to be fully present and engaged in what is going on right now. The remaining part of engagement is stepping up to participate in projects, committees, and activities in the workplace. Do not sit on the sidelines and watch others get things done—be an active participant at work or school. Keep in mind that your first responsibility in the workplace is to do your job the best way possible, and you cannot ignore that in favor of additional tasks which may be fun but are secondary to the job for which you were hired. The key is finding the right balance.

5. Leadership

In virtually all our organizations, there are persons who possess formal leadership titles and are responsible for the function and operation of the whole organization or parts thereof. The likelihood is that most of you reading this book aspire to a leadership role that you hope will come with a nice office, impressive title, and comfortable salary. There is nothing wrong with this, but we recommend that you not wait until you are given the formal title, and, instead, begin acting like a leader while you are still in school or are in your first professional position.

What does it mean to act like a leader when you do not have the title to serve as a public pronouncement of your position? For us, leadership is a verb and not a noun. It is something that you do, rather than just think about. While there are literally thousands of books and articles written about leadership, and there are countless leadership development courses available, leadership at this stage of your career requires you to step up and take action. If you see something that needs to be done, do it. Do not wait for someone else to identify a problem and ask you to participate. If you see a patient or visitor looking lost in the halls of your organization, do not just walk past them and head to your next meeting. Instead, stop and ask if they need help. Rather than just point them in the right direction, escort them to their destination. Doing this reduces the fear and uncertainty of the patient and helps to enhance their experience with your organization. Besides, you never know which senior executive might be watching you at that moment.

6. Mentors

Identifying one or more mentors is vital for professionals at every stage of their career. The person who serves as a mentor early in your career might not necessarily be the right person as you move forward in your career journey. The essential role of the mentor is to give you honest and candid advice. The mentor serves as a sounding board for you particularly when you have professional questions and concerns. The choice of a mentor is one of the more important decisions you will make. Typically, family members should not serve as mentors because they are too close to you emotionally, and they might not be able to give you the information and feedback you require, or you might not be able to hear and accept that feedback.

When thinking about a professional mentor, it is useful to consider someone who is experienced in the same part of the health sector as you. The reason for this is that they understand the context in which you are working. The mentor can serve one or more roles for you including coach, source of support, supplier of resources, or personal champion. While many mentors and mentees prefer to meet face to face, that might not always be possible, so a telephone call or video teleconference (using Skype or other technology) might be required. When working with a mentor, come prepared to have a productive conversation. Be clear about what you want and need from the mentor, and if he or she offers advice, suggestions, or observations, make notes and be ready to act on them. Remember that in virtually all cases, mentors are not being compensated for their time, energy, and effort. Unlike professional coaches who are typically paid on an hourly rate, mentors are persons who are giving you their time. The minimum you can do is be fully present and engaged during every meeting with your mentor, come prepared with a short set of questions, and (most important) listen carefully to what your mentor shares with you. Be sure to provide a small token of appreciation for your mentor. Handwritten thank you notes are particularly effective. An effective mentor has your best interests at heart, and is there to help you navigate your career path.

7. **Networking**

One of the most commonly used maxims in our program is "Network or no work." What does this mean and why is this important? Networking is fundamentally about marketing yourself. This does not mean that you should make wild and extravagant claims about yourself and your abilities. What networking does mean is getting out and meeting people in the field, asking insightful and intelligent questions about others, and demonstrating a genuine interest in others and the organizations they represent.

There are two reasons why personal networking is so vital to professionals in the health sector. The first reason revolves around finding your first job, or identifying new career opportunities. In many cases, job openings are advertised through traditional means including newspaper ads, online job boards, and through the human resources departments in individual organizations. However, many jobs (including entry-level positions) are first circulated internally. Candidates who are already known by decision leaders in the organization are likely to have a better chance at being seriously considered for those positions than those who are known just by a resume and cover letter.

The second reason for personal networking is grounded in the foundation of healthcare management. Despite the presence of multiple forms of technology, large and complex organizational structures, and immense amounts of money flowing into and out of the system, healthcare is fundamentally a relationship-based business. The most effective healthcare leaders know that their ability to effectively relate to multiple stakeholder groups is central to their personal and organizational success. Growing your professional network through participation in one or more membership associations such as the American College of Healthcare Executives (ACHE), Medical Group Management Associations (MGMA), Health Information and Management System Society (HIMSS), and others is a key part of professional networking. Meeting other healthcare leaders provides a tremendous opportunity to share, learn, and grow as a professional.

8. Professionalism

Success in healthcare management and professionalism are tightly coupled. Fair or not, you will be under a virtual microscope where everything that you do and say will be evaluated and measured against the cultural norms of the organization. The point here is not to categorize the cultures of all the various organizations making up the health sector, but it is fair to say that healthcare managers operate in what might be referred to as "conservative" and "traditional" organizations. We are not referring to political conservatism, but rather a set of attitudes and values that are frequently found in the health sector. For example, one of the common terms used to describe hospital- and clinic-based nonphysician managers are "suits," simply because most persons in this role come to work every day in a business suit.

There are several behaviors that help to define professionalism in the health sector including dress, speech, grooming, and posture. Think about the impression you make on others when you consider these four criteria. While your friends may not be bothered by your wrinkled and dirty clothes, mumbling when you talk or excessive use of profanity, uncombed hair and bad breath, and slouched shoulders when you walk or stand, the odds are that these behaviors will certainly work against you in a professional environment. In addition to the behaviors mentioned, consider timeliness, honesty, and consideration of others as part of your professional makeup.

Finally, in an era of almost ubiquitous use of social media, think about what your virtual profile says to current or prospective employers. You may have had a great time at a party and someone posted a picture of you throwing back tequila shots. Is this the image you want portrayed to your future or current organization? Carefully consider what you write in an e-mail before pressing the ENTER key. Ask whether you would be comfortable if that rather uncomplimentary e-mail that you just wrote about a coworker or your boss were to be published on the front page of your local newspaper. Our recommendation to you is that you begin working on your professional behavior while you are still in school. Do not wait until the first job to begin acting in a professional manner.

9. Risk Taking

In the previous section, we noted that health sector organizations tend to be somewhat conservative by nature. Taking risks with patient care and finances is done rarely, if ever. However, we also know that growth (personal and organizational) often comes about as the result of failure. How many of you have never failed at anything in your life? While failure is never fun, it provides a wonderful opportunity to grow and change, though it might not feel that way at the time. By definition, taking a risk involves the chance of failure. In this context, we are not talking about risks that put yourself or others in harm's way. Our intention here is to encourage you to do things that intentionally move yourself out of your comfort zone and take the opportunity to learn and grow.

In this context, we are recommending that you be bold but smart about taking risks. As the great sage, Yogi Berra, once said, "When you come to the fork in the road, take it." We are always provided opportunities to serve on committees, participate in projects, or take on assignments that are new, unfamiliar, and maybe even a bit scary. Taking a risk and taking advantage of these opportunities gives you a chance to learn, grow, and change for the better. Yes, you might fail, but so what? Pick yourself up, dust yourself off, and take the lessons learned to try again. Persistence and determination are embodied within taking risks and failing. You will never succeed unless you are willing to keep trying even after you have been knocked down.

10. Self-Awareness

Another important attribute of preparation and professionalism is self-awareness. This is ancient wisdom and is at the heart of effective leadership. Who are you? What are your core values? What do you stand for? It is essential to uncover the answers to these somewhat existential questions in a fair and honest manner. Many of you heard while growing up that you can be anything to which you set your mind. While this sentiment is noble and often inspiring, it may not always be true. Perhaps you grew up wanting to be an astronaut, sports star, physician, or a supreme court judge. Wait a minute—I thought that you could do anything you set your mind to do. Perhaps the better approach would be to have a clear and unvarnished understanding of your personal strengths and weaknesses.

In their book, *First, Break All the Rules*, Buckingham and Coffman make a clear and convincing argument that all of us possess certain strengths and weaknesses. Rather than trying to fix our weaknesses and improve upon them, it makes much more sense to identify those attributes that make up our strengths and develop those to the fullest. Take those strengths and find professional opportunities to bring them to the surface. The question for many of you might be, how can you identify your strengths? There are many psychometric instruments available that can help you determine and give voice to both strengths and weaknesses. This is also where a mentor or coach can be of assistance.

One final element of self-awareness is understanding your emotional intelligence. In our experience, EQ is more important than IQ in predicting success in healthcare leadership. While the IQ is fixed (and not altogether that critical a number), your emotional intelligence is a measure of how aware you are of your own set of emotions and how they affect others. Do not ever discount the role that emotions play on how you function in your personal and professional lives. Unlike IQ, with a combination of awareness and coaching, you can "move the needle" of your EQ. Self-awareness of your strengths, preferences, and your emotions can have a profound impact on your effectiveness as a healthcare leader.

11. **Teamwork and Team Performance**

For those of us who have worked directly or indirectly in healthcare organizations, we know that teams and team performance are at the heart of organizational effectiveness. Our question for you is: How well do you work as part of a team, whether at school or work? When you are part of a team are you fully engaged, or is your mind drifting somewhere else? Do you fully participate in team decisions or do you default to whatever the majority has to say? If there is prework required for the team, do you come prepared or do you have excuses for not doing the work ahead of time? Do you play "devil's advocate" just to be provocative, or do you question assumptions of the team to help it reach good decisions? Do you step up to help the team accomplish its goals, or do you sit back and allow others to do the work? Our recommendation to you is that given the importance of teams in healthcare, you start working now to improve your team skills.

12. **Serving Others**

Healthcare is a service business. While every healthcare organization is filled with the latest technological innovations, the basic business model exists to serve the needs of others. The majority of the time, the focus of our service is the patient. If you have any question about this assertion, take a few minutes to walk through the halls of a typical hospital. Spend some time in your local emergency department. Talk with the physicians, nurses, and other caregivers to understand their perspectives on what it means to serve others.

Beyond serving the needs of our patients, healthcare management acts to serve all our myriad stakeholder groups. Think about the service that we provide to those who work with us. What sort of colleague are you? When others ask you to help with a project or activity, are you willing (within reason) to give of yourself for the greater good, or do you find reasons why you cannot participate? Are you the type of person on whom others can depend? Do you follow through with commitments? At your heart, do you enjoy working with and being of service to others?

In summary, this chapter has worked to provide you with 12 important attributes essential to the success of persons in healthcare management and leadership. This is not an all-inclusive list, but is intended to be a starting point for your professional growth and development. We invite you to expand on the ideas provided here and share with us your thoughts and observations.

PART II

HEALTHCARE MANAGEMENT CAREERS

CHAPTER 6
CAREERS IN ACUTE CARE HOSPITAL

CHIEF COMPLIANCE OFFICER

JOB DESCRIPTION

The chief compliance officer (CCO) serves as the point person for all hospital compliance activities. The CCO needs to be a person of high integrity, and any other duties the CCO has should not be in conflict with the compliance goals of the hospital. Coordination and communication are the key functions of the CCO with regard to planning, implementing, and monitoring the compliance program.

EDUCATION AND EXPERIENCE

Many CCOs at larger hospitals possess a law degree, although a master's degree in business administration or health administration are frequently seen. CCOs typically have 5 or more years of experience in healthcare compliance. CCOs frequently are certified in healthcare compliance.

CORE COMPETENCIES AND SKILLS

- Outstanding interpersonal skills including the ability to effectively communicate with persons throughout the organization including clinicians
- Excellent verbal and written communication skills
- Experience with Centers for Medicare & Medicaid Services (CMS) Conditions of Participation for acute care hospitals and CMS survey processes
- In-depth knowledge of external clinical quality reporting requirements
- Current knowledge of The Joint Commission, state, and federal guidelines, regulations, and standards
- Experience in coordinating, preparing, and participating in state, The Joint Commission, and CMS surveys within past 3 years
- Current statistical knowledge and skill in developing statistical data displays
- Experience in the use of statistical and quality software
- Ability to analyze and resolve complex issues

COMPENSATION

The median salary for a CCO is $110,000. The range of salaries earned is $96,000 to $231,000, although, with incentives and bonus pay added on, the salary can be as much as $300,000.

EMPLOYMENT OUTLOOK

The employment outlook for CCOs in large hospital settings is generally good. Smaller hospitals typically cannot afford a CCO, and that responsibility is distributed among other staff members.

FOR FURTHER INFORMATION

■ Health Care Compliance Association (http://www.hcca-info.org)

2

CHIEF EXECUTIVE OFFICER

JOB DESCRIPTION

As a member of the hospital's senior management team, the chief executive officer (CEO) will participate in operational decision-making processes necessary for the successful attainment of the hospital's mission in addition to maintaining an awareness of changes in healthcare matters that could have an impact on the success of the hospital. The CEO works with system management to develop and implement policies and procedures, short- and long-range goals, objectives, and plans. He or she provides leadership to hospital managers, directors, and officers who will enroll support, create ownership of goals, and encourage active participation in decisions that impact the hospital. The CEO develops and maintains positive relations with the community in which the hospital is located, as well as the community leaders.

EDUCATION AND EXPERIENCE

- A master's degree in hospital administration and / or business administration
- A minimum of 5 years of demonstrated successful leadership in a healthcare facility, which includes, but is not limited to, building relationships with board members, physicians, hospital employees, and community; growing hospital revenue to meet budgetary goals and objectives; and meeting necessary regulatory and compliance approvals and quality accreditations

CORE COMPETENCIES AND SKILLS

- Ability to develop a long-range course of action or set of goals to ensure successful realization of the organization's vision
- Ability to establish clear goals that align a unit's efforts with the organization's vision
- Ability to synergize between people, processes, and strategies to drive execution of business objectives
- Ability to build a competitively superior organization by attracting, developing, and retaining talent to ensure that people with the right skills and motivations are in the right place at the right time to meet business needs
- Ability to build and drive sustained revenue growth
- Ability to build strategic alliances outside the organization to create business opportunities and execute business strategies
- Ability to develop an organizational culture that leads to ongoing excellence and effective growth of the business while maintaining the highest integrity

■ Ability to ensure that affordable healthcare is provided by the acquisition, utilization, and organization of human, financial, and physical resources, and develop improved techniques and practices

■ Ability to organize hospital functions through delegation of duties, appropriate departmentalization, and maintaining accountability from managers

■ Relevant knowledge to recommend on hospital policy positions to the governing board regarding legislation, government, administrative policy and other public policies

■ Relevant knowledge to recommend personnel policies to support patient care, and ensure that accurate and complete personnel records are maintained

■ Ability to review and act on inspecting agencies' reports

■ Financial skills to prepare annual budget including internal financial controls

■ Effective communication and public relation skills to integrate the hospital with the community

■ Ability to maintain professional affiliations to enhance professional growth and remain current with the latest trends in hospital administration

■ Proven leader, strong work ethic, strategist/visionary, strong interpersonal skills, team builder

■ Ability to build physician/provider, employee, and community relationships

■ Strong financial knowledge

■ Experience and knowledge in quality initiatives

COMPENSATION

The average salary for hospital CEOs is just over $400,000, although, at the top end, the base salary can exceed $5 million per year. This figure varies depending on the size of the hospital and the region in which the hospital is located. CEOs of smaller hospitals located in rural communities tend to earn less than their contemporaries in large, urban hospitals.

EMPLOYMENT OUTLOOK

The overall outlook for hospital CEO jobs is expected to slowly decline over the next several years. The reason for this is found in the reduction of the number of acute care hospitals in the United States. There continues to be a number of hospitals that are closing in rural communities, and urban hospitals that are either merging with competitors or closing altogether. The average acute care hospital CEO remains in the position for approximately 5 years so there is a regular turnover of persons in these positions.

FOR FURTHER INFORMATION

■ Visit local universities offering the Master of Health Administration (MHA) degree or equivalent. A list of these university-based programs can be found at the Association of University Programs in Health Administration (www .aupha.org)

■ American College of Healthcare Executives (www.ache.org)
■ Department of Labor, Bureau of Labor Statistics (https://www.bls.gov/ooh/management/medical-and-health-services-managers.htm)

 NAME: DEBORAH ADDO

Title: Chief Executive Officer, Senior Vice President
Organization: Inova Loudoun Hospital, Inova Health System

1. Briefly describe your job responsibilities.

- Serve as top administrator for the organization
- Determine and formulate policies and provide overall direction
- Deliver the highest quality of patient care
- Lead while creating a positive and productive culture
- Set and follow standards for operational excellence
- Hire and retain qualified staff
- Implement clinical procedures and policies
- Safeguard required compliance with state, federal, and Centers for Medicare & Medicaid Services (CMS) regulations as well as hospital policies
- Develop a relationship with outside organizations, including the medical community, referring physicians, and the media
- Deliver strong financial performance

2. What would you consider to be a "typical" day for you?

- Early morning safety huddle with key leaders
- Rounding in various service areas
- Meetings with leaders, staff, board, or community
- Lunch with physicians, donors, or community leaders
- Coaching and developing leaders
- Phone calls
- E-mails
- Planning and preparing for both short-range and long-range initiatives
- Networking

3. What education or training do you have? Is it typical for your job?

- Bachelor of Arts in Psychology
- Master of Public Health (MPH)

Continued

NAME: DEBORAH ADDO Continued

Yes, most hospital CEOs have a master's degree of some kind. It may be a Master of Health Administration (MHA), Master of Business Administration (MBA), MPH, and so on. I chose public health because it helped me to bridge both the acute care experiences with those of the rest of the human experiences, which include environment, demographics, beliefs, norms, and so forth. Our health is a result of so many things, and public health helped to provide that context for me.

4. What is the most challenging part of your job?

Motivating and encouraging young people to continue to come into the field. There are so many options for jobs and opportunities that candidates sometime feel what we have to offer in healthcare is not as glitzy as some other line of work. We need to continue to make our work relevant and appealing to the limited job pool.

5. What do you consider to be the best part of your job?

What we do absolutely makes a difference. We are a conduit to health and healing. We are fortunate enough to be there at the beginning of life for some, as well as at the end of life for many. We have the ability to help shape and influence the quality of life for those we serve. For me, what we are blessed to do is a mission, a calling, and a privilege. I have never regretted choosing healthcare.

6. What path did you take to get to the job you are in today?

I worked in hospitals even when I was in college, and just worked my way up. As an employee, I looked for opportunities to grow and contribute. I volunteered for new initiatives and hard tasks. I watched what others did, who were in leadership positions, and learned from their successes and mistakes. Whenever I was promoted, I always looked for ways to expand the role or scope to meet an unmet need. Once I was given the opportunity, I made sure that my team performed with excellence. Hiring the right people; setting the appropriate goals; mentoring and developing and surrounding myself with the right people all contributed to my success.

I began as a unit manager for support services. My path from there consisted of roles of assistant director for support services; director of support services; continuous quality improvement (CQI) director; executive for reengineering; director for care management; executive for health management; vice president (VP) for patient care services;

Continued

NAME: DEBORAH ADDO Continued

chief operating officer (COO); and CEO. Along the way, I also studied to become a licensed minister and now serve as an associate minister for my church.

7. What advice do you have for someone who is interested in a job such as yours?

- Examine your motives about why you want to be a CEO in healthcare. It will help to sustain you during the tough times.
- Don't be afraid to let people know along the way that you want to be a CEO. While some may doubt or put up barriers, many will help you along the way.
- In every role that you are in, operate, perform, and carry yourself as if you are at the next level. People need to be able to envision you in the level you are aiming for before you get there.
- Study and learn about the field. It is always changing and you can always improve.
- Surround yourself with strong performers. When they succeed, you succeed.

NAME: **CHRISTINE CANDIO**

Title: President and Chief Executive Officer
Organization: St. Luke's Hospital

1. Briefly describe your job responsibilities.

My responsibilities are to lead, direct, and ensure our operations and overall health ministry are consistent with our mission, philosophy, and objectives in serving our patients, community, and team members with safety and the highest quality of care.

2. What would you consider to be a "typical" day for you?

Although no 2 days are the same, there are important responsibilities and oversight that I strive to ensure is part of my typical day. These include rounding on the inpatient units and departments throughout the hospital, as well as visiting all of our off-site locations on a regular basis; meeting with senior staff, whether as a formal group for strategic or operational matters, and/or individually for functional responsibilities; employee and physician relations, community and legislative relations (local and state); and quality and financial measures, program development, system strategic initiatives.

3. What education or training do you have? Is it typical for your job?

I hold a Bachelor of Science in Nursing and a master's degree in public health administration with a concentration in healthcare management. The industry, in general, has seen an increased number of individuals with clinical backgrounds, especially physicians, obtaining postgraduate degrees in healthcare and/or business management programs.

4. What is the most challenging part of your job?

Today, the healthcare industry is presented with many challenges. Primary among these is the delicate balancing of maintaining high-quality

Continued

NAME: CHRISTINE CANDIO Continued

affordable healthcare services to meet patient and community needs in an environment of rising healthcare costs, decreased reimbursement to providers, the looming question of insurance coverage for all, in light of our changing administration, and an aging population. The impact is significant to all concerned, that is, patients, community, healthcare facilities, and physicians. As such, CEOs must face these challenges as opportunities in the reevaluation of our strategic vision, while remaining nimble and ready to adjust/course-correct on the basis of patients/community needs.

5. What do you consider to be the best part of your job?

The best part of my job is providing a helping/guiding hand in creating the type of services and environment expected of us from our patients, community, and team members. Chief among this is interacting with our patients, families, and working with staff and physicians to ensure positive experiences to all whom we serve.

6. What path did you take to get to the job you are in today?

I began my healthcare career as an RN at the bedside. Management was always of great interest to me. I realized that in order to progress on my career path, as well as my desire to continue my education, it was necessary to obtain a master's degree. Over the course of several years, I held progressive leadership positions: manager of ambulatory services; administrative director of women's & children's services; system director of women's & children's services; vice president patient services/chief nurse executive; executive vice president; president and CEO.

7. What advice do you have for someone who is interested in a job such as yours?

It is very important to have focus and a true passion for the profession. Always keep the patient at the center of everything you do. Embrace ongoing education and lifelong learning. Our professional association, the American College of Healthcare Executives, is the premier organization to assist us in our ongoing educational journey.

CHIEF FINANCIAL OFFICER

JOB DESCRIPTION

The chief financial officer (CFO) is responsible for the operational and financial performance of assigned communities. He or she is responsible for the development of an effective operational referral network in surrounding counties and areas in support of the Hospital Services critical access objectives, and ensure safe, evidence-based, compassionate care for patients. General responsibilities include the development of relationships with providers and facilities within the Hospital Services for the purposes of potential collaboration and/or shared services. Responsibilities also include planning/directing and the delivery of services consistent with strategic plans, providing leadership for the development of health-care services, promoting physician and community relationships, and promoting management/employee behaviors that contribute to the achievement of the goals and objectives of the hospital. The CFO: ensures that clinical support services are coordinated across staff, functions, and activities in order to improve patient care and clinical outcomes; leads the operations and maintains accountability for the overall administration and management of providing efficient, high-quality, patient-/family-focused care; leads in the development of Hospital Services as state and national leaders of quality and safety standards for Critical Access Hospitals.

EDUCATION AND EXPERIENCE

- Certification as a public accountant is required, preferred master's degree (or equivalent years of experience) from an accredited college or university
- Previous CFO level, or equivalent experience, within an acute care environment required
- Previous experience with a proprietary healthcare system highly preferred
- Minimum 5 years' financial/accounting progressive managerial experience in acute care environment

CORE COMPETENCIES AND SKILLS

- Ability to monitor hospital performance with all financial performance ratios such as day's cash on hand, accounts receivable (AR) days, full time equivalents (FTE) ratios, and so forth
- Ability to coordinate Medicare and Medicaid cost reports with cost report consultant
- Ability to coordinate with auditors and financial consultants

- Relevant knowledge to serve as a resource to the Pension Committee and Finance Committee
- Relevant skill to develop new revenue sources and financial proforma of services to include a business plan
- Ability to assist departmental managers with financial performance of their departments
- Ability to establish and implement a process to develop the annual operating and capital budgets
- Ability to assist in the development of the hospital's strategic plan and explain financial trend analysis
- Experience handling overall financial operations of the acute care facility including accounting, budgetary, audits, tax, and other financial planning activities within the hospital organization; including management of respective departmental heads
- Experience working with system management to develop and implement policies and procedures, short- and long-range goals, objectives, and plans
- Ability to provide financial leadership to hospital managers, directors, and officers that will enroll support, create ownership of goals, and encourage active participation in decisions that impact the hospital
- Ability to ensure the hospital meets necessary financial regulatory and compliance requirements
- Financial expertise in the planning of new services that generate additional sources of profitable revenue
- Expertise in managing costs by continually seeking data that will identify opportunities, and take action to eliminate nonvalue costs in conjunction with the hospital's chief executive officer and chief nursing officer
- Ability to represent the hospital at meetings including medical staff, hospital board of director meetings, as well as relevant community meetings as needed
- Ability to participate in the hospital's monthly operation reviews as well as participate in corporate office meetings as deemed necessary
- Ability to build a culture of fiscal responsibility and accountability, including developing and implementing rigorous budget planning and monitoring processes across all departments; develop the operational infrastructure for effective fiscal management
- Expertise to ensure smooth functioning of all operating departments in the finance division: revenue cycle, financial planning/budget, general accounting, payroll, accounts payable, patient registration, financial counseling, inpatient accounts, business office, investigations, managed care office, internal audits, admitting and contract management control/audit
- Ability to develop long-range financial forecasts built on a sound operating model and provide adequate funding for meeting long-term capital needs; hold lead responsibility for budget planning and reporting at the system level, working very closely in preparing for board of director meetings

- Ability to serve as chief advisor to the president on matters of budget, strategy, and financial planning; participate with senior leadership team on a range of issues relating to day-to-day management of the system
- Ability to develop effective tools for institutional analysis and research, including serving as a leader and resource for scenario planning for various internal departments and optimizing efficiency with limited resources
- Ability to lead continuous efforts to maximize the hospital's financial status, such as developing and planning initiatives that create operating efficiencies, improve revenue cycle performance, and build greater business volumes for the hospital
- Ability to actively seek out new and strategic opportunities to enhance revenues, including working with internal and external partners to institute new programs; directly oversee capital expenditure projects
- Ability to oversee internal audit function and direct audit activities, creating an annual audit plan to do the same
- Ability to oversee compliance with federal, state, and local governmental agency laws and regulations and compliance to the standards, rules, and regulations of various accrediting and approving bodies
- Must be proficient in written and verbal communication skills
- Ability to establish and maintain effective working relationships with hospital staff and community
- Ability to maintain confidential information concerning personal, financial, or medical matters

COMPENSATION

The average salary for hospital CFOs is $106,000 per year. This figure varies depending on the size of the hospital and the region in which the hospital is located. CFOs of smaller hospitals located in rural communities tend to earn less than their contemporaries in large, urban hospitals.

EMPLOYMENT OUTLOOK

The overall outlook for hospital CFO jobs is expected to slowly decline over the next several years. The reason for this is found in the reduction of the number of acute care hospitals in the United States. There continue to be a number of hospitals that are closing in rural communities and urban hospitals that are either merging with competitors or closing altogether. The average acute care hospital CFO remains in the position for approximately 5 years so there is a regular turnover of persons in these positions.

FOR FURTHER INFORMATION

- Healthcare Financial Management Association (www.hfma.org)
- Department of Labor, Bureau of Labor Statistics (https://www.bls.gov/ooh/management/financial-managers.htm)

CHIEF INFORMATION OFFICER

4

JOB DESCRIPTION

The chief information officer (CIO) provides technology vision and leadership in the development and implementation of the hospital-wide information technology (IT) program. The CIO will lead the organization in planning and implementing enterprise information systems to support both distributed and centralized clinical and business operations, and achieve more effective and cost-beneficial enterprise-wide IT operations. Additionally, the CIO's responsibilities are the following:

- Provides strategic and tactical planning, development, evaluation, and coordination of the information and technology systems for the hospital
- Facilitates communication between staff, management, vendors, and other technology resources within the organization
- Oversees the back-office computer operations of the affiliate management information system, including local area networks and wide-area networks
- Manages multiple information and communications systems and projects, including voice, data, imaging, and office automation
- Designs, implements, and evaluates the systems that support end users in the productive use of computer hardware and software
- Develops and implements user training programs
- Oversees and evaluates system security and back-up procedures; supervises the network administrator

EDUCATION AND EXPERIENCE

Most acute care hospitals' CIOs require a bachelor's degree in computer science, business administration, or a related field or equivalent experience. A master's degree in health/hospital administration, public health, or business administration, or related field, is highly desirable. A minimum of 3 years of experience with increasing responsibilities for management and support of healthcare information systems and information technology and direct management of a major IT operation are preferred. Significant experience in a healthcare setting is desirable, specifically in technology and information systems planning to support business goals.

CORE COMPETENCIES AND SKILLS

- Outstanding interpersonal skills including the ability to effectively communicate with persons throughout the organization including clinicians

- Excellent verbal and written communication skills
- Significant experience in data-processing methods and procedures, and computer software systems
- Knowledge of systems design and development process, including requirements analysis, feasibility studies, software design, programming, pilot testing, installation, evaluation, and operational management
- Ability to oversee the management and coordination of all fiscal-reporting activities for the hospital
- Familiarity with the design, management, and operation of health IT systems
- Proven ability to link and apply complex technologies to business strategies
- Experience in negotiating contracts with vendors, contractors, and others
- Ability to analyze and resolve complex issues, both logical and interpersonal

COMPENSATION

Most hospital based CIOs earn salaries in the range of $125,000 to $310,000 per year. However, this figure varies depending on a number of variables including the size of the hospital and the region of the country in which the hospital is located. CIOs of smaller hospitals in more rural areas tend to earn less than their counterparts at large, urban hospitals.

EMPLOYMENT OUTLOOK

The overall outlook for hospital CIO jobs is expected to increase over the coming years. The reason for the increase is due to the need for hospitals to make health technology an increasing part of clinical and administrative operations. There remains a number of federal financial and regulatory incentives to vigorously move into health IT. CIO is a relatively new occupation, and it is difficult to assess turnover, but anecdotal reports indicate that CIOs turn over at a brisk pace to accept roles with increasing salary and responsibility.

FOR FURTHER INFORMATION

- Visit local universities offering the Master of Health Administration (MHA) degree or equivalent, particularly those that offer concentrations in health IT (www.aupha.org)
- Health Information Management System Society (www.himss.org)
- Department of Labor, Bureau of Labor Statistics (https://www.bls.gov/ooh/management/computer-and-information-systems-managers.htm)

CHIEF LEARNING OFFICER

JOB DESCRIPTION

The chief learning officer (CLO) is a comparatively new position in hospitals. The goal of the CLO is to help facilitate and accelerate learning throughout the organization. The CLO directs the organization's educational, training, and development programs to empower staff and ensure their maximum effectiveness and contribution to meeting organizational goals. As part of the senior leadership team, the CLO will perform the following:

- Partner with organizational leaders to identify needs for training and organizational development; will develop and implement new trainings as needed
- Advise senior leadership regarding initiatives and activities that promote maximum staff effectiveness and create a positive impact on service quality
- Develop and evaluate employee development programs, and ensure that programs have a beneficial impact on service delivery
- Plan, launch, monitor, and act on long-range learning initiatives that are aligned with the organization's strategic goals
- Design and establish benchmarks that measure the impact and effectiveness of organizational development programs on the organization's overall performance
- Forge relationships with internal and external stakeholders, including but not limited to, universities/colleges, public schools, and governmental entities

EDUCATION AND EXPERIENCE

Hospital-based CLOs require a master's degree, a doctoral degree preferred, in education, organizational development, human resources, or comparable fields of study, and a minimum of 5 years of leadership experience, preferably in the areas of human resources management, academic and/or professional development, or comparable areas.

CORE COMPETENCIES AND SKILLS

- A minimum of 10 years' progressive experience in adult learning and e-learning
- A minimum of 5 of the 10 years in a strategic leadership role
- Experience with accreditation and certification organizational criteria, policies, standards, and processes

- Data-driven, systems thinking to generate and execute ideas at strategic and tactical levels
- Ability to thrive in a fast-paced environment, integrating disparate activities, new technologies, and agendas while adhering to deadlines and budgets
- Instinctive collaborator with strong staff management experience who values teamwork and the input of others
- Creative visionary with a passion for learning and professional development, and the ability to clearly articulate ideas and concepts
- Strong analytical and problem-solving skills, with the ability to understand the big picture
- Strong computer skills including Microsoft Office applications; Internet and technology savvy

COMPENSATION

Most hospital-based CLOs earn salaries in the range of $150,000 to $300,000 per year.

EMPLOYMENT OUTLOOK

The overall outlook for hospital CLO jobs is expected to increase over the coming years. The reason for the increase is due to need for hospitals and health systems to develop the capacity to create learning organizations that can respond effectively to continuous environmental change.

FOR FURTHER INFORMATION

- Visit local universities offering the Master of Health Administration (MHA) degree or equivalent, particularly those that offer concentrations or courses in organizational learning (www.aupha.org)
- American College of Healthcare Executives (www.ache.org)
- Department of Labor, Bureau of Labor Statistics (https://www.bls.gov/ooh/management/medical-and-health-services-managers.htm)

6

JOB DESCRIPTION

The chief medical information officer (CMIO) is a new position in hospitals. The goal of the CMIO is to help facilitate and accelerate the clinical use of information technology throughout the organization, and serve as the bridge between the clinical staff and information technology department. The CMIO directs the effective use and implementation of information technology, particularly as it applies to physicians, nurses, and other clinical staff. As part of the senior leadership team, the CMIO will do the following:

- Serve as a liaison between medical and technical departments and executive leadership
- Head studies for the design and integration of IT systems and infrastructure in the medical department
- Study trends in health informatics to develop applications that increase efficiency in patient care
- Develop standards and "rules" in medical terminology and application to increase efficiency in patient care
- Advise steering committees on subject of health informatics and policymaking within the organization

EDUCATION AND EXPERIENCE

Hospital-based CMIOs generally require an MD degree, although some smaller hospitals might employ an advanced practice nurse in this role. It is also expected that the CMIO have experience in medical informatics.

CORE COMPETENCIES AND SKILLS

- Outstanding interpersonal skills including the ability to effectively communicate with persons throughout the organization including clinicians
- Excellent verbal and written communication skills
- Knowledge of the process and tools for capturing, organizing, and using individual and departmental intellectual assets, such as competencies, best practices, and so on
- Ability to work collaboratively to create meaningful use of health information technology
- Familiarity with the legal and regulatory elements of health information technology

■ Outstanding project management skills
■ Ability to educate and influence other clinicians around the adoption of health information technology
■ Familiarity with the full spectrum of electronic medical records systems
■ Ability to analyze and resolve complex issues

COMPENSATION

CMIOs earn in the range of $50,000 to $400,000, although many of these persons do continue to practice medicine. Small hospitals would typically not be able to employ a CMIO so these positions would be expected to be found at large, urban hospitals or academic health centers.

EMPLOYMENT OUTLOOK

A growing number of hospitals are expanding their traditional information systems roles to include persons whose primary training and experience is in medicine or nursing. Most traditionally trained chief information officers do not have the clinical expertise that makes the CMIO role particularly important as healthcare organizations grow and develop their IT infrastructure.

FOR FURTHER INFORMATION

■ Health Information Management Systems Society (www.himss.org)
■ Chief Medical Information Officer (www.cmio.net)

JOB DESCRIPTION

The chief medical officer's (CMO's) responsibilities include promoting concepts and practice of quality improvement; establishing and maintaining effective working relationships with medical staff; participating in reviews of qualifications, credentials, performance, and professional competence and character of medical staff applicants and members; working within the appropriate facility or operational leadership model (chief executive/nursing/medical officer or chief of medical staff) to establish, monitor, and improve aggregate clinical outcomes.

EDUCATION AND EXPERIENCE

The majority of acute care hospital CMOs possess a medical doctorate or doctor of osteopathy degree. They possess board certification or qualification and level of expertise typically gained through 5 years' experience in clinical practice; they must be eligible for or hold a current state license to practice medicine; and they must be eligible for medical staff privileges. Persons in this capacity typically have 3 years of medical staff leadership experience.

CORE COMPETENCIES AND SKILLS

- Proven track record of partnering with medical staff to achieve desired facility-specific and organizational outcomes
- Knowledge of modern national trends in hospital technology, quality, and patient safety
- Skilled in effectively handling multiple conflicting assignments, demands, and priorities
- Skilled in influencing physician behaviors; partnering and problem solving with physicians and administrative leaders within multiple clinical areas and among members of the medical staff; navigating a highly matrixed organizational structure with skill and efficiency; analyzing complex financial/statistical data; maintaining a high level of organization with strong attention to detail in order to respond quickly to varying situations
- Proven experience implementing a continuous improvement culture

COMPENSATION

Most hospital CMOs earn between $326,000 and $434,000 per year. However, this figure varies depending on a number of variables including the size of the hospital and the region of the country in which the hospital is located. CMOs of smaller hospitals in more rural areas tend to earn less than their counterparts at large, urban hospitals.

EMPLOYMENT OUTLOOK

Job opportunities for CMOs will continue to soar through 2020. Greater demand for CMOs will focus on improving physician relationships, coupled with quality improvement, patient safety, cost controls, changing reimbursement strategies, and meeting the needs of patients as a result of population health measures.

FOR FURTHER INFORMATION

- Department of Labor, Bureau of Labor Statistics (https://www.bls.gov/ooh/management/medical-and-health-services-managers.htm)

 NAME: AMIT POWAR

Title: Chief Executive Officer (CEO)
Organization: Reading Health Physician
Network (RHPN)

1. Briefly describe your job responsibilities.

- Direct, lead, and manage all aspects of the physician enterprise
- Responsible for the quality and service delivery of care for patients
- Oversee and manage the fiscal and operational aspects of RHPN
- Accountable for the short- and long-term strategy and tactical plans

RHPN has over 500 providers, 60 locations, 900,000 visits annually, and over $300 million in gross revenues.

2. What would you consider to be a "typical" day for you?

- Breakfast at 7 a.m. with an RHPN doctor, or group of doctors, to learn about ongoing challenges, opportunities, and so on (if I am not meeting with one of my own doctors, I am likely meeting a doctor who is perhaps interested in joining us or I am meeting a colleague/competitor from the local or regional market).
- Review calendar for the day and the next with my assistant
- Meeting with my management team
- Review of daily, weekly, and monthly dashboard for RHPN
- Spend time reviewing news articles of interest
- Attend meetings that require decision making, strategy considerations, and tactics deployment
- Site visit to an RHPN location (once a week at least)
- Random call to an RHPN physician or staff member
- Dinner meetings (once or twice a week) with doctors discussing new initiatives, ideas, and so on

Continued

NAME: AMIT POWAR Continued

3. **What education or training do you have? Is it typical for your job?**

   ■ I am by training an obstetrician and gynecologist, and I received my Master of Health Administration (MHA) from the George Washington University.

   ■ Given that the role is of the CEO of a physician enterprise, I'd say a clinical degree/background with management education is typical. However, there are many instances of those who are in a similar role without the typical background and experience. As long as you can build relationships, surround yourself with smart people, and motivate and lead a group, your skills are transferable.

4. **What is the most challenging part of your job?**

   ■ Prioritization. With so many competing priorities, it is quite a challenge to continually make decisions and solve problems that are most pressing and time sensitive.

5. **What do you consider to be the best part of your job?**

   ■ Walking away every day from work and feeling decisions made would positively impact the delivery of care.

6. **What path did you take to get to the job you are in today?**

   ■ The path I took may seem quite atypical, but I think it provided me with the right experience and learnings to lead and manage.

   ■ I started as a Six Sigma black belt manager and worked on many process improvement projects. This experience enabled me to learn quickly about many areas in the hospital, work with many different individuals, and learn how to rally a group of people from different areas to work on improving a process.

   ■ In my next role as the associate executive director of ancillary and support services, I oversaw and managed all ancillary and support areas in a hospital. This experience provided me with an in-depth understanding of how nonclinical and ancillary areas support the clinical side of healthcare.

   ■ Following this experience, I worked at the corporate office of a large health system with the CEO and chief operating officer (COO) as the senior director of health system operations, and

Continued

NAME: AMIT POWAR Continued

gained experience in strategy and tactics. I learned the importance of being patient and the ability to look long term.

■ Next, I worked in the ambulatory and physician enterprise side of the organization as the senior director of ambulatory operations, and learned about ambulatory and physician operations. Given the movement of healthcare from inpatient to ambulatory, this was a timely move.

■ Following this, I spent some time on the community and public health side as the vice president of community and public health of the enterprise as we were preparing for and putting a structure around population health and the launch of an insurance company.

■ Thereafter, I started focusing on building a network of aligned organizations for the health system in the role of vice president of affiliated network and regional operations.

■ Last but not the least, I moved into my current role as CEO of RHPN.

7. What advice do you have for someone who is interested in a job such as yours?

■ Building and managing relationships, excellent interpersonal skills, communicating clearly and concisely in a consistent manner, ability to adapt and change, willingness to make tough decisions and take risks, being able to look long term and create strategy, but also apply tactical steps to make day-to-day progress.

8   CHIEF NURSING OFFICER

JOB DESCRIPTION

The chief nursing officer's (CNO's) primary responsibility is to provide leadership and guidance around quality patient care and other patient care services delivered in the hospital. As part of the senior leadership team, the CNO will perform the following:

- Assume ultimate administrative responsibility for nursing standards and practice regardless of the practice area or reporting relationship of the nurse
- Direct hospital nursing activities within the context of hospital policies and procedures
- Ensure continuous and timely nursing services to patients
- Ensure nursing standards, practices, policies, and procedures, in accordance with all applicable laws as well as regulatory and accreditation requirements, are consistent with current research findings and national professional standards
- Direct nursing service performance improvement activities
- Actively participate in hospital leadership functions
- Collaborate with hospital leaders to design and provide patient care and services, including availability of sufficient, qualified nursing staff
- Develop, present, and manage budgets for nursing services

EDUCATION AND EXPERIENCE

Bachelor's degree in nursing and a current RN license are the minimum clinical training required, although, in most cases, a master's degree in nursing, a Master of Business Administration (MBA), Master of Health Administration (MHA), or related master's degree is preferred. A minimum of 3 to 5 years' experience at the CNO level is desired.

CORE COMPETENCIES AND SKILLS

- Outstanding interpersonal skills including the ability to effectively communicate with persons throughout the organization including clinicians
- Excellent verbal and written communication skills
- Outstanding physician relationship skills
- In-depth knowledge of external clinical quality reporting requirements
- Current knowledge of The Joint Commission, state and federal guidelines, regulations, and standards

- Demonstrated expertise in negotiation, coaching, and interpersonal skills
- Ability to develop, implement, and administer nursing services budget and expense control system
- Ability to prepare master nursing services staffing plan
- Ability to analyze and resolve complex issues
- Ability to recruit, interview, evaluate, and hire qualified personnel to meet patients' needs

COMPENSATION

CNOs earn in the range of $85,000 to $192,000, although the salary will vary depending on the size, location, and complexity of the hospital.

EMPLOYMENT OUTLOOK

Every hospital in the nation requires a CNO, and jobs in nursing administration are likely to keep pace with the overall growth of hospitals.

FOR FURTHER INFORMATION

- Bureau of Labor Statistics (https://www.bls.gov/ooh/management/medical-and-health-services-managers.htm)
- American Organization of Nurse Executives (www.aone.org)

NAME: MEGHAN YEAGER

Title: Clinical Nurse/Claims Administrator
Organization: Yale New Haven Hospital/Yale New Haven Health System

1. Briefly describe your job responsibilities.

Clinical nurse—ortho/trauma
As a core member of the care delivery team, my role as a clinical nurse on the orthopedics trauma unit involves collaborating with the multidisciplinary team to facilitate coordination of patient care. Through utilization of the nursing process, the clinical nurse diagnoses and treats patient and family responses to actual or potential health problems. I use the nursing process of assessment, planning, intervention, and evaluation while caring for my patients, maintaining confidentiality and dignity.

Claims administrator—Legal and Risk Services Department
As the claims administrator, I am responsible for the investigation of general and professional liability claims. I monitor compliance with certain litigation procedures and regulatory requirements related to malpractice claims. I also manage the administration of the legal hold process and support the team in response to subpoenas. In addition to other insurance administrative assignments, I participate in risk mitigation projects in collaboration with quality improvement and patient safety nurses.

2. What would you consider to be a "typical" day for you?

Clinical nurse—ortho/trauma
As a clinical nurse, my day always begins with a safety huddle. The charge nurse leads the huddle and highlights the unit census, high-risk patients, those heading to the operation room (OR) and patients on bed alarms and at risk for falls, those with pressure ulcers/drains/telemetry/drips, and so forth. Following huddle, we begin our bedside report where the nurses and patient/family are involved in the handoff of care. Following report, I begin my assessments and medication administration. About 1.5 hours into the shift, the team meets again for discharge rounds which include care management, nurse management, physical/

Continued

NAME: MEGHAN YEAGER Continued

occupational therapists, and the nurses to discuss discharge plans for the shift. Following discharge rounds, I continue my patient care duties. I am constantly rounding between patients, assessing pain, reviewing telemetry monitors, repositioning patients, and completing scheduled neurological checks. My 12-hour shift ends with another huddle, followed by the bedside handoff.

Claims administrator—Legal and Risk Services Department
Doesn't everyone's day begin with their phones? Voicemails and e-mails are the start of my claims administration day! Claims come into our hospitals/physician offices/corporate offices via mail, e-mail, or our most favorite way—personally served by a marshal. The claims are logged and distributed to the litigation team. Another nurse or I review the claim, write a summary including alleged damages, and then assign each claim to an internal attorney, nurse administrator, and a legal secretary. After assignment, the claims investigation process begins. This incorporates gathering a variety of information such as medical records and films, sequestering pathology specimen, obtaining incident/security reports, patient relations files, policies/procedures, contacting witnesses, notifying departmental chairs/administration, and establishing legal holds in collaboration with IT. The litigation team then meets to develop a plan and discuss strategies including hiring expert clinicians to review the medical care, hiring outside counsel for defense in a filed suit, and establishing case reserves. Whether we are reviewing medical records, answering discovery responses, meeting with witnesses, or reviewing coverage and financial issues, there is always something to do. The "typical day" involves a lot of moving parts as cases are all in various stages of development, and, of course, these cases last for years. When I'm not handling claim-related activities, I am involved in risk mitigation projects including root cause analysis, and sentinel event review committees in collaboration with quality improvement and patient safety nurses.

3. What education or training do you have? Is it typical for your job?

I obtained a Bachelor of Science in Business Administration (BSBA) in entrepreneurship and a minor in natural sciences (premedicine). I went straight to graduate school and obtained my Master of Health Science Administration (MHSA) in the quest to be a hospital administrator. While I was completing my administrative fellowship, I realized how helpful it would be to understand clinical medicine, and decided to pursue nursing school at night. I obtained my Associate of Science in Nursing (ASN), and began working as a clinical nurse in combination with my legal and

Continued

risk services position. As we are a Magnet® hospital, I am back in school working on my Master of Science in Nursing (MSN).

Certainly a clinical nursing position requires a nursing degree and license. As it relates to the claims administrative position, I definitely have advanced education that is not necessarily required. However, my education brings a unique perspective and an elevated level of experience to the team.

4. What is the most challenging part of your job?

The most challenging part of nursing is balancing these complex illnesses and high-acuity patients while trying to keep up with documentation. We love charting! In addition to documentation, I'd say adjusting staffing according to a fluctuating census is a challenge.

The most challenging part of claims administration is navigating a very large health system to identify witnesses, and gather applicable records/policies/procedures from an alleged event that may have occurred years prior. Plus, when employees hear "legal department" they want to run in the other direction!

5. What do you consider to be the best part of your job?

The best parts of nursing are the interactions with patients/families, and the bonds that are formed while taking care of a person during his or her most vulnerable time. It is very satisfying to be part of a team that is passionate about healing and works to ensure that our patients, families, and communities we serve benefit from the very best healthcare.

The best part of being the claims administrator is the people I interact with and the variety of cases and experiences I encounter on a daily basis. While most people want to run far away from litigation, working with the team to identify risk exposure, reduce adverse events, and increase patient safety allows us to work toward fulfilling our mission and taking care of the patients we are privileged to serve.

6. What path did you take to get to the job you are in today?

After grad school, I completed an administrative fellowship, which revolved around a lot of risk management/quality improvement–related projects. Though I really didn't like my legal classes in grad school, and never had a desire to attend law school, my mentor (a healthcare system general counsel) opened new doors to this risk/legal part of healthcare.

Continued

NAME: MEGHAN YEAGER Continued

She offered me my first "real job" as a risk manager for a large community teaching hospital. I quickly realized that having some clinical experience would be beneficial to many areas in hospital administration, so I pursued a nursing degree. Though completely unexpected, I ended up being able to blend both positions by working as a clinical nurse while also working as a claims administrator.

7. What advice do you have for someone who is interested in a job such as yours?

The best piece of advice is to not be afraid to take chances. Find a mentor—someone you admire, who will support you and push you outside your comfort zone. You never know what doors will open, and if they do, take the risk, it's worth it.

CHIEF OPERATING OFFICER

JOB DESCRIPTION

The chief operating officer (COO) assumes line responsibility and authority for the administrative direction, evaluation, and coordination of the functions and activities of assigned departments within the hospital organization to ensure operation objectives and results are in accordance with overall hospital needs. In the absence of the hospital chief executive officer (CEO), the COO represents the CEO in the coordination of entire portions of the hospital organization, speaking and acting within the scope of objectives set forth in the practice and/or policy of the hospital.

EDUCATION AND EXPERIENCE

- A master's degree in hospital administration and/or business administration
- A minimum of 5 years of demonstrated successful leadership in a healthcare facility, which includes, but is not limited to, building relationships with board members, physicians, hospital employees, and community; growing hospital revenue to meet budgetary goals and objectives; and meeting necessary regulatory and compliance approvals and quality accreditations

CORE COMPETENCIES AND SKILLS

- Ability to ensure the consistent and effective execution of key systems and processes that make effective use of organizational resources
- Ability to lead a team or unit to enhance product or service quality; drive the business toward enhanced product or service quality
- Ability to create a work environment in which employees are committed to their organization and feel pride and job ownership
- Ability to build strategic alliances and partnerships within the organization to collaboratively execute business strategies
- Ability to create an environment in which products and processes are designed to ensure customer satisfaction; effectively incorporate customer perspectives in all business activities
- Ability to manage the day-to-day operations in the hospital; assume responsibility for hospital administration in the absence of the senior vice president (SVP) and area manager
- Leadership skills in building a team and an organization that will assume responsibility and accountability for achieving both the mission and financial/operational objectives

- Ability to maintain open channels of communication and foster information sharing
- Ability to ensure the integration of quality, service, and efficiency improvements into day-to-day operations
- Ability to establish clearly defined goals and objectives and ensure follow-through in a timely manner
- Ability to provide leadership and guidance in the development and implementation of ongoing programs to improve performance and manage costs, while improving the quality of patient care delivery
- Ability to achieve/exceed performance expectations throughout the hospital's operations; establish an environment that supports caregivers and enhances growth, communication, and job satisfaction
- With human resources (HR), direct the implementation of integrated HR strategies to ensure quality results in the identification, recruitment, retention, and development of key human resources
- Ability to manage the operating and capital budgets of areas of responsibility
- Ability to aggressively mitigate all variances to budget
- Relevant knowledge to make sound decisions on best use of resources in support of regional priorities and strategies
- Proven leader, strong work ethic, strategist/visionary, strong interpersonal skills, team builder
- Ability to build physician/provider, employee, and community relationships
- Strong financial knowledge
- Experience and knowledge in quality initiatives

COMPENSATION

The average salary for hospital COOs is $285,000 per year. This figure varies depending on the size of the hospital and the region in which the hospital is located. COOs of smaller hospitals located in rural communities tend to earn less than their contemporaries in large, urban hospitals.

EMPLOYMENT OUTLOOK

The overall outlook for hospital COO jobs is expected to slowly decline over the next several years. The reason for this is found in the reduction of the number of acute care hospitals in the United States. There continue to be a number of hospitals that are closing in rural communities and urban hospitals that are either merging with competitors or closing altogether. The average acute care hospital COO remains in the position for approximately 5 years, so there is a regular turnover of persons in these positions.

FOR FURTHER INFORMATION

- Visit local universities offering the Master of Health Administration (MHA) degree or equivalent. A list of these university-based programs can be found at the Association of University Programs in Health Administration (www .aupha.org)

- American College of Healthcare Executives (www.ache.org)
- Department of Labor, Bureau of Labor Statistics (https://www.bls.gov/ooh/management/medical-and-health-services-managers.htm)

 NAME: ANGIE BASS

Title: Chief Operating Officer
Organization: Missouri Health
Connection, a health information
exchange firm

1. Briefly describe your job responsibilities.

The Missouri Health Connection (MHC) is the state of Missouri's largest and most productive health information exchange (HIE), and was given the designation of Missouri's State Designated Entity by the Department of Health and Human Services Office of the National Coordinator (ONC). It is one of the most mature statewide HIEs in the country. Established in 2009, MHC's purpose is to facilitate the safe and secure delivery of medical results and health-related information among healthcare providers, hospitals, public health facilities, and others to improve the quality and efficiency of healthcare services for patients in Missouri and our border states. MHC is a rapidly growing nonprofit organization (501c3) on the forefront of HIE and health information technology.

The chief operating officer (COO) is an executive-level position and is responsible for the coordination of staff and their ability to carry out assignments and tasks. In addition, commercial strategy and development of MHC is also a primary responsibility of the COO. The COO focuses on all strategies and activities relating to marketing, brand development, sales, product development, operational stability, and customer service; ultimately aiming to drive business growth and increase engagement of MHC's customers and stakeholders. The COO reports directly to the chief executive officer (CEO) and is concerned primarily with ensuring the integrated commercial success of MHC. The role combines technical knowledge of the organization and the healthcare industry, with strong marketing and business development skills.

Duties and Responsibilities

- Work with the MHC CEO and board of directors and executive staff to prepare annual departmental- and organizational-level goals, and the mechanisms to benchmark progress against these goals

Continued

NAME: ANGIE BASS Continued

- Perform market analysis to identify opportunities to broaden MHC's reach within Missouri's healthcare community and beyond
- Develop strategies to recruit healthcare providers, data senders, and other industry-relevant vendors to engage with MHC and diversify its membership and product suite
- Own all aspects of the customer relationship through leadership of three key segments: provider relationship management, operational and technical support, and customer service
- Lead a team of relationship managers responsible for representing MHC to healthcare providers and the healthcare community, within Missouri and beyond, including goal setting, training, and overall performance management
- Lead a team of operational technicians to ensure the performance of MHC's results delivery operation is properly monitored and protected, realizing the operational infrastructure of MHC's viability as a dependable, reliable, and stable source of medical information is paramount
- Lead a team of customer support specialists, developing and implementing best practices for addressing customer issues, and collecting information that drives a cycle of continuous improvement
- Serve as one of the public-facing leaders of MHC, protecting the brand reputation of the organization and delivering key messages that serve the broader interests of the organization and the ultimate goal for improving healthcare in the state of Missouri
- Help develop new product roll-out plans, including marketing and training requirements
- Maintain operating policies as necessary to ensure high levels of customer satisfaction among MHC users
- Establish and maintain relationships with key stakeholder organizations to promote MHC and identify new business opportunities
- Conduct all MHC business with the highest levels of customer service, integrity, and professionalism

2. **What would you consider to be a "typical" day for you?**

- Internal meetings: team meetings, project meetings, contractor meetings
- External meetings: industry calls, public relations

Continued

II ■ Healthcare Management Careers

NAME: ANGIE BASS Continued

- Governance: meetings with board members, governmental relations, strategic planning
- Business development: calls, proposals, demonstrations, assessments
- Customer relationship management: meetings/calls with customers, addressing customer needs
- Operations: policy development, compliance audits, staff development/training, product/service development and maintenance

3. What education or training do you have? Is it typical for your job?

Master of Health Administration from University of Missouri, Columbia, December 2006

Bachelor of Science in Business Administration from University of Missouri, Columbia, May 2002

Acceptable background and training for a senior operations-level position could include experience in healthcare administration or operations, health policy, health informatics, electronic health record system training/certifications, information technology, engineering, project management, and compliance/legal operations. There are many different professional tracks that can lead to a senior-level operations position with an HIE.

4. What is the most challenging part of your job?

The HIE industry is dynamic because the ball is always moving currently. The most challenging aspect of my responsibilities is to continually ensure that the HIE's operations and strategic plan are up to date and on target with the ever-changing industry requirements and needs of our members. The sheer number of multithreaded decision points that need to be managed, investigated, and decided upon quickly on a daily basis makes for a challenge and requires organization and an ability to prioritize matters appropriately.

5. What do you consider to be the best part of your job?

Never a dull moment. The work to operate an HIE is notably intense and an incredible amount of work. Working across several technology sectors, you gain experience and knowledge about companies, technology, products/services, and processes, which expands your knowledge base

Continued

NAME: ANGIE BASS Continued

and introduces you to contacts that all result in better outcomes in my ability to carry out my duties more effectively.

Also, I am passionate about using technology to improve patient care. Ultimately, saving a life or making a patient healthier or more comfortable as a result of the of information being made available is one of the most powerful things I can be proud of.

6. What path did you take to get to the job you are in today?

My path started in health policy. With my master's in health administration, I leveraged the policy aspects of that education and training to begin my policy career working in state government and for the state legislature. As a policy analyst, I became several layers of knowledge deep in a vast number of health and public policy topics. As such, when I learned about HIE in my state, I was immediately interested and pursued a job opening as a program manager. Over a few years, I worked my way up to the senior operations leader of the firm.

7. What advice do you have for someone who is interested in a job such as yours?

In order to be successful, you must be nimble and adapt to stress, pressure, and change easily and quickly. You must be passionate about the work in order to sustain the intensity. Having a leadership style that is inclusive and motivates your team is essential. Having training in healthcare compliance or electronic medical record system is very helpful.

 NAME: **BAHAA WANLY**

Title: Chief Operating Officer
Organization: OHSU Partners:
Salem Health

1. Briefly describe your job responsibilities.

As COO and vice president of Salem Health Medical Group, I am responsible for operations of Salem Hospital, West Valley Hospital, and the medical group. My responsibility is for developing its strategic direction and to ensure the effective implementation of all approved strategies, tactics, policies, and procedures in all practices that constitute the integrated provider network.

2. What would you consider to be a "typical" day for you?

Strategic planning, review of health system performance, one-on-ones, rounding, contracting, meetings that cover all the above

3. What education or training do you have? Is it typical for your job?

Master of Health Administration (MHA) degree and operations background

4. What is the most challenging part of your job?

Understanding the political landscape

5. What do you consider to be the best part of your job?

Making team members successful and achieving high performing results

6. What path did you take to get to the job you are in today?

Health administration undergrad, any work experience I could get such as internships, fellowships, master's in health administration, lots of

Continued

NAME: BAHAA WANLY Continued

networking, clinical management, process improvement, strategic planning, are examples

7. What advice do you have for someone who is interested in a job such as yours?

Exceed expectations in your role; network; you need an MHA; get as much experience as possible; and volunteer to take on special projects

JOB DESCRIPTION

The chief patient experience officer will drive and foster a culture of patient- and family-centered care and service excellence, while improving patient and family experience and patient relations across the organization. The chief patient experience officer will work directly with other executives to assess and communicate performance and to create change at all levels of the organization. This position will also be accountable to supporting and managing the organizational needs, as well as the design, implementation, and evaluation of programs that facilitate the professional development and continuous learning of all team members. Tasked with translating the concepts of service excellence, patient experience, and patient relations into actionable behaviors, this individual will take a culture steeped in clinical excellence into the ever-evolving world of patient- and family-centered care.

EDUCATION AND EXPERIENCE

Chief patient experience officers require an advanced degree in nursing, medicine, organizational development, public health, health administration, business, or related field. Additionally, 10 years of related experience with progressive levels of responsibility are required.

CORE COMPETENCIES AND SKILLS

- Outstanding interpersonal skills including the ability to effectively communicate with persons both inside and outside the organization
- Excellent verbal and written communication skills
- Strong leadership and consensus-building skills
- Advanced knowledge of various Consumer Assessment of Healthcare Providers and Systems (CAHPS®) surveys, patient satisfaction survey tools, the field of consumer research, and complaint and grievance management
- A proven track record of results and working with process management
- Advanced data analysis and interpretation skills to lead the service improvement effort and to create the credibility needed for interaction with hospital leaders and faculty
- Ability to articulate challenges and be proactive and aggressive in thinking about new ways to do things, and create enthusiasm for new initiative
- Performance in patient satisfaction surveys in the upper tier (75 percentile or higher)

- Ability to work in a team environment and ensure high-quality, compassionate patient care
- Exceptional problem-solving skills

COMPENSATION

Chief patient experience officers will earn between $153,000 and $222,000 per year, although the total salary will vary depending on the size and location of the hospital, and the education and experience of the candidate.

EMPLOYMENT OUTLOOK

Virtually every hospital in the United States has someone in the role of the chief patient experience officer, so the employment outlook for this job is strong. The demand for persons with these skills will continue to increase, given the shift in hospital reimbursement to attaining high patient satisfaction scores.

FOR FURTHER INFORMATION

- Association for Patient Experience (www.patient-experience.org/About.aspx)

JOB DESCRIPTION

The chief quality officer (CQO) is responsible for planning, administration, and monitoring of consistent readiness of all quality management, regulatory requirements, and quality improvement processes. The CQO will oversee and coordinate all hospital efforts to monitor and maintain compliance with all regulatory, state, federal government, and The Joint Commission. As a member of the senior management team, the CQO initiates and oversees the development of a comprehensive quality/performance improvement program. In collaboration with hospital leadership, staff, medical staff leadership, and board of trustees, the CQO directs and coordinates quality/performance improvement and hospital initiatives.

EDUCATION AND EXPERIENCE

A master's degree in health administration, nursing, public health, or business administration is typically required. Most CQOs have a minimum of 10 years of experience in quality management.

CORE COMPETENCIES AND SKILLS

- Outstanding interpersonal skills including the ability to effectively communicate with persons throughout the organization including clinicians
- Excellent verbal and written communication skills
- Experience with Centers for Medicare & Medicaid Services (CMS) Conditions of Participation for acute care hospitals and CMS survey processes
- In-depth knowledge of external clinical quality reporting requirements
- Current knowledge of The Joint Commission, state, and federal guidelines, regulations, and standards
- Experience coordinating, preparing, and participating in state, The Joint Commission, and CMS surveys in the past 3 years
- Current statistical knowledge and skill in developing statistical data displays
- Experience in the use of statistical and quality software
- Ability to analyze and resolve complex issues

COMPENSATION

CQOs earn in the range of $90,000 to $136,000, although with incentives and bonus pay added on, the salary can be as much as $150,000.

EMPLOYMENT OUTLOOK

The employment outlook for CQOs in large hospital settings is generally good. Smaller hospitals typically cannot afford a CQO and that responsibility is distributed among other staff members.

FOR FURTHER INFORMATION

- Bureau of Labor Statistics (https://www.bls.gov/ooh/management/medical-and-health-services-managers.htm)
- National Association for Healthcare Quality (www.nahq.org)

 NAME: DENNIS R. DELISLE

Title: Executive Project Director
Organization: Thomas Jefferson
University and Hospitals

1. Briefly describe your job responsibilities.

I am responsible for overseeing the implementation of a comprehensive electronic health record (EHR) (Epic Systems) system across ambulatory and inpatient settings (130+ physician offices, three hospitals, three emergency departments, four urgent care centers). The project team for which I am responsible consists of more than 140 staff and 80 consultants, and has a 2-year implementation time period.

The scope of the project is complex; it includes 61 EHR applications across 1,700+ physicians, 800+ house staff, and 3,000+ nurses. In my role, I am responsible for planning, organizing, directing, and managing the project teams and the tasks to achieve goals within budgeted funds and available personnel. I work with executive leadership to establish policies and ensure the project goals and objectives are met through the planning and decision-making processes. I oversee and facilitate a robust governance structure that includes academic, provider, interprofessional, access and revenue cycle, and executive steering committees.

On a daily basis, my leadership team, comprising eight directors, evaluates actual project progress against plans and directs corrective actions. My role serves as an advocate and liaison between stakeholder groups across the organization (clinical, financial, and technical). The project team must analyze end user needs, create clinical workflows, develop strategies tailored to the organization, and provide guidance throughout the scope of implementation for the Epic EHR and associated projects.

2. What would you consider to be a "typical" day for you?

My days can be highly variable owing to the short timeline, complexity, and intensity of the project. On average, I spend 7 to 10 hours in

Continued

NAME: DENNIS R. DELISLE Continued

meetings each day. Meetings vary in content and participants from day-to-day problem solving with project staff, to weekly planning with leadership, or monthly executive report outs. As my scope is broad, the depth and breadth of topics is equally diverse, which makes for a very dynamic role. The project follows a 2-week cadence of meetings, meaning that the specific meetings we have tend to repeat in 2-week cycles to ensure timely progress is made. Given the long hours in meetings, my weeks are accompanied by early mornings in the office for "time to work" and weekends for additional catch-up.

3. What education or training do you have? Is it typical for your job?

What I have: Doctor of Science in Health Systems Management, Master of Health Services Administration, Certified Lean Master, Certified Project Management Professional, Certified Lean Six Sigma Black Belt, Certified Change Agent, and Certified Pennsylvania State Baldrige Examiner.

This broad educational/training background provides me a solid foundation of operational excellence, change management, and leadership.

What is typical: For EHR implementations, the core skill set should embody project management, change leadership, and operational or technical experience. Project directors will vary across organizations. Depending on the organization's culture among other factors, the make-up of the project director will change based on need. For example, in an organization with a weak track record for project execution and success, executives may seek a project director with extensive project management expertise; whereas an organization with a gap between the clinical operations and information technology (IT) departments may want someone who has experience in both areas.

4. What is the most challenging part of your job?

The most challenging part is balancing priorities and resources throughout the duration of the project. The implementation timeline is fixed (in terms of the go-live dates); therefore, the project requires diligent, disciplined oversight on a daily basis. Resource constraints impact the project significantly. We are constantly pressed with reallocating resources (time, money, people) to meet new or changing priorities. The dynamic nature of the project requires a high degree of agility and responsiveness.

Continued

NAME: DENNIS R. DELISLE Continued

5. What do you consider to be the best part of your job?

To me, the best part is working with teams. Within the project, we have over 80 individual workgroups and committees made up of project team and clinical/operational/financial staff. We also engaged over 1,000 staff to contribute to the project. It is amazing to see the amount of progress teams can make. The culture of the organization is starting to shift to a team-based model for getting things done. It is exciting to be a part of something far greater than what any individuals can do on their own.

6. What path did you take to get to the job you are in today?

In my prior job I led Jefferson's Operational Excellence program, which included the education and project execution of Lean Six Sigma, change management, and Baldrige projects. I am currently an adjunct faculty member of the Thomas Jefferson University (TJU) College of Population Health where I teach three courses on operational excellence and Lean thinking. These experiences offered opportunities to work with people throughout the organization on strategic projects and quality improvement initiatives. I spent a lot of time building meaningful relationships with frontline staff up to executives, and committed myself to being open to different ways of thinking and solving problems. By building a strong, diverse network and an expertise in operational excellence, I think it helped position me for the executive project director role.

7. What advice do you have for someone who is interested in a job such as yours?

Executive leadership support is essential to a successful EHR implementation. There are significant barriers and complexities that will challenge the team and organization. In these situations, you need to have strong leaders to help remove obstacles, allocate required resources, and hold everyone accountable to achieve the stated goals. Be aware of the level of commitment a job like this demands. The work hours are very long and intense; it is not for everyone. However, the end result is highly rewarding.

CHIEF TECHNOLOGY OFFICER

JOB DESCRIPTION
The chief technology officer (CTO) is responsible for overseeing all technical aspects of a stand-alone or multihospital system. The CTO works with executive management to grow the organization using technological resources. Using an active and practical approach, the CTO will direct all employees in information services (IS) departments to attain the company's strategic goals.

EDUCATION AND EXPERIENCE
- Bachelor of Science degree in related field with significant experience in the information technology arena, including management and strategic planning. MBA/Master of Health Administration (MHA)/Master of Science degree in related field highly desirable
- Minimum 10 years of experience in healthcare technology

CORE COMPETENCIES AND SKILLS
- Exceptional project management and organizational skills
- Proven track record of success in leadership and high-impact positions
- Ability to establish the hospital's technical vision and lead all aspects of its technological development
- Ability to envision the hospital's strategic direction, development, and future growth
- Ability to work in a consultative fashion with other departmental heads, as an advisor of technologies that may improve their efficiency and effectiveness
- Leadership in a fashion that supports the hospital's culture, mission, and values
- Subject matter expertise for technology platforms and ability to create plans of redundancy for each
- Ability to track, analyze, and monitor technology performance metrics
- Ability to oversee all system design and changes in system architecture
- Ability to conduct research and case studies on leading-edge technologies and make determinations on the probability of implementation
- Ability to act as a good steward of hospital resources and ensure control budgets
- Ability to maintain current knowledge of technology landscape and developments

- Ability to oversee all system design, capacity planning, and changes in system architecture
- Exceptional verbal and written communication skills

COMPENSATION

CTOs earn in the range of $110,000 to $290,000, although many of these persons do continue to practice medicine. Small hospitals would typically not be able to employ a CTO so these positions would be expected to be found at large, urban hospitals or academic health centers.

EMPLOYMENT OUTLOOK

Hospital technology is an essential part of clinical and administrative operations. In his or her role on the senior leadership team, the CTO is a crucial member of hospital operations. The employment outlook for CTOs is good, given the recognition that technology strategy needs to be centralized and given high organizational priority.

FOR FURTHER INFORMATION

- Health Information Management Systems Society (www.himss.org)
- College of Healthcare Information Management Executives (www .chimecentral.org)

 NAME: **JUSTIN O. KUPREVICH**

Title: Telehealth Program Manager—
Jefferson Community Physicians
Organization: Jefferson Health

1. Briefly describe your job responsibilities.

I oversee the development and expansion of a program that combines real-time video and mobile applications of virtual health and education between healthcare providers and their patients or other providers. As part of a nine-hospital system, I am responsible for inpatient and ambulatory applications of synchronous (live-video) specialist consults for hospital patients, and routine and urgent video visits for patients with their primary care, OB/GYN, or an emergency physician across a network of two hospitals, almost 300 physicians and advanced practice providers, as well as an online scheduling platform and several related applications.

2. What would you consider to be a "typical" day for you?

The lack of a truly typical day drew me to this role, but I spend my time meeting with medical practices and hospital departments to promote the adoption of telehealth in new capacities, working with physicians and patients to guide them through the processes associated with a telehealth visit, helping expand the use and capabilities of our online appointment scheduling program, and troubleshooting any and all of the above.

3. What education or training do you have? Is it typical for your job?

Official education: Bachelor of Science in Business from Pennsylvania State University and a Master of Health Administration from the George Washington University. Between college and grad school, I worked in several capacities in a health system that helped build my familiarity with electronic medical records, hospital service lines and departments, and processes. Typical backgrounds for my colleagues range from similar to my own, to having previous work in nursing, medicine, and information technology.

Continued

4. What is the most challenging part of your job?

The most challenging part of my job is also my favorite. I start my day in any of a variety of locations, and may or may not know what I'm going to be working on until everything starts happening. The variety and ambiguity take some getting used to, but keep me on my toes and as flexible as possible.

5. What do you consider to be the best part of your job?

Aside from enjoying the variety and challenge of my position, being part of something new, exciting, and challenging that benefits patients and providers of care is unbelievably rewarding.

6. What path did you take to get to the job you are in today?

I kind of stumbled into healthcare with an internship in college, and fell in love with the excitement of hospitals. After graduation, I worked for a few years in clinical support and administrative roles before grad school. Upon completion of my graduate program, I spent a year in healthcare consulting, which allowed me to get involved in different aspects of care delivery and transformation across geographies, ownership models, and belief systems. When presented with the offer to join Thomas Jefferson University and Health System, it was an opportunity I couldn't refuse.

7. What advice do you have for someone who is interested in a job such as yours?

My best advice would be to remain open to new opportunities, even when they don't seem to fit with your "plan"; the healthcare field is unbelievably vast and the scope of jobs is continuously growing and changing.

13 CLINICAL DEPARTMENT MANAGER

JOB DESCRIPTION

Clinical department managers typically have responsibilities in one department and, therefore, have matching experience in the respective field. This position will work with clinicians and administrative staff to ensure optimization and meeting of departmental goals. Clinical department managers will develop and implement policies, plans, and procedures that aim to meet departmental objectives. They will develop and evaluate key financial reports, while maintaining the respective departmental budget. This position is further responsible for reporting these findings to top management, as well as educating medical staff during operational transition periods. Clinical department managers must also hire necessary staff and develop a team geared toward achieving departmental goals.

EDUCATION AND EXPERIENCE

- Bachelor's degree, preferably in healthcare management or administration
- Master's degree strongly preferred
- No special certification, registration, or licensure is required
- Active membership in such organizations as American College of Healthcare Executives (ACHE), Medical Group Management Associations (MGMA) and/or American College of Medical Practice Executives (ACMPE) strongly preferred
- A minimum of 5 to 7 years of experience in clinical operation management to include planning and programmatic development, fiscal and personnel management, and marketing and public relations expertise

CORE COMPETENCIES AND SKILLS

- Skills to coordinate and manage clinical care operations, business planning, program development, and marketing
- Ability to manage daily operations and budgets and supervise staff; work with clinical leadership, senior management, and others to advance the strategic and operational interests of the department
- Ability to oversee the timely and accurate submission of professional charges, for working through the billing edits and denial processes with the departments and Physicians' Billing Services, for providing regular reporting and analysis of relevant metrics, and for ensuring the overall fiscal health of practice management within the Neurosciences program

- Relevant knowledge to ensure these functions are performed in accordance with all applicable laws and regulations and hospital's philosophy, policies, procedures, and standards
- Ability to effectively respond to imperatives and to develop and analyze planning initiatives
- Proven experience in revenue maximization
- Demonstrated experience in compliance management
- Administrative experience in a hospital setting; experience in an academic medical environment preferred
- Ability to work well and communicate with people on all levels
- Strong computer skills and strong organizational skills
- Knowledge of office automation, human resource management, and financial analysis skills
- Knowledge of Health Maintenance Organization (HMO)/Preferred Provider Organization (PPO) insurance regulations preferred

COMPENSATION

Most clinical department managers earn between $70,000 and $180,000 per year, with the middle 50% falling between about $85,000 and $120,000. Earnings for this position are dependent upon the location and type of facility, as well as the type of department. For example, clinical managers at general medical hospitals earn nearly $110,000, while managers at nursing care facilities would make only about $75,000.

EMPLOYMENT OUTLOOK

The need to optimize efficiency and achieve departmental goals has never been more important in healthcare facilities. Clinical department managers will continue to play a crucial role in helping departments meet necessary objectives in the rapidly evolving industry of healthcare. From 2016 to 2022, this position is expected to grow 17%, which is much faster than most fields. Opportunities will be plentiful in relation to other fields, especially for those who already have relevant experience in healthcare.

FOR FURTHER INFORMATION

- Visit local universities offering the BS in Health Administration, master's in Health Administration (MHA) degree or equivalent. A list of these university-based programs can be found at the Association of University Programs in Health Administration (www.aupha.org)
- American College of Healthcare Executives (www.ache.org)
- Department of Labor, Bureau of Labor Statistics (https://www.bls.gov/ooh/management/medical-and-health-services-managers.htm)

 NAME: DAVID NITKIN

Title: Chief of Staff/Senior Director of Administration
Organization: Howard County General Hospital/Johns Hopkins Medicine

1. Briefly describe your job responsibilities.

I am responsible for coordinating the senior leadership team at the hospital, which includes researching and following through on important issues that cross silos, and setting the agenda for weekly team meetings and projects. I keep the president apprised of issues by preparing briefings for meetings and appearances, and correspondence. I also track the hospital's performance on strategic metrics, and make sure projects and action plans stay on track.

2. What would you consider to be a "typical" day for you?

A typical day would include several meetings of important committees, such as Quality and Safety or Master Planning. It would involve preparing briefing materials for upcoming meetings and events, and working directly with the president several times a day as he offloads questions and tasks.

3. What education or training do you have? Is it typical for your job?

My bachelor's degree is in government and I have a master's in public policy. Most in my position would hold a master's in health administration.

4. What is the most challenging part of your job?

I am a newcomer to healthcare, having transitioned from government and politics, and, before that, journalism. It has been a challenge to climb the learning curve on issues and nomenclature in a hospital setting.

5. What do you consider to be the best part of your job?

I love being part of the mission of improving the health of our patients and the community, and I embrace the opportunity to do so in the most compassionate and cost-effective way.

Continued

NAME: DAVID NITKIN Continued

6. What path did you take to get to the job you are in today?

After a two-decade career in journalism, I switched paths and went into the world of local government and politics, working for two prominent elected officials in my home state of Maryland, in communications and policy. I have deep knowledge of the community I am in, and many players, and those within the hospital knew of my experience and strengths and thought I could add value here.

7. What advice do you have for someone who is interested in a job such as yours?

An administrative residency program would probably be the most direct path to this position.

 NAME: **ERIKA SCHOUTEN**

Title: Director, Neuroscience Institute
Hartford Region
Organization: Hartford HealthCare

1. Briefly describe your job responsibilities.

The Neuroscience Institute pulls together expertise in several disciplines across Hartford HealthCare, including neurology and neurosurgery. I'm the director of the Neuroscience Institute for the Hartford region. I head up the development and maintenance of the comprehensive, integrated, multidisciplinary neuroscience service by improving clinical outcomes, customer satisfaction, growth, and financial performance. I am focused on the day-to-day operations of the service line. I am responsible for increasing the coordination of care, enhancing access to treatment, improving quality and safety, and developing innovative programs.

2. What would you consider to be a "typical" day for you?

I start my day by attending one of the several neuroscience areas' daily huddles. I rotate which huddle I attend every day. After the huddle, I typically take the time to walk around and interact with the staff. I spend a great deal of my day in meetings that cover many topics and agendas, such as coaching staff members, reviewing quality initiatives, and monitoring key performance metrics. I also spend time traveling to our satellite locations and ambulatory practices. However, I don't really have typical days. Each day brings unique challenges and opportunities. I am thankful to be working in an area that has dedicated clinicians and staff, and is interesting and constantly evolving. Every day I learn something new that I did not know before.

3. What education or training do you have? Is it typical for your job?

I received my bachelor's degree in health management and policy from Oregon State University, and a master's in health services administration

Continued

from the George Washington University. I completed my Administrative Fellowship at Hartford Hospital in 2012. The fellowship provides great exposure and the ability to see and do things you would otherwise not experience until much later in your career, such as attending board meetings, chief executive officer (CEO) cabinet meetings, and so on. The ability to learn from strong leaders and gain knowledge through actively participating in projects and mentorship is a unique opportunity. In short, the fellowship presents the chance to apply the theories and knowledge acquired in the classroom.

It's typical at my level to have a master's degree in healthcare administration or business with experience in strategy and operations within the acute care setting.

4. What is the most challenging part of your job?

The most challenging part of my job is staying abreast of the rapid changes and advances taking place in healthcare. Finding the time to stay current on the news and pertinent literature that impacts our industry is difficult but critical. As technology and research are rapidly improving and expanding, I hope to leverage new advances to improve the level of patient care received.

5. What do you consider to be the best part of your job?

The opportunity to be responsible for designing, improving, and implementing processes and services is both rewarding and exciting. It is fulfilling to witness the positive impact successful systems have on the quality of care received by patients at Hartford Hospital and within the system. Listening to our patients and their families, and hearing their stories are the best part of my job. Working at Hartford HealthCare has allowed me the opportunity to further my desire to improve patient care and services.

6. What path did you take to get to the job you are in today?

I started my career by interning at Samaritan Hospital in Lebanon, Oregon in 2006. I was drawn to healthcare because it is all about serving others and relationships. After graduating with my bachelor's degree, I completed a year-long internship at St. Joseph's Hospital in Orange, California. This experience confirmed my interest in healthcare. I was

Continued

fascinated by the operations of a hospital and I decided the next step was gradu-ate school.

After completing my fellowship and master's degree, I was offered the role of project manager for academic affairs at Hartford Hospital. I was responsible for managing departmental staff, as well as planning and directing the administrative, financial, and operational activities of the academic and research department. I also served as a primary liaison on behalf of the vice president of academic affairs and the chief academic officer between physicians, management, and administrative staff, and other key stakeholders. My previous education and expe-rience prepared me to accept my current role as a neurosciences administrator.

7. What advice do you have for someone who is interested in a job such as yours?

It's important early in your career to learn the importance of organizational prepa-ration, teamwork, and tenacity. These skills are the requisite foundation for strong leadership. I recommend taking the time to reflect and create a road map for your career with goals and objectives. Focus on what you truly want to accomplish, then work really hard and do your best. Be willing to take risks and compete with yourself. If you always do your best you will feel satisfied and the results will follow.

It is also important to find strong mentors and build meaningful relationships. You should also mentor others when you are in a position to help others. I have begun to mentor the incoming Administrative Fellows at Hartford Hospital as I feel strongly about giving back, as so many others do for me.

 NAME: CHARLES M. ZOLLINGER

Title: Director, Clinical Services
Organization: Intermountain Donor Services

1. Briefly describe your job responsibilities.

- Provide direction and support to the four clinical managers of organ recovery, surgical services, tissue referral, and tissue recovery departments.
- Ensure the clinical departments have the appropriate training and staffing to meet regulatory guidelines.
- Be a resource to frontline organ donation staff regarding organ donation eligibility.
- Work closely with the other departmental directors to promote collaboration toward constancy of organizational purpose.

2. What would you consider to be a "typical" day for you?

When covering calls as administrator on call, I field queries 24/7 from frontline staff and clinical managers regarding patient eligibility as organ donors, advice regarding organ allocation, clarification on regulatory compliance, and/or staffing issues. I participate in weekly case review meetings with our four clinical departments. Many of my days are filled with a variety of meetings with internal and external departments with a focus on process improvement, strategic planning, project management, problem solving, training, and innovation.

3. What education or training do you have? Is it typical for your job?

My role requires a bachelor's degree; a master's degree is preferred. I am currently working on my executive master's in health administration from Milken Institute School of Public Health at the George Washington University. Key to this role is attending and participating in educational offerings with other organ procurement organizations (OPO) across the United States in an effort to share knowledge, network, and identify best practices.

Continued

4. What is the most challenging part of your job?

From an administrative standpoint, managing and prioritizing the many competing priorities on a daily basis. Clinically, making the tough decisions that may impact whether an organ is transplanted or not.

5. What do you consider to be the best part of your job?

Working with high-performing professionals who are passionate about realizing families' wishes to donate their loved ones' organs and tissues.

6. What path did you take to get to the job you are in today?

I already had my bachelor's degree when I started working for my current employer in 1996. Within a couple of years, I was promoted to the role of organ donation coordinator and subsequently went back to school to obtain my nursing degree. After several years, I was promoted to supervisor, and then manager. Later on, I was promoted to administrative director overseeing the day-to-day operations of the organ recovery department. After some organizational restructuring, I was promoted to director of clinical services.

7. What advice do you have for someone who is interested in a job such as yours?

Having a clinical background is key to understanding what the frontline clinical staff deal with on a daily basis. Ideally, the clinical experience should include having worked for an OPO. One of the most important skills to possess is effective communication—it is vital to leading and navigating interpersonal relationships within and between teams/departments and with other organizations.

COMMUNITY RESOURCE ADVISOR/ OPTIONS COUNSELOR

JOB DESCRIPTION

Community resource advisors play an integral role in providing information for services to patients during and after their inpatient stay. This position works with elderly patients aged 60 years and older, disabled patients aged 22 years and older, and the respective patients' families. These advisors offer free, unbiased information so that patients and their caregivers can make informed decisions after the patient's stay. This role involves making recommendations to the patient about available options for long-term care, housing services, and even home care services. Community resource advisors will meet patients and their caregivers at the hospital, in physician offices, rehabilitation centers, community settings, and at home.

EDUCATION AND EXPERIENCE

This position will often require a bachelor's degree in a related field, such as social work or nursing. Individuals considering this position should be willing to obtain a social work license. Five to ten years of previous experience working as a case manager with the elderly and disabled populations is desirable. Knowledge of home care resources and the services associated with these populations is also helpful.

CORE COMPETENCIES AND SKILLS

- Excellent communication skills, as this position requires working with patients, patients' family members, and medical staff
- Familiarity with long-term care service options and community resources
- Ability to travel to various locations within a community
- Superior writing skills to develop information packets
- Comfort for working in various medical environments
- Demonstrated ability to research relevant services for patients on websites
- Knowledge of state and federally subsidized programs and resources
- Ability to work with a multidisciplined team of doctors, nurses, and patients

COMPENSATION

Community resource advisors should expect to make $40,000 to $65,000 annually. Experience and the level of responsibility will affect the position's salary. Those working in for-profit organizations will tend to make more than advisors in not-for-profit organizations.

EMPLOYMENT OUTLOOK

Community resource advisors can prevent nursing home placements, saving the state and federal government thousands of dollars per patient each month. Realizing these savings will be integral if these positions will continue to receive financial support.

FOR FURTHER INFORMATION

- ■ Executive Office of Elder Affairs—Massachusetts Association of Councils on Aging (www.mcoaonline.com/member-services/pages/eoea)
- ■ Case Management Society of America (www.cmsa.org)

Title: Senior Director of Government Programs

Organization: Providence Health & Services

1. Briefly describe your job responsibilities.

My systemwide role (across 34 hospitals/4,500 patient care providers) is to direct all aspects of hospital and provider eligibility, education, registrations, and attestations related to governmental incentive programs. This includes assessing eligibility for quality programs, monitoring performance, responding to audits, and providing appropriate reports to executive and operational leaders, and escalating risks as necessary so we achieve success and receive the appropriate governmental incentives that are critical to our operating budget. This includes the enormous changes that are part of MACRA (Medicare Access and CHIP [Children's Health Insurance Program] Reauthorization Act). The responsibilities within this role have a direct impact on a significant portion of our organization's net operating income.

Sustaining success with these complex programs is challenging. While we participate in these programs, it is critically important we understand the impact to all clinicians so that the care that we provide is not negatively impacted. We want to minimize any extra burden to our patient-facing care teams as much as possible. This proves challenging because most governmental programs will require changes to existing workflows.

2. What would you consider to be a "typical" day for you?

My day is often composed of online meetings (conference calls). Although I participate in in-person meetings, we try to be cost effective, being conscious of our geographic footprint (spread across five states, including Alaska). Collaboration must be coordinated. My days often get so filled with meetings that I have to block off "desk time," so that I can catch up with important work.

I have a very matrixed work environment; although I have a team that directly reports to me, our success requires strong collaboration with others (clinicians, technical resources, executive leaders, et al.).

Continued

NAME: RAY MANAHAN Continued

3. What education or training do you have? Is it typical for your job?

I have a bachelor's degree in biology and advanced training in pharmacy. Rarely do I apply those years of education to my current job. However, what I have learned from my postbaccalaureate education in healthcare administration (Master of Health Administration [MHA]) plays a significant role in my current activities—inside and outside my organization.

My MHA degree has helped me better appreciate my role, and has also nurtured me to be a more forward-thinking leader while being sensitive to those who are part of my team. It may not be required for similar jobs that function like mine, but I believe an advanced degree is important.

4. What is the most challenging part of your job?

Healthcare is undergoing a tremendous transformation. My organization, like many, must be agile in order to survive the massive changes. I find interpreting the external forces outside our organization and thoughtfully applying them to our day-to-day activities to be very challenging. There are times when these may be in disagreement with our core mission and values. My role is to help us find a respectful translation to minimize any negative impacts to our caregivers, while at the same time keep us financially viable.

I have a very efficient team who know how to get the job done. I find that shielding them from interferences (internal and external) is key to our success. There is a certain amount of transparency needed, but an effective leader should be tactful and know when and where the appropriate content should be shared.

5. What do you consider to be the best part of your job?

Our organization's core values keep me at my job. Leaders are taught to connect the work that we do to our mission. I believe this has been key to our longevity. Each division within our large enterprise is required to have respectful dialogue with their employees so they don't lose focus of why we are here, which is to thoughtfully serve the poor and needy in our communities. Having been formed by strong religious women whose lives were about serving the most vulnerable, it is important that we not lose sight of this. Connecting our team to our mission and core values has led to our many successes.

In addition, my organization invests time and money in nurturing leaders on our humble background, helping them to put concept into

Continued

NAME: RAY MANAHAN Continued

practice. Our "leadership formation" efforts provide me the opportunity to deepen my appreciation for our heritage, mission, and core values with my own sense of mission and values. I work on applying this values-based thinking daily.

6. What path did you take to get to the job you are in today?

Although I've been in the healthcare industry since graduating from college, I would never have imagined that I would end up with the job that I have now; honestly, there were years when I thought healthcare was mind numbing. However, new opportunities in healthcare information technology (IT) project management, and the ever-changing healthcare IT landscape, helped me to regain my focus. I remained a project/program manager for many years, working for both profit and nonprofit organizations, and working on IT projects, before I landed my current role as director.

Certainly, my current job would be extremely more challenging if I had not passed through the journey that I have taken. Like many, we need years of challenging experiences and many lessons learned. This journey continues today.

7. What advice do you have for someone who is interested in a job such as yours?

As I'm sure many would understand, it takes significant maturity to take on an administrative role that deals with the changing healthcare landscape. This is not a job for someone right out of college. It took me over 15 years after getting my bachelor's degree to "find my stride."

While there are many trials, I find tremendous self-fulfillment in my job and I credit my organization and our leaders for this. Outside of maturity, if there is additional solid advice I would give, it is to take some time to understand *why* change in healthcare is needed—perhaps, find a deep personal connection like a negative experience either you or a loved one experienced in a hospital or other healthcare setting. I have no doubt that this will not be a difficult exercise.

DIRECTOR OF BUSINESS DEVELOPMENT

JOB DESCRIPTION

The director of business development is responsible for planning, developing, implementing, and evaluating new clinical outreach opportunities at the hospital in collaboration with key service line and departmental leaders. The director provides support to leadership in strategic planning, project facilitation, productivity and operations improvement, strategic analysis, space planning, and other strategic activities within the hospital.

EDUCATION AND EXPERIENCE

Master's degree in health administration, business, or an analytical field is required along with 3 to 5 years' experience in healthcare planning, management, or consulting.

CORE COMPETENCIES AND SKILLS

- Outstanding interpersonal skills including the ability to effectively communicate with persons throughout the organization
- Excellent verbal and written communication skills
- Demonstrable knowledge of healthcare industry trends and hospital business structure
- Ability to build and maintain appropriate peer relationships to facilitate organizational objectives
- Ability to drive the development of major strategic and capital projects, and determine volume projections for inpatient and outpatient services; facilitate annual strategic review and goal-setting process
- Ability to participate in hospital's master space plan development, hospital budget development, and provide data support on scheduled and ad hoc projects
- Experience in leading and motivating work teams with the intent to create and articulate a vision and direction; ability to inspire, encourage, and influence others toward shared vision and optimal outcomes
- Demonstrated ability to quickly understand an issue, to identify alternatives, to quantify and assess, and to objectively present recommendations that are in the best interest of the system, the region, and the hospital
- Ability to facilitate group discussions and to work broadly with administration, hospital, and medical staff
- Capability to analyze financial, volume, and market data

COMPENSATION

Business development directors earn in the range of $147,000 to $190,000, although the total salary will vary depending on the size and location of the hospital, and the education and experience of the candidate.

EMPLOYMENT OUTLOOK

Typically, only larger hospitals and health systems can afford to have the position of director of business development. It is reported that this is a position that is frequently used to develop persons who plan to move into senior management positions; therefore, the turnover of business development professionals is very brisk.

FOR FURTHER INFORMATION

■ Healthcare Financial Management Association (www.hfma.org)
■ American College of Healthcare Executives (www.ache.org)

NAME: FAIZA HASEEB

Title: Physician Business Development Manager
Organization: Cleveland Clinic Abu Dhabi (CCAD)

1. Briefly describe your job responsibilities.

Develop and implement the growth strategy for Cleveland Clinic Abu Dhabi, including facilitating integration within the partnering organizations, expanding provider networks, both locally and internationally, cultivating new service lines, fostering excellent marketing and public relations with community physicians. Direct the operational, strategic, and business planning for any assigned enterprise initiatives, as well as for designated affiliates and business lines. Identify opportunities for business and product expansion, complete with feasibility studies and risk analysis in collaboration with operating executives. In addition, partner with senior management, affiliate executives, and the corresponding institutes/departments to cascade strategies and direct linkages through business plans and budget processes. Function as an effective resource to executives, management teams, and board of directors. Coordinate and align market-driven growth across assigned affiliates and corresponding operational unit (OU), while aligning with the enterprise growth strategy.

The role also works with the office of clinical staff affairs on physician recruitments, physician engagement, and retention.

2. What would you consider to be a "typical" day for you?

We kick off the day with a morning huddle to understand the "state of the house."

On the strategy and business development side of the role, the day includes meeting internal and external stakeholders to mitigate potential issues, discuss opportunities, and build/foster relationships with existing and new clients.

Another aspect of the position involves managing the operations of all incoming referrals, both locally and internationally. As a result, there are numerous times where I am "putting out fires" with referring

Continued

NAME: FAIZA HASEEB Continued

providers, patient issues/complaints, provider schedules, and other operational necessities.

The last key function of my job is to ensure we are recruiting the right/quality physicians for our institute and that their onboarding is seamless and as efficient as possible. This includes overseeing the physician recruitment process, licensing and credentialing process, and finally onboarding the physician.

3. What education or training do you have? Is it typical for your job?

- Bachelor of Science in Health Science Studies, Pre-Physical Therapy with a Management Minor, Baylor University
- Master of Health Services Administration, The George Washington University
- Executive Education Certificate in Leading Change in Complex Organization, Massachusetts Institute of Technology

4. What is the most challenging part of your job?

CCAD is an organization with over 65+ nationalities and over 70 different languages spoken. The most challenging part of the job is to understand the needs of different stakeholders and articulate them to our caregivers (CCAD employees) in the best way possible, while acknowledging the cultural and political sensitivities of the region, health structure, and government.

5. What do you consider to be the best part of your job?

The most rewarding part of the job is working with the different people from all across the world, who are putting in their best efforts to bring the highest quality of care to the population of United Arab Emirates (UAE) and the Gulf region.

6. What path did you take to get to the job you are in today?

I kicked off my career working in an outpatient practice, as an administrative assistant, right after my bachelor's from Baylor University. A year into the role, I moved to Washington, DC for my Masters in Health Services Administration at the George Washington University (GWU). During my time at GWU, I had the opportunity to work closely with other alumni as

Continued

NAME: FAIZA HASEEB Continued

a graduate assistant and intern at the Emory Clinics, Emory Healthcare, in Atlanta, Georgia.

Upon completing my theoretical part of the master's program, I did my Healthcare Administrative Fellowship with ARAMARK Healthcare, in conjunction with the Institute of Diversity, at their client healthcare system named Virtua. This was the first time Virtua was hosting an administrative fellow at their facility, and even though I had a structured guideline from ARAMARK regarding the aspects of the program, I really had the opportunity to develop the fellowship as I wanted. With the buy-in from all the executives, I gained exposure in the different parts of the hospital, including standing in the parking lot at 5 a.m. with security to manage the parking lots, 3 days in the kitchen to understand the kitchen operations, and 2 days with facilities resolving issues throughout the facility. These experiences, along with working on vital project work with human resources (HR), finance, operations and strategic growth, and other functions provided me with a holistic perception of how different functions come together to provide high quality of care. The fellowship also gave me insight on accountability, stakeholder buy-in, and ownership of projects and initiatives. It also enabled me to draw connections between seemingly disparate subjects and people to balance ARAMARK relationships with Virtua Health relationships, and to foster the best interests of both organizations.

As the fellowship was coming to an end, Virtua Leadership created a position for me within the system, as the administrative project manager for population health of Virtua South (covering three facilities). The time spent at Virtua set me up for success; from the skills I developed, to the hands-on experiences of managing multiple major projects, such as:

■ Establishment of the Virtua Hub and Spoke Pharmacy
■ Consolidation of the Berlin facility
■ Coordinating the insourcing of the surgical instruments
■ Consolidation of the Central Sterile Department into a centralized operations
■ Multiple renovations project
■ Extensive market analysis and service line growth plans
It was at an American College of Healthcare Executives (ACHE) congress where I met my current manager, Ryan Cork, senior director of clinical staff affairs, and Jonathan McGowen, senior director of clinical operations. I was introduced to Jonathan by one of the vice presidents at Virtua, and he shared the CCAD

Continued

project with me. It wasn't until another year and a half that I found myself traveling half-way across the world to open a complex multispecialty, state-of-the-art hospital in Abu Dhabi, UAE.

From May 2104 until now, I have had responsibility to operationalize the Heart & Vascular Institute at CCAD, which started with 20 physicians and grew to a team of 40 physicians by the end of 2016. The services comprise outpatient clinic, echo and stress labs, vascular lab, cath and electrophysiology labs, and the operating rooms. As it was a greenfield project, I had the opportunity to work on a number of different projects along with my main responsibility of managing the Heart & Vascular Institute. The depth of knowledge I gained in the past two projects, combined with my previous experiences and skills, opened new doors for me at CCAD. As a result, about 6 months ago I was appointed as the physician business development manager for the organization. The physician business development manager is responsible for identifying and developing strategic business relationships and physician referral networks with community partners and physicians, healthcare organizations, and other potential customers, both locally in the UAE and in the international market. In this key position, I work closely with the strategy and business development department, the marketing department, and, most of all, the individual institutes to ensure all efforts are made to support CCAD's overall growth strategy and long-term vision.

Additionally, this position will also be required to oversee all physician recruitment and on-boarding for CCAD's staff physicians, clinical associates, and nurse practitioners. This position reports directly to the senior director of clinical staff affairs.

7. What advice do you have for someone who is interested in a job such as yours?

- Change is a constant in healthcare
- Healthcare is an industry of people—so you have to enjoy people and get comfortable working with people who are very different from you
- Be careful not to focus so much on your next promotion, or title or salary; most times the experience and excelling in your current role should be everything
- Don't wait for advancement opportunities to come to you. Get involved in projects unrelated to or in addition to your current job. Open doors and opportunities for yourself!
- Network or NO work
- Keep it simple and concise
- Healthcare is a very small industry, everyone knows everyone!

16

JOB DESCRIPTION

The director of development heads the development department and is responsible primarily for philanthropy and fund raising in her/his respective not-for-profit hospital. Frequently the director of development is also in charge of the hospital's foundation. This position is often referred to as "the executive director of the hospital foundation." In every case, this person is in charge of leading all fund-raising activities. There is extensive work and interaction with real and potential donors.

EDUCATION AND EXPERIENCE

A bachelor's degree in business administration is the minimum academic qualification, although a master's degree in either business or health administration is becoming the standard level of education for development directors. A minimum of 5 years of progressive fund-raising responsibilities in a healthcare environment or comparable complex organization is required.

CORE COMPETENCIES AND SKILLS

- Outstanding interpersonal skills including the ability to effectively communicate with persons both inside and outside the organization
- Excellent verbal and written communication skills
- Experience working with medical visionary leaders and the corporate sector in regards to philanthropic and strategic partnerships
- Familiarity with development program data management systems
- Skills to work with volunteer groups and community leaders
- Significant experience in planned giving, annual fund campaigns, and other philanthropic activities
- Experience with the various state and federal laws surrounding fund-raising and development
- Ability to build and maintain a strong employee communication program
- Ability to build appropriate major and planned giving, annual giving, grant writing, donor stewardship and recognition programs; gift processing and use of volunteers
- Capability to analyze financial, volume, and market data

COMPENSATION

Development directors earn in the range of $86,000 to $140,000, although the total salary will vary depending on the size and location of the hospital, and the education and experience of the candidate.

EMPLOYMENT OUTLOOK

The U.S. Department of Labor projects steady growth of development directors in the coming years. Job growth is projected to be good throughout the hospital industry. Virtually all not-for-profit hospitals are involved with fund-raising and development work, and given the shrinking levels of reimbursement from commercial and governmental payers, these professionals will play an ever-important role for the foreseeable future.

FOR FURTHER INFORMATION

- Association of Fundraising Professionals (www.afpnet.org)
- Association for Healthcare Philanthropy (www.ahp.org)

NAME: **ANDREA ZWISCHENBERGER**

Title: Senior Director, Executive Administration

Organization: Cleveland Clinic

1. Briefly describe your job responsibilities.

At Cleveland Clinic, we partner administrators with each physician leader to execute their vision, and I work directly with our chief executive officer. As senior director of executive administration, I drive implementation and project management for enterprise-wide, strategic projects, including the Care Affordability cost structure realignment program. I support the strategic priorities of the chief executive officer and executive team.

2. What would you consider to be a "typical" day for you?

We start at 7 a.m. most days, as we work with surgeons and physicians. I am in meetings most of the day, varying from large group meetings to one-on-ones. Often, we are working on large projects that take months, or years, to implement, so we'll do work to progress in those projects. I spend a great deal of time working on slides—primarily for our CEO's internal and external presentations and key meetings. I actually love doing slides—I'm one of those strange people who enjoy making pre-sentations. And I try, to no avail, to manage my inbox throughout the day.

3. What education or training do you have? Is it typical for your job?

I have a Master of Health Services Administration from the George Washington University, and a Bachelor of Science in Public Health, magna cum laude, from the George Washington University. I completed graduate internships at a community hospital in Washington, DC and a large academic medical center in Kentucky. I came to the Clinic for a 1-year postgraduate administrative fellowship. That's a very typical path for healthcare administrators.

Continued

4. What is the most challenging part of your job?

I have been at the Clinic for 5 years, which seems like a long time to me, but it's a relative nanosecond compared to most Clinic employees and physicians with 40-year tenures. As a newbie, it's challenging to understand the history and navigate the years of relationships that have been developed.

5. What do you consider to be the best part of your job?

I work on projects across the organization, and am able to be creative and learn every day. I feel like I know a little bit about a lot of topics working in executive administration. I'm able to look at information, suggest ideas, and think creatively about new ways to do work. No one day is ever the same as the next. And our CEO is constantly challenging me to learn new content each day.

6. What path did you take to get to the job you are in today?

I was very fortunate to have great mentors in my internships, fellowship, and throughout undergrad and graduate school. I listened when they recognized my strengths and weaknesses and trusted their advice. They guided me from a pre-med track to public health focus to healthcare administration.

7. What advice do you have for someone who is interested in a job such as yours?

Do a really good job in your current role, whether it's school or work. I advise young professionals to truly excel in the job they're doing today. If you focus on your current role and not the next role, people will recognize your competency and proficiency. Don't be afraid to ask questions, ask for advice, and demonstrate that you're a learner.

17

DIRECTOR OF EMERGENCY SERVICES

JOB DESCRIPTION

The director of emergency services assumes 24-hour fiscal, clinical, and operational responsibility for his/her assigned area incorporating the hospital's mission, goals, and strategic plan. The director of emergency services ensures quality patient care and oversees patient flow processes within the emergency department. The director of emergency services, in collaboration with the director of security, fire and safety, and deputy safety officer, is responsible to provide clinical support for the emergency management plan.

EDUCATION AND EXPERIENCE

Most directors of emergency services are RNs who have additional education in business or health administration. Persons in this role typically have 5 or more years of emergency department nursing experience.

CORE COMPETENCIES AND SKILLS

- Outstanding interpersonal skills including the ability to effectively communicate with persons both inside and outside the organization
- Excellent verbal and written communication skills
- Strong leadership and consensus-building skills
- Familiarity with emergency services data management systems
- Ability to manage the flow of patients and information to expedite care, collaborating with physicians and healthcare professionals
- Ability to ensure regulatory compliance with Department of Health Services (DHS), Occupational Safety and Health Administration (OSHA), and all other regulatory agencies
- Proven experience in creating staffing models for both full- and part-time professional employees
- Proven abilities to build and manage budgets
- Ability to work in a team environment and ensure high-quality compassionate patient care
- Exceptional problem solving skills

COMPENSATION

Emergency services directors earn in the range of $64,000 to $107,000, although the total salary will vary depending on the size and location of the hospital, and the education and experience of the candidate.

EMPLOYMENT OUTLOOK

Virtually every community hospital in the United States has a functioning emergency department that requires the skill and talent of an administrative director. This job is becoming more complex as hospitals are required to maintain high-quality emergency services 24 hours a day, 365 days a year.

FOR FURTHER INFORMATION

■ Association of Healthcare Emergency Preparedness Professionals (www .ahepp.org)

18

DIRECTOR OF ENVIRONMENTAL SERVICES

JOB DESCRIPTION

The director of environmental services plans, administers, and directs all activities related to environmental services, complying with the standards established by the hospital and various regulatory agencies. He or she leads environmental services staff and assistant managers and works to establish and maintain effective working relationships with other departments to provide a unified approach to patient care.

EDUCATION AND EXPERIENCE

Directors of environmental services generally possess a bachelor's degree in business administration or environmental health. To become eligible for one of these positions, the candidate must also have 4 to 6 years of hospital housekeeping experience.

CORE COMPETENCIES AND SKILLS

- Outstanding interpersonal skills including the ability to effectively communicate with persons inside the organization
- Excellent verbal and written communication skills
- Ability to develop and maintain environmental services in accordance with state and federal regulations, accepted standards, professional practices, and hospital policies
- Familiarity with environmental services data management systems
- Experience at creating and maintaining job descriptions and completing annual performance reviews on all employees in a timely manner
- Working knowledge of infection control techniques
- Experience in supervising departmental personnel including hiring, orientation, determining workload and delegating assignments, training, monitoring, scheduling and evaluating performance, and initiating corrective and disciplinary actions.
- Skilled in supporting and motivating staff at both the supervisory and hourly level
- Proficient in computer skills including word processing and spreadsheet applications
- Ability to build and manage budgets

COMPENSATION

Environmental services directors earn in the range of $37,000 to $103,000, although the total salary will vary depending on the size and location of the hospital and the education and experience of the candidate.

EMPLOYMENT OUTLOOK

Job prospects for directors of environmental services are reported to be good across the country. Every hospital must maintain a highly effective environmental services department that needs to be run by persons who are dedicated to providing a safe and clean setting for patients, clinicians, and visitors.

FOR FURTHER INFORMATION

■ Association for the Healthcare Environment (www.ahe.org)

19 DIRECTOR OF FOOD AND NUTRITION SERVICES

JOB DESCRIPTION

The director of food and nutrition services directs and integrates all aspects of food and nutrition service for patients, employees, and cafeteria customers, including clinical nutrition services, retail, and catering services. The director provides leadership and direction, and is responsible for planning, organizing, and staffing the department in accordance with the mission, values, and vision of the hospital.

EDUCATION AND EXPERIENCE

Bachelor's degree is required with a minimum of 3 years of experience in food service management, or a recognized culinary diploma with a minimum of 5 years of demonstrated management experience. Most hospitals prefer someone with a Registered Dietician (RD) qualification.

CORE COMPETENCIES AND SKILLS

- Outstanding interpersonal skills including the ability to effectively communicate with persons both inside and outside the organization
- Excellent verbal and written communication skills
- Strong leadership and consensus-building skills
- Ability to direct and integrate all aspects of food and nutrition service for patients, employees, and cafeteria customers, including clinical nutrition services, retail, and catering services
- Ability to ensure that there are ongoing in-service and educational training programs for staff, and policies and procedures in place to guide the staff in their duties that address safety for food handling, emergency supplies, orientation for new employees, work assignments, and job descriptions
- Ability to deal with multiple project demands and tight deadlines
- Ability to oversee proper menu planning, purchasing of food and supplies, schedules, sanitation, and the retention of essential records
- Demonstrated initiative, follow-through, and ability to work independently
- Ability to build and manage budgets

COMPENSATION

Food and nutrition service directors earn in the range of $86,000 to $116,000, although the total salary will vary depending on the size and location of the hospital and the education and experience of the candidate.

EMPLOYMENT OUTLOOK

The employment outlook for directors of food and nutrition service is somewhat complicated. Each and every hospital must be able to meet the precise dietary requirements of all inpatients and, therefore, must have an operational on-site food service. Food and nutrition services for inpatient care will continue to require a director. However, hospitals also maintain a cafeteria for employees and visitors, as well as catering for hospital events. In a number of cases, hospitals outsource their food service operations for these service lines to an outside vendor. In other cases, hospitals have actively tried to improve the quality of their food service by working to improve and upgrade internal operations. In either case, food and nutrition services directors will continue to be an important role at all hospitals.

FOR FURTHER INFORMATION

■ Association for Healthcare Foodservice (www.healthcarefoodservice.org)

20   DIRECTOR OF GRANTS AND CONTRACTS

JOB DESCRIPTION

Under the general supervision of the chief financial officer, the director manages the Grants and Contract Management Office (GCMO), which provides both preaward and postaward administration of grants and contracts in order to assist the faculty/staff in obtaining and utilizing financial support from extramural sources, and ensures compliance with rules and regulations of various awarding agencies. This position: acts as an advisor to scientific staff regarding grants and contracts; creates new accounts, monitors all expenses, verifies availability of funds and allowable expenses as dictated by the funding agency; communicates new regulations and procedures; forecasts future funding and associated expenses; acts as liaison between labs and other departments at the hospital; provides administrative and technical guidance and support to faculty and staff.

EDUCATION AND EXPERIENCE

This position will often require a bachelor's degree in a related field, such as business or health administration. A master's degree is preferred. Ten years of federal and nonfederal grants and contracts experience is required. Experience must include 5 years of supervisory/management experience. Strategic planning, preaward/postaward management, and compliance experience are strongly preferred.

CORE COMPETENCIES AND SKILLS

- Excellent communication skills, as this position requires working with researchers, granting agencies, and governmental regulators
- Familiarity with contract and grant activities
- Ability to travel to various locations within a community
- Superior writing skills to develop information packets for principal investigators
- Comfort in working in various medical environments
- Demonstrated ability to manage a team of contract and grant staff
- Knowledge of state and federally subsidized programs and resources
- Ability to work with a multidisciplined team of doctors, nurses, and patients

COMPENSATION

Directors of grants and contracts should expect to make $56,000 to $98,000. Experience and the level of responsibility will affect the position's salary. Another important variable is the size of the hospital and the volume of funded research taking place.

EMPLOYMENT OUTLOOK

Academic health centers and large teaching hospitals depend on a constant flow of contract and grant income. Directors of grants and contracts are highly sought after, particularly in the competitive environment that surrounds obtaining governmental and nongovernmental funding for research.

FOR FURTHER INFORMATION

- ■ National Grants Management Association (www.ngma.org)
- ■ National Contract Management Association (www.ncmahq.org)

21

DIRECTOR OF HUMAN RESOURCES

JOB DESCRIPTION

The director of human resources (HR) heads the HR department in a hospital, overseeing the entire functioning of the department. This position typically reports directly to the chief executive officer (CEO) of a hospital. Recruitment of employees, training, development, setting the salaries and benefits of employees, and managing employee–employer relations, are some of the primary duties of a hospital HR director.

EDUCATION AND EXPERIENCE

A bachelor's degree in business administration is the minimum academic qualification, although a master's degree in either business or health administration is becoming the standard level of education for HR directors. Most hospitals require a minimum of 5 years of senior HR experience. Experience in working with labor unions is also critical for HR directors.

CORE COMPETENCIES AND SKILLS

- Outstanding interpersonal skills including the ability to effectively communicate with persons throughout the organization including clinicians
- Excellent verbal and written communication skills
- Thorough knowledge of all aspects of HR administration including applicable local, state, and federal regulatory requirements, Fair Employment Practices Act, the National Labor Relations Act, Title VII of the Civil Rights Act, Rehabilitation Act, wage and hour and employee benefits–related regulations
- In-depth knowledge of external clinical quality reporting–requirements
- Current knowledge of The Joint Commission, state, and federal guidelines, regulations and standards
- Experience coordinating, preparing, and participating in state, The Joint Commission, and Centers for Medicare & Medicaid Services (CMS) surveys within past 3 years
- Current statistical knowledge and skill in developing statistical data displays
- Experience in the use of statistical and quality software
- Experience in leading and managing change

COMPENSATION

HR directors earn in the range of $76,000 to $131,000, although the total salary will vary depending on the size and location of the hospital.

EMPLOYMENT OUTLOOK

The employment outlook for directors of HR is generally good. This is a position that all hospitals must fill. There is no specific information relating to turnover in this position, but HR directors at smaller hospitals typically move into positions with larger salaries and additional opportunities.

FOR FURTHER INFORMATION

■ Society for Human Resource Management (www.shrm.org/Pages/default .aspx)

 NAME: **ROBY A. HUNT**

Title: Vice President of Human
Resources
Organization: MedStar Medical Group/
MedStar Health

1. Briefly describe your job responsibilities.

As a member of the executive team of MedStar Medical Group, I am responsible for ensuring that we acquire, train, develop, reward, and engage all physicians, associates, and management in our organization. I also have responsibility for ensuring that our physicians and associates provide excellent experience and service excellence to our patients and their family members. Along with my colleagues on the executive team, I am responsible for the strategic development and overall effectiveness of our medical group across a large geography, which includes 85 locations and 10 hospitals in Washington DC, Maryland, and Virginia. These responsibilities include profit and loss of our many medical practices, patient satisfaction results, compliance with many federal and local regulations, quality and safety measures, and associate satisfaction.

2. What would you consider to be a "typical" day for you?

A typical day includes interacting with executive team members on a number of subjects regarding recruitment, performance management, compensation of our physicians, and other associates. I also work with physician leaders and operations management on improving patient satisfaction, employee engagement, and physician engagement. I very often interact with system human resources and physician leaders regarding various physician employment issues. I also spend a good amount of my day interacting with and developing my direct reports to the director of human resources, director of physician recruitment, and manager of clinical education, to be sure they are succeeding in executing the plans and tactics we all share.

3. What education or training do you have? Is it typical for your job?

I possess a Bachelor of Arts in Organizational Communications with an emphasis in Human Resources Development. I also have a certificate

Continued

NAME: ROBY A. HUNT Continued

as a Senior Specialist in Human Resources from the Human Resources Certification Institute. These are fairly typical degrees and certifications in human resources; however, it is probably more common for a vice president to also possess a master's degree in human resources, business, or healthcare administration.

4. What is the most challenging part of your job?

As a member of senior management, there are times when the head of human resources needs to be an employee advocate in addition to advocating on behalf of the business. This can be challenging when trying to quantify employee-related activities or decisions. The most challenging of these is whether to close an office, service, or whether to do an economic layoff. Other challenges often involve whether to discipline or terminate a physician who may be the source of a significant amount of revenue.

5. What do you consider to be the best part of your job?

The best part of my job is when I get to see or read about positive patient experiences from physicians or associates I have been involved in hiring or mentoring. The best part of my current job is when I am able to see the financial outlook, patient satisfaction, safety and quality, and employee satisfaction all improve in an organization. It is also great to see associates and management develop skills that positively affect their employees' lives.

6. What path did you take to get to the job you are in today?

Following college, I took a number of positions that allowed me to round out my career in human resources. While many follow paths that lead to specialization, I followed a path that allowed me to become a human resources generalist. Early in my career, I began working for healthcare-related organizations, and for the past 25 years, I have led the human resources function for a number of different healthcare organizations. The one constant has been with transforming the human resources function from a transactional department ensuring compliance with various labor laws, to a function that supports the organization's mission and strategy. Because that is what I have mainly focused on, and that happens to be where human resources has been moving during those years, I have been relatively successful at achieving those goals.

Continued

NAME: ROBY A. HUNT Continued

7. What advice do you have for someone who is interested in a job such as yours?

I tell others all the time, "to be successful in human resources in healthcare you must be agile." Healthcare and human resources have changed tremendously over the past two decades, and you must be able to change with them. It is also terribly important to understand how the business operates and what drives success. You cannot be a successful executive in any organization if you don't understand what makes it successful. To do so, you must study the business of healthcare, be involved in lifetime learning, and be willing to take some risks. It is also important to understand that your voice is just as important as the others in the room. As one of my mentors taught me, it is not enough to "be at the table," you need to be able to "play at the table."

JOB DESCRIPTION

The director of marketing for an acute care hospital is responsible for a wide range of activities including helping to develop and execute a strategic plan for marketing the hospital's services to the community. He or she will also help market the hospital's services and activities to other groups including patients, employees, and physicians. Guiding the hospital's interactions with the media will also be critical, as will helping to train other senior leaders within the hospital to interact with members of the media. Other responsibilities include advertising, internal communications, hospital publications, community relations, and helping to manage special events. He or she will also work closely with the hospital's senior leadership to help manage successful implementation of the hospital's vision and strategic plan.

EDUCATION AND EXPERIENCE

A bachelor's degree is a minimum expectation for most marketing director positions, and a master's degree is preferred. Educational background should be in marketing, communications, public relations, journalism, or another related field. Prior experience in healthcare, hospital, or service line marketing is crucial. Many employers expect marketing directors to have at least 5 to 7 years of relevant prior experience.

CORE COMPETENCIES AND SKILLS

- Ability to use good judgment in potentially difficult political situations
- Excellent written and oral communication skills
- Excellent editing skills
- Outstanding interpersonal skills, as this position will be responsible for working with top management
- Ability to work under pressure and deal effectively with crises
- Solid understanding of computer applications (Microsoft Word, etc.)
- Ability to understand the impact of market forces on hospital strategy
- Ability to promote cross-departmental collaboration
- Experience working with social media and web design

COMPENSATION

The majority of marketing directors make between $42,000 and $144,000 annually. Marketing directors with broader responsibilities at larger hospitals will likely earn a higher salary. Similarly those working in a busier, urban area, stand to make more than someone living in a rural setting.

EMPLOYMENT OUTLOOK

As the number of hospitals in the United States decreases slightly over the next several years, the demand for hospital marketing directors will decrease slightly as well. However, the outlook for these jobs remains high as the use of social media and other types of communication increases among hospitals.

FOR FURTHER INFORMATION

■ Society for Healthcare Strategy & Market Development (www.shsmd.org)

JOB DESCRIPTION

The director of materials management implements and administers the hospital supply chain function under general supervision and within corporate guidelines. The director is responsible for purchasing, inventory control, material systems, and financial controls. Materials management works closely across hospital departments to assure that medical technology of all types is available to clinicians and patients.

EDUCATION AND EXPERIENCE

Minimum of a bachelor's degree in business or healthcare administration, or other related field is required. Five or more years of healthcare materials management experience with at least 3 years of supervisory experience are required.

CORE COMPETENCIES AND SKILLS

- Outstanding interpersonal skills including the ability to effectively communicate with persons both inside and outside the organization
- Excellent verbal and written communication skills
- Ability to analyze and recommend policies and procedures relative to supply chain's technology practices and suppliers
- Ability to maintain cost/revenue ratios in accordance with budget; maintain adequate inventory levels; assist with negotiation of contracts with suppliers for the purchase of capital and noncapital products and services
- Ability to develop and prepare reports and presentations on usage statistics, purchasing trends, marketing data, and savings relative to competitive bidding and national agreements
- Ability to deal with multiple project demands and tight deadlines
- Ability to create a team environment and exhibit appropriate quality service behaviors in meeting and/or exceeding the needs of employees, customers, coworkers, and others
- Demonstrated initiative, follow-through, and ability to work independently
- Ability to build and manage budgets

COMPENSATION

Directors of materials management earn in the range of $38,000 to $116,000, although the total salary will vary depending on the size and location of the hospital and the education and experience of the candidate.

EMPLOYMENT OUTLOOK

The employment outlook for directors of materials management is good now and into the foreseeable future. Hospitals must remain technologically sophisticated in order to be competitive, and it is up to the director of materials management to help guide the hospital to make the best technology acquisition decisions possible.

FOR FURTHER INFORMATION

- ▓ Association for Healthcare Resource & Materials Management (www .ahrmm.org)

24

JOB DESCRIPTION

The director of medical records is responsible for maintaining the records of patients in accordance with federal governmental regulations regarding patient privacy. Administration and oversight of the medical records program along with an understanding of the latest computer software and technology are key responsibilities of the position.

EDUCATION AND EXPERIENCE

A Bachelor of Science in Health Information Management is a degree aimed at preparing one for a career in information and data management, among other areas. Following the completion of this degree, graduates are eligible to sit for the Registered Health Information Administrator Certification (RHIA). Although not required, a master's degree in health information management or a similar area will provide one with the knowledge and skill set needed.

CORE COMPETENCIES AND SKILLS

- Outstanding interpersonal skills including the ability to effectively communicate with persons throughout the organization including clinicians
- Ability to plan, direct, and evaluate staff
- Ability to read, analyze, and apply laws, regulations, and procedures as related to medical records
- Excellent verbal and written communication skills
- Ability to understand and use the latest computer software and security
- Ability to hold subordinates accountable for organizational goals
- Ability to develop and maintain a departmental budget
- Attention to detail

COMPENSATION

A director of medical records may earn in the range of $73,000 to $98,000. However, this figure varies depending on a number of variables including the size of the hospital and the region of the country in which the hospital is located. Directors of medical records of smaller hospitals in more rural areas tend to earn less than their counterparts at large, urban hospitals.

EMPLOYMENT OUTLOOK

The outlook for directors of medical records is expected to increase in the coming years. The consistently changing landscape of health information technology will require this position to adapt and grow.

FOR FURTHER INFORMATION

■ Department of Labor, Bureau of Labor Statistics (www.mcoaonline.com/member-services/pages/eoea)

■ American Health Information Management Association (www.ahima.org/Default.aspx)

25

JOB DESCRIPTION

The director of patient accounts is responsible for promoting and maximizing the revenue cycle throughout the organization. This includes oversight of all processes involved in the capture, management, and collection of patient revenues.

EDUCATION AND EXPERIENCE

A bachelor's degree in finance or accounting is required, but a master's degree is preferred. Three to five years of experience in healthcare accounting and finance are required.

CORE COMPETENCIES AND SKILLS

- Outstanding interpersonal skills including the ability to effectively communicate with persons throughout the organization and in the community
- Ability to plan, direct, and evaluate staff
- Ability to understand and adapt to the changing regulatory environment
- Excellent verbal and written communication skills
- Excellent understanding of hospital billing, coding, registration, and financing
- Ability to hold subordinates accountable for organizational goals
- Ability to develop and maintain a departmental budget

COMPENSATION

A director of patient accounts may earn in the range of $117,000 to $168,000. However, this figure varies depending on a number of variables including the size of the hospital and the region of the country in which the hospital is located. Directors of patient accounts of smaller hospitals in more rural areas tend to earn less than their counterparts at large, urban hospitals.

EMPLOYMENT OUTLOOK

Job prospects for directors of patient accounts are reported to be good across the country. This is a crucial position in maintaining and improving the financial standing of any hospital.

FOR FURTHER INFORMATION

- Healthcare Financial Management Association (www.hfma.org)

26 DIRECTOR OF PHYSICIAN RELATIONS

JOB DESCRIPTION

The director of physician relations directs and oversees programs designed to foster positive relations between physicians and the hospital or healthcare facility. The director promotes the organization among members of the medical community in order to establish partnerships and affiliations. The physician relations manager is responsible for planning and implementing outreach efforts focusing on physicians, community groups, and other potential referral sources in the hospital's target markets. The position focuses primarily on developing and improving hospital referral relationships with physicians in the service area, with the goal of maximizing referral and redirection opportunities for both inpatient and outpatient services.

EDUCATION AND EXPERIENCE

Directors of physician relations are required to possess a bachelor's degree in business, healthcare administration, or related field; a master's degree is generally preferred. Most candidates for the director of physician relations have 3 years of progressively responsible experience in hospital marketing or business development.

CORE COMPETENCIES AND SKILLS

- Outstanding interpersonal skills including the ability to effectively communicate with persons both inside and outside the organization
- Excellent verbal and written communication skills
- Strong leadership and consensus-building skills
- Familiarity with physician relations data management systems
- Skills to enhance communication between community physicians and hospital specialists
- Proven ability to monitor needs and respond to concerns of community physicians
- Demonstrated skill at relationship management promoting clinical services, programs, and facilities in order to enhance referral volume and ensure the success and growth of the hospital
- Experience at communicating with current and potential referring physicians, enhancing awareness of hospital offerings, identifying provider issues, monitoring and reporting on referral trends, and serving as a general customer contact for referring entities

- ■ Proficiency in developing and maintaining computerized databases
- ■ Ability to build and manage budgets

COMPENSATION

Physician relations directors earn in the range of $99,000 to $163,000, although the total salary will vary depending on the size and location of the hospital and the education and experience of the candidate.

EMPLOYMENT OUTLOOK

Managing the relationship with physicians is an important activity at every hospital. Given the changes envisioned by health reform, there is no question that effective directors of physician relations are going to be in high demand in the near-term future.

FOR FURTHER INFORMATION

- ■ American Association of Physician Liaisons (www.physicianliaison.com/default.cfm)

NAME: JONATHAN T. BROWN

Title: Pharmacy Assistant Director
Organization: Good Shepherd Medical
Center (GSMC)

1. Briefly describe your job responsibilities.

As pharmacy assistant director, I am responsible for pharmaceutical services for two stand-alone emergency rooms (ERs), as well as a physician-owned ambulatory surgical center. At the main hospital, I support my direct supervisor, the director of pharmacy, in various ways by working on the pharmacists' schedule, change management, clinical initiatives, and communication between the management and our employees. My direct reports are the staff pharmacists, the tech supervisor and her subordinates, and the pharmacy technicians.

2. What would you consider to be a "typical" day for you?

A typical day would start off with me greeting staff and catching up with people regarding their weekend, or what shifts they are working today. This starts at 9 a.m. and ends around 9:15 a.m. I get in later than my director, but I also stay later. We do this so there is a manager around for a larger part of the day. Then I check my e-mail and respond to urgent messages for approximately 20 to 30 minutes. After that, I will examine variances from the weekend or previous day, and, if Pharmacy is involved, I will investigate and be ready to present resolutions by the variance meeting at 10:20 a.m. After that meeting, I usually eat an early lunch. I always get lunch in the cafeteria and know a majority of the employees in the cafeteria by name. This helps me have a more enjoyable and personable experience.

After lunch, I run reports on our automated dispensing machine software that tells me if I need to sell narcotics from the main hospital to our ancillary ERs. If I need to fill out Drug Enforcement Administration (DEA) forms for those narcotics, I will, and then if I need to go to these ERs thereafter, I will. Once I get back to the Longview campus, a pharmacy technician and I head over to the ambulatory surgical center where we fill medications for their new automated dispensing machines. While over there, and throughout the day, I stop and communicate with people as necessary.

Continued

Last thing that I do in the day is check my e-mail one last time to see if there is anything urgent.

Random issues occur frequently. These are mini projects that need to be resolved and they require extra attention throughout the day. These may include employee issues, attendance problems, working on the schedule, a medication error, or complaints from a different department.

3. What education or training do you have? Is it typical for your job?

I have a Doctorate in Pharmacy (PharmD), and a Six Sigma Green Belt Certificate from Villanova. To practice pharmacy, the PharmD has become the standard, but people who graduated from school before the late 1990s practice with a bachelor's degree in pharmacy. The Six Sigma Green Belt is not typical for my job, but has helped me keep efficiency as a primary focus for my projects. For assistant directors and directors of pharmacy, a Master of Business Administration (MBA) or Master of Health Administration (MHA) is desired.

4. What is the most challenging part of your job?

The most challenging part of my job is defining roles and keeping communication channels open. Healthcare is such a dynamic arena that it is unwise to keep doing the same thing for too long. Trying to figure out a more efficient, yet safe, process is extremely taxing, but can reap rewards. Communicating with one another is the only way change can become permanent. Different initiatives within a hospital have a diverse group of stakeholders, so the impact is difficult to gauge.

5. What do you consider to be the best part of your job?

The best part of my job is to be able to create positive change that will overall lead to increased performance of the Pharmacy department, and positively impact patient care.

6. What path did you take to get to the job you are in today?

The path I took to get to my current job has been an interesting one. I graduated with my PharmD in late April 2012; I was hired at GSMC the next February. This was due to the job market for hospital pharmacists being especially congested in Florida. Snowbirds would come

Continued

NAME: JONATHAN T. BROWN
Continued

down from various locations for seasonal work and it was difficult for new graduates to be hired at hospitals. I was stubborn in the fact that I refused to work at a retail chain pharmacy such as Walgreens or CVS. While in Florida studying for my boards, a headhunter reached out to me and told me about an opportunity in East Texas in a city called Longview, which I had never heard of.

Once at GSMC, I worked there as a staff pharmacist for about a year and a half. I was called about an opportunity as a pharmacy manager for the CHRISTUS Spohn network in Corpus Christi, Texas, but did that only for about 3 months, and came right back to GSMC. I then applied for the pharmacy assistant director position once it was available in another 4 months. I have been in my current role as pharmacy assistant director since September 2015.

7. What advice do you have for someone who is interested in a job such as yours?

My advice would be first to be sound at what you do. For me, that was being a pharmacist. This allowed me to be ready for the promotion within my department because I was already proven. Secondly, I would say, it is beneficial to meet other employees in completely different departments to get a feel of how what you do affects them. Finally, I would keep bridge burning to a minimum. Sometimes, it is necessary if people aren't acting with integrity, but you never know when you will need somebody. Respect goes a long way.

JOB DESCRIPTION

The director of social services functions as the main figure within the social services department, which is often in a rehabilitation center. It is this person's responsibility to identify and provide for the needs of each patient in order for the patient to reach his or her potential. While adhering to federal, state, and local guidelines and regulations, the director of social services will additionally work with patients' families to ensure the smoothest possible transition beyond the hospital admission. This position will lead teams of social workers that help patients readjust to a new environment, whether it is in a rehabilitation center, a nursing home, or the patient's house.

EDUCATION AND EXPERIENCE

A bachelor's degree in social work is often the only educational requirement for becoming a director of social services at smaller clinics. At larger rehabilitation centers, however, a master's in social work is the minimum. Experience in an acute or long-term care facility, or a license that fulfills state and federal regulations, is expected. Most directors of social services have experience in management.

CORE COMPETENCIES AND SKILLS

- Outstanding interpersonal and communication skills in order to work with residents and residents' families
- Demonstrated ability to successfully counsel residents and assist them in achieving their maximum potential
- Familiarity with gathering and evaluating admissions reports, as well as preadmission screenings
- Excellent management skills including the ability to lead staff toward achieving the goals of the social services department
- Ability to train staff when required
- Superior understanding of local, state, and federal requirements
- Exceptional writing skills

COMPENSATION

The director of social services is the head of the social services department. This individual should expect to receive a salary that reflects this position's leadership. Typically, the director of social services will receive a salary between $95,000 and $129,000, with $112,000 being an appropriate average.

EMPLOYMENT OUTLOOK

The director of social services plays a critical role in coordinating teams to offer services to the families of patients. This position is responsible for ensuring that patients and their families have a smooth discharge from the hospital. Social services workers provide information about postadmission services that could prevent readmissions, which save hospitals millions of dollars each year. Hospitals will continue to utilize social workers, making the director of this department a coveted position.

FOR FURTHER INFORMATION

- National Association of Social Workers (www.socialworkers.org)
- Society for Social Work Leadership in Health Care (www.sswlhc.org)

28

JOB DESCRIPTION

The executive director is responsible for leading and strengthening a comprehensive fund-raising program in support of the foundation's mission and goals. Specific emphasis is focused on annual giving, major giving, planned giving, grants, and fund-raising events. The executive director will strive to build a greater understanding and support for both the hospital's and foundation's mission, vision, and goals in the region.

EDUCATION AND EXPERIENCE

Bachelor's degree is required; advanced degree is preferred. A degree in marketing/business/public relations/communications may be helpful. Minimum of 5 years of increasingly responsible fund-raising experience, preferably in a healthcare setting, with evidence of continued growth through education and participation in professional fund-raising organizations is necessary.

CORE COMPETENCIES AND SKILLS

- Outstanding interpersonal skills including the ability to effectively communicate with persons throughout the organization
- Excellent verbal and written communication skills
- Ability to develop annual measurable objectives in the areas of annual giving, special events, capital projects and campaign donations, planned giving and grant awards to support reaching the 5-year strategic plan goals
- Ability to establish and oversee policies and procedures related to the implementation and management of an effective and professional fund-raising program
- Ability to develop and manage a program to integrate the hospital chief executive officer (CEO), the foundation board chair, board members, and key volunteers into the foundation fund-raising process; work with the hospital CEO to effectively inform the hospital board of directors on foundation activities
- Ability to be aware of grant opportunities and effectively respond to them with requests and proposals
- Experience in leading and motivating work teams with the intent to create and articulate a vision and direction; ability to inspire, encourage, and influence others toward shared vision and optimal outcomes

- Demonstrated ability to quickly understand an issue, to identify alternatives, to quantify and assess, and to objectively present recommendations that are in the best interest of the system, the region, and the hospital
- Ability to facilitate group discussions and to work broadly with administration, hospital, and medical staff
- Capable of analyzing financial, volume, and market data

COMPENSATION

Marketing directors earn in the range of $147,000 to $190,000, although the total salary will vary depending on the size and location of the hospital and the education and experience of the candidate.

EMPLOYMENT OUTLOOK

Typically, only larger hospitals and health systems can afford to have the position of foundation executive director. It is reported that this is a position that frequently is used to develop persons who plan to move into senior management positions; therefore, the turnover of business development professionals is very brisk.

FOR FURTHER INFORMATION

- Healthcare Financial Management Association (www.hfma.org)
- American College of Healthcare Executives (www.ache.org)

29

JOB DESCRIPTION

The medical staff coordinator is responsible for providing administrative and credentialing support for the activities of the medical staff of the hospital. The medical staff coordinator assists with all medical staff requirements, and maintains records and systems that result in efficient program operation.

This role supports the medical/dental/allied health credentialing process, including the processing of new applications, requests for temporary privileges, and biennial reappointments. The medical staff coordinator works to coordinate referrals, authorizations, and payments for patient care services. The coordinator must ensure compliance with all guidelines and policies of the managed care organizations.

EDUCATION AND EXPERIENCE

The position requires an associate degree or equivalent; bachelor's degree in health-related field is desired. At least 1-year credentialing and privileging experience in a medical setting is preferred.

Familiarity with the Continuing Medical Education (CME) process is highly encouraged. Certified Provider Credentialing Specialist (CPCS) is preferred; willing to be certified within 2 years of hire is required.

CORE COMPETENCIES AND SKILLS

- Ability to verify competence, medical and/or professional education, residency, internships, fellowships, additional formal training, relevant board certifications, healthcare affiliations, work history, military experiences, professional references, licensure and certifications, Drug Enforcement Administration (DEA) certificates, malpractice coverage, and privileges the applicant is requesting
- Ability to query the National Practitioner Data Bank as appropriate
- Ability to manage expenses as appropriate
- Ability to maintain the credentialing database assuring accuracy and completeness
- Ability to act as a liaison between the medical staff and other departments of the hospital, and provide assistance in the coordination of the duties of the medical staff
- Ability to organize and maintain credentials files in the medical staff office

■ Ability to present completed files to the credentials committee for recommendation of approval of appointments and privileges

■ Ability to maintain a working knowledge of the Medical Staff Bylaws and applicable hospital policies to ensure the medical staff's compliance with stated parameters

■ Familiarity with the current Joint Commission standards, state and federal law pertaining to the medical staff, and apply them to the credentialing process as needed

■ Ability to facilitate medical staff committee meetings as requested, which includes committee notification, drafting agendas, taking and drafting minutes; any follow-up as required

■ Ability to take on other related responsibilities as required

COMPENSATION

Medical staff coordinators earn in the range of $39,000 to $51,000, although the total salary will vary depending on the size and location of the hospital and the education and experience of the candidate.

EMPLOYMENT OUTLOOK

The employment potential for medical staff coordinators is very strong. Every hospital must maintain current records of their medical staff members as mandated by governmental and nongovernmental accrediting bodies. There is regular turnover in this position, resulting in a continuing need for well-trained professionals.

FOR FURTHER INFORMATION

■ National Association of Medical Staff Services (www.namss.org)

30

JOB DESCRIPTION

The volunteer services coordinator is responsible for working with and overseeing volunteers of the hospital, which can range in number from ten to hundreds, based on the size of the facility. Volunteers participate in a multitude of tasks throughout the hospital, from patient transport to working at the front desk. The coordinator must make sure the volunteers have the proper training, the state-mandated records, conduct the interviewing and hiring process, and be the point person for these employees. The coordinator will also work to create policies, job descriptions, and funding events.

EDUCATION AND EXPERIENCE

Volunteer services coordinators typically have a bachelor's degree, with a minimum of 3 years of experience in nonprofit fund-raising, recruiting, marketing, and leading groups of people.

CORE COMPETENCIES AND SKILLS

- Outstanding interpersonal skills including the ability to effectively communicate with persons throughout the organization and in the community
- Ability to plan, direct, and evaluate staff
- Ability to think critically and provide reliable advice
- Excellent verbal and written communication skills
- Understanding of the regulations associated with volunteers working within hospitals
- Ability to hold subordinates accountable for organizational goals
- Ability to develop and maintain a departmental budget

COMPENSATION

A volunteer services coordinator may earn in the range of $37,000 to $78,000. However, this figure varies depending on a number of variables including the size of the hospital and the region of the country in which the hospital is located. Volunteer services coordinators of smaller hospitals in more rural areas tend to earn less than their counterparts at large, urban hospitals.

EMPLOYMENT OUTLOOK

Volunteers are essential for the function of hospitals throughout the country, and economic challenges increase the importance of these individuals. This position is going to remain stable and a part of all healthcare organizations.

FOR FURTHER INFORMATION

■ Association for Healthcare Volunteer Resource Professionals (www.ahvrp .org)

JOB DESCRIPTION

The administrator serves as the chief administrative officer of the clinic. The role of the administrator is to develop and implement the clinic's strategic plan in collaboration with physician owners. The position includes oversight of all clinical operations including human resources, finance, compliance with legal and regulatory requirements, information technology, medical records, accreditation, and reimbursement by third-party payers. The clinical administrator has overall responsibility for nonphysician staff members.

EDUCATION AND EXPERIENCE

Education and experience vary depending on the size and complexity of the physician practice. Smaller practices will frequently hire persons with a bachelor's degree in either business or (preferably) healthcare administration for the role of administrator. Large physician practices typically require a master's degree in business or healthcare administration. Most of the larger physician practices require a minimum of 3 years of physician practice management experience in a leadership role.

CORE COMPETENCIES AND SKILLS

- Exceptional interpersonal skills, including the ability to effectively communicate with persons throughout the organization
- Responsibility toward developing and implementing the clinic's mission and strategic vision
- Ability to provide leadership in developing, planning, and implementing the clinic's business plans to the physicians
- Ability to recommend, develop, and implement improvements for the practice
- Ability to communicate to the board about current trends, problems, and medical activities to facilitate policy making
- Ability to establish, secure approval, and oversee clinical operating policies and procedures
- Ability to participate in and coordinate physician recruitment
- Ability to oversee efforts for recruitment, development, and performance evaluation of employees

- Financial skills to oversee the business and financial affairs of the clinic and fiscal management in conjunction with the practice of the certified public accountant (CPA)
- Ability to oversee and manage the billing and collection processes/department
- Skills to enhance operational effectiveness, emphasizing cost containment without jeopardizing important innovation or quality of care
- Ability to ensure clinical compliance with all regulatory agencies governing healthcare delivery and the rules of accrediting bodies
- Ability to continually monitor operations, programs, physical properties, and initiate appropriate changes
- Ability to encourage community education through participation in health fairs and events to promote awareness, and take responsibility for managing the overall marketing activities of the practice
- Ability to represent the clinic in its relationships with other health organizations, governmental agencies, and third-party payers
- Ability to manage all practice-related managed care relationships, including related reimbursement, negotiation with third-party payers, provider credentialing, and maintenance of contracts
- Ability to serve as liaison to and channel of communication among the hospitals, health plans, insurance companies, and regulatory bodies
- Ability to resolve any medical–administrative problems and keep lines of communication open with staff to ensure high employee morale and a professional, healthful clinical atmosphere
- Ability to maintain professional affiliations and enhance professional development to keep current in the latest healthcare trends and developments
- Ability to maintain the strictest confidentiality

COMPENSATION

Administrators can expect to earn between $75,000 and $150,000 per year, although large, complex practices can pay upward of $350,000. This salary will vary depending on the size, location, and medical specialty of the practice.

EMPLOYMENT OUTLOOK

The U.S. Department of Labor projects a strong, faster-than-average growth of administrators. A significant part of this growth is due to changes projected to occur as a result of healthcare reform that will shift the focus of care from the hospital to the physician clinic.

FOR FURTHER INFORMATION

- Medical Group Management Association (www.mgma.com)
- American Medical Group Association (www.amga.org)

- Ability to identify trends and motivate workforce toward changes needed to adapt and remain competitive
- Ability to identify opportunities for improvement and change
- Ability to utilize standard computer-related applications
- Skill in analyzing financial, volume, and market data

COMPENSATION

Associate administrators can expect to earn between $55,000 and $110,000 per year. This salary will vary depending on the size, location, and medical specialty of the practice. Small practices will typically use the CEO/administrator to fill this role. Only mid- to large-size physician practices can afford to have their own associate administrator.

EMPLOYMENT OUTLOOK

The U.S. Department of Labor projects strong, faster-than-average growth of associate administrators. A significant part of this growth is due to changes projected to occur as a result of healthcare reform that will shift the focus of care from the hospital to the physician clinic.

FOR FURTHER INFORMATION

- Medical Group Management Association (www.mgma.com)
- American Medical Group Association (www.amga.org)

 NAME: **APRIL D. SABADO**

Title: Strategic Projects Coordinator
Organization: Virginia Hospital Center
Physician Group

1. Briefly describe your job responsibilities.

I work directly under the chief operations officer of Virginia Hospital Center (VHC) Physician Group to complete special projects and rapid-improvement initiatives, including workflow mapping, process improvement, creating project proposals, managing the patient experience line, managing the employee recognition program, collating data and creating slides for two executive-level presentations per month (quality council and physician administrative council), and coordinating the content and agenda items for 10 director/executive-level meetings per month. I also manage the COO's calendar, and prepare physician compensation employment agreements for review.

2. What would you consider to be a "typical" day for you?

- 5%: I answer patient calls that come through the COO's Patient Experience Line. I resolve complaints, or record positive comments, if applicable. Employees who are positively recognized are given accolades on a monthly basis.
- I spend 20% of my day preparing physician employment contracts. I am informed regularly when a new physician is hired, or an existing physician needs a new contract or an amendment. These requests come directly from the physician recruiter or the COO, and require multiple reviews by the director of legal services and the COO before I send the final draft to the physician.
- 20%: I coordinate 10 meetings per month, in total. I keep track of the COO's agenda items for each meeting, and collate all data/slides/distributions as requested by the COO.
- 25%: I attend meetings. During these meetings, I am facilitating a project discussion, taking meeting minutes, or discussing projects with a director.
- 20%: I assist the directors with projects, write project proposals, help with administrative tasks, or coordinate resources.
- 10%: scheduling and other administrative duties.

Continued

NAME: APRIL D. SABADO Continued

3. What education or training do you have? Is it typical for your job?

I have a Master of Business Administration (MBA), Master of Science (MS) in Healthcare Management and a Bachelor of Science (BS) in Business Administration. I don't believe a graduate degree is required for my position, but I sincerely believe that I am able to take on as much as I do (though it is overwhelming) because of my education and experience.

4. What is the most challenging part of your job?

- Working for six directors who all have competing priorities.
- This is a very "high-pressure" position because there are unpredictable deadlines (e.g., same-day requests for data, new physician contracts must be finalized within 3 days, patients require a call back before the end of the day).

5. What do you consider to be the best part of your job?

I like feeling as though I'm helping people (patients, the COO, the directors, the hospital, the practice managers, et al.).

6. What path did you take to get to the job you are in today?

I am a military spouse who has always worked in administrative positions (mostly the governmental sector), and decided I wanted to work in a field where I was able to serve the active duty military community and its veterans. I decided to study healthcare management with the intention of becoming a medical service corps officer as an administrator.

I went to Marymount University for my MBA and MS in Health Care Management and accepted a position at VHC as a practice administrator halfway through my graduate program. After I graduated, I moved into my position as strategic projects coordinator.

7. What advice do you have for someone who is interested in a job such as yours?

Physician group operations takes persistence. The environment is always changing (workflows, policies, staff, etc.), and it is difficult to see the benefits of your labor. It is important to maintain a positive attitude and focus on the "small wins."

 NAME: MATTHEW JURON

Title: Project Manager, Business
Development, Ambulatory Services
Organization: Northwell Health

1. Briefly describe your job responsibilities.

My role at Northwell Health (formerly North Shore-LIJ Health System) is
to support the growth of the ambulatory network through physician/prac-
tice alignment via employment models. I manage the due diligence process and develop business plans by working with relevant stakeholders
(including the service line, finance, hospital administration, legal, human
resources). We have the common goal of closing clinical and market
gaps, improving access, and supporting Northwell's market expansion.

2. What would you consider to be a "typical" day for you?

A typical day can involve data inventory, business plan development/
review and meetings with the service line/finance/legal teams. Other
days are spent in the field meeting with physicians and discussing
next steps. Daily, we use Microsoft Excel for business planning and
Salesforce to track the steps of our active physician alignments.

3. What education or training do you have? Is it typical for your job?

I have an undergraduate degree in sociology/global health from Emory
University. I then went on to receive my Master of Health Administration
(MHA) from the George Washington University. This degree is fairly typical
in my line of work. The other project managers with whom I have worked
have had either an MHA, Master of Public Administration (MPA) (some with
specialization in healthcare) or Master of Business Administration (MBA).

4. What is the most challenging part of your job?

The most challenging aspect of my job is driving forward a portfolio
of 50 active projects and maintaining contact with all of our relevant

Continued

stakeholders, all while appropriately managing expectations. This has sharpened my communication, time management, and follow-up skills.

5. What do you consider to be the best part of your job?

The best part of my job is working on such a motivated and collegial team. I also really enjoy the aspect of the job that allows me to interface with so many different members of the health system, as well as directly with community physicians.

6. What path did you take to get to the job you are in today?

After completing a postgraduate fellowship with Northwell Health (at the time, North Shore-LIJ), I accepted a full-time role in business development, and have been working in this capacity since June 2015. The fellowship was rotational based and I had spent 3 months in business development from July to September 2014.

7. What advice do you have for someone who is interested in a job such as yours?

Familiarize yourself with tax returns and profit-and-loss statements. Demonstrate a high level of engagement, a positive attitude, an ability to balance numerous active projects, and a propensity to perform well in a team setting.

 NAME: RODNEY VANDERWARKER

Title: Vice President of Primary Care, Behavioral Health and Institute Operations

Organization: Fenway Health

1. Briefly describe your job responsibilities.

I am responsible for the programmatic operations related to our three largest clinical departments. These departments include about 75% of the agency's staff from a variety of disciplines. The four departmental directors of these departments report to me. Our Primary Care division includes all on-site specialty care, digital radiology and clinical support staff, in addition to the primary care providers. Behavioral Health includes group and individual therapy, substance abuse treatment, and psychiatry. The Fenway Institute houses a roughly $9 million research and professional educational portfolio which is funded mostly through federal grants. The Institute also houses a data management and health informatics core that supports all programs at Fenway Health, including management of our electronic medical records. The manager of the core reports directly to me. Additionally, a social services agency, AIDS Action Committee of Massachusetts, is a controlled affiliate of Fenway Health. The programmatic work of that agency is also in my portfolio. Finally, our Sponsored Program staff and one staff member focused on strategic initiatives (also known as "special projects") are housed in the Executive Office and report directly to me.

2. What would you consider to be a "typical" day for you?

Typically I arrive at the office by 6:30 a.m. so that I can have time to complete administrative work, read applicable news and other literature, and prepare for various discussions. I am generally in meetings with either direct reports or focused work groups throughout the day. I try to schedule lunch meetings as often as possible to maximize that time. Afternoon meetings generally stop by 5 p.m. Assuming I don't have an evening responsibility (e.g., board meeting, agency event, networking dinner), I

Continued

NAME: RODNEY VANDERWARKER
Continued

try to leave the office by 5:30/6:00 p.m. After dinner, I try to clear out any unanswered e-mails and get to bed by 9:30 p.m. Repeat.

3. What education or training do you have? Is it typical for your job?

My undergraduate degree is in history/education. I also have a Masters of Public Health (MPH) with a focus on policy and management. My training, through various positions at Fenway Health and at other organizations, has been in leadership and management. It isn't unusual for MPHs to work in healthcare administration—especially in operations. However, I work with many clinically trained people in administration—mostly physicians and various levels of nurses (nurse practitioner, RN, etc.). People with clinical training are most common in my type of job.

4. What is the most challenging part of your job?

Resources—whether time, money, space, or other—are limited within any organization. Given this, resources need to be prioritized. I find it most challenging to figure out how to navigate the system to get the right resources to my direct reports so that they can be successful.

5. What do you consider to be the best part of your job?

I get to work with some of the smartest, most mission-driven people in the world—especially in the area of lesbian, gay, bisexual, and transgender (LGBT) health. As a gay man, I know that the work Fenway Health does has a real impact on the lives of people in my community. This is rewarding beyond belief.

6. What path did you take to get to the job you are in today?

I went to school to be a history teacher and, late in my training, realized that it wasn't a fit for me. I had several leadership roles on my college campus and decided to give higher education a try. I worked in student services after college. While at that job, I started volunteer work for an AIDS service agency. The early 1990s was a difficult time when many people with HIV died rather quickly. I felt a calling to work in this field both because it was my community being heavily impacted, and because I wasn't afraid like so many others were. I leapt at the opportunity to be executive director of a small AIDS service agency. I learned a lot during

Continued

my 3 years on the job, and I was ready to have less responsibility. I took a job as a research associate at Fenway Health—an entry-level position, but still working on HIV/AIDS issues. I came to Fenway at the beginning of what continues to be an immense wave of growth. I was the ninth person hired in the research division. Five years later, I cycled through three management positions and finally became the departmental director when the position became vacant. By that time, the department was made up of 35 staff and the projections were that growth would continue. I remained the departmental director and served on the agency's senior team for 10 years. I helped grow the department to about 100 staff and expanded our work into new areas. The entire agency saw similar growth. In 2013, I was asked to take a position in the Executive Office to take on my current role. Some of this was indeed about coming into the agency at the right time and some of this was about having many opportunities to learn and to demonstrate capability.

7. What advice do you have for someone who is interested in a job such as yours?

Work hard, network, and be curious.
Also, always be humble.

 NAME: JUSTIN DEAN ZAKIA

Title: Practice Group Administrator
Organization: The George Washington
University Medical Faculty Associates
(MFA)

1. Briefly describe your job responsibilities.

I am responsible for the operations and management of the academic departments of surgery and urology, including oversight of all staff, hiring/firing, and contract negotiations in coordination with the departmental chairs: finances, business development, and growth.

2. What would you consider to be a "typical" day for you?

Each day is a balancing act of putting out the fires of the day and figuring out why they were burning in the first place, leaving time every day for consideration of long-term goals and strategy. There is a great deal of e-mail and several meetings. Rarely does a day go by without at least touching upon a human resource/employee issue. I make it a point to interact with individual physicians every day in order to keep them updated on the fiscal side of their practice. It is important to me that I make time for leadership training and professional development of my staff on a regular basis. We are currently undergoing a significant culture change, so, when able, I try to spend some time most days walking around in relatively informal conversations trying to draw out any concerns or anxieties that might be keeping the staff from fully engaging and transparently discussing the issues.

3. What education or training do you have? Is it typical for your job?

I have a Bachelor of Science degree in environmental science from Cornell, and a Master of Healthcare Delivery Science from Dartmouth. I was trained as a naval officer, a surgical device salesman, and a hospital administrator. I'm not terribly typical.

Continued

NAME: JUSTIN DEAN ZAKIA
Continued

4. What is the most challenging part of your job?

It is a constant, and worthwhile, challenge to prioritize the issues that arise every day. I work to rise above the minutia, align with the organization's strategy, and keep an eye on the big picture every day, because there is always a temptation to get into the weeds, fix the problem in front of you, jump at the short-term gain, and dive deeper. I was trained under the principle of innovation, that change is constant, and that if we don't do everything we do better each year, we are doing worse; and it is a challenge to not focus all of my resources on the here and now; but I enjoy the challenge and it dovetails nicely with my passion for developing and empowering leaders.

5. What do you consider to be the best part of your job?

I work with good people, doing good works. By that I mean that any of my staff or peers could make a better living in another industry. Everyone wants to make money, of course, but people in healthcare want something else as well. I come to work each day surrounded by people who, at least to some degree, want to make the world a better place; and my job is to make them better. It is very rewarding to watch persons grow and take on new challenges that they aren't sure they can handle and to see them excel, and to know you were a small part of that. I don't see many patients; I know that we are healing the sick and fixing the broken every day and that is a wonderful thing to know, but it is abstract for me. My reward is seeing a stronger, more capable, more confident, higher functioning team.

6. What path did you take to get to the job you are in today?

I was a naval officer for 8 years, then a minimally invasive spine surgery rep for 4 years. After seeing the inside of the U.S. healthcare system first hand, I desired to try to help fix it and I became a hospital administrator in a nonprofit community hospital. Now, I am an administrator for a multispecialty academic physician group. The path led from Florida, to Virginia, to Florida, to California, to Virginia, to New Hampshire, to DC— not a straight path.

Continued

NAME: JUSTIN DEAN ZAKIA
Continued

7. What advice do you have for someone who is interested in a job such as yours?

A system is perfectly designed to get the results it's getting; the U.S. healthcare system is in a state of disrepair, so don't assume that just because an organization was successful in the past, it has the secret to being successful in the future. Don't think outside the box; know that there aren't any boxes. For this system to become sustainable, we will need to find new ways to connect patients, providers, and information; but we'll need to move beyond that. If our mission becomes maintaining and improving the health of a population, we will need to connect the system with all aspects of patients' lives: jobs, homes, families, built environment, virtual environment, leisure, education with doctors, providers, clinics, hospitals, pharmaceuticals, devices, records; and someone has to pay for it. My best advice is to keep an open mind; any one of us can create the future of healthcare because no one has any idea what the day after tomorrow will look like.

33

JOB DESCRIPTION

The chief information officer (CIO) provides vision and leadership in the development and implementation of the clinic-wide information technology (IT) program. The CIO will lead the clinic in planning and implementing enterprise information systems to support both distributed and centralized clinical and business operations, and achieve more effective and cost-beneficial enterprise-wide IT operations. Additionally, the CIO provides the following: strategic and tactical planning; development, evaluation, and coordination of the IT systems for the healthcare network. The CIO also oversees the back office computer operations of the affiliate management information system, including local area networks and wide-area networks; designs, implements, and evaluates the systems that support end users in the productive use of computer hardware and software; develops and implements user-training programs; and oversees and evaluates system security and back up procedures.

EDUCATION AND EXPERIENCE

Most medical clinics require a bachelor's degree in computer science, business administration, a related field, or equivalent experience. A master's degree in health/hospital administration, public health, business administration, or related field is highly desirable. A minimum of 3 years' experience with increasing responsibilities managing and supporting healthcare information systems and IT is required; direct management of a major IT operation is preferred. Significant experience in a healthcare setting is desirable, specifically in technology and information systems planning to support business goals.

CORE COMPETENCIES AND SKILLS

- Outstanding interpersonal skills, including the ability to effectively communicate with persons throughout the organization (including clinicians)
- Excellent verbal and written communication skills
- Significant experience in data-processing methods and procedures and computer software systems
- Experience with the systems design and development process, including requirements analysis, feasibility studies, software design, programming, pilot testing, installation, evaluation, and operational management
- Ability to oversee the management and coordination of all fiscal reporting activities for the clinic

- Familiarity with the design, management, and operation of health IT systems
- Proven ability to link and apply complex technologies to business strategies
- Experience negotiating contracts with vendors, contractors, and others
- Ability to analyze and resolve complex issues, both logical and interpersonal

COMPENSATION

Physician practice CIOs can expect to earn between $100,000 and $250,000 per year, with some CIOs in very large practices earning significantly more. This salary will vary depending on the size, location, and medical specialty of the practice. Small practices will typically use the chief executive officer (CEO)/administrator to fill this role. Only mid- to large-size physician practices can afford to have their own CIO.

EMPLOYMENT OUTLOOK

There exists an ongoing demand for persons skilled in clinical information systems management. There are a multitude of new clinical and administrative IT and informatics applications that require skilled and dedicated professionals.

FOR FURTHER INFORMATION

- American Medical Group Association (www.amga.org)
- Healthcare Information and Management Systems Society (www.himss.org)
- Medical Group Management Association (www.mgma.com)

DIRECTOR OF UTILIZATION AND CASE MANAGEMENT
34

JOB DESCRIPTION

The director of utilization and case management is responsible for strategic direction, leadership, planning, organization, and general management for all aspects of the managed care department. The director is responsible for ensuring effective utilization of services. Working with the clinical departments, the director of utilization and case management directs the design, implementation, and evaluation of a standardized case management model that results in standardizing a care coordination model throughout the clinic, with ongoing metrics for evaluation and improvement of patient care. The director is responsible for ensuring maximum incentive payments are received for various case management programs.

EDUCATION AND EXPERIENCE

A bachelor's degree in health or business administration is required, and a master's degree in one of these disciplines is the preferred educational preparation. Typically, 5 years' experience in a medical care delivery organization is required. Four years of experience in peer review with quality management responsibility is also required. Five years of nursing or patient care experience is preferred. Some clinics prefer nationally recognized certification as a risk/compliance officer.

CORE COMPETENCIES AND SKILLS

- Outstanding interpersonal skills including the ability to effectively communicate with persons throughout the organization
- Excellent verbal and written communication skills
- Regular communication with physicians and providers regarding quality and risk management problems, issues, and potential resolutions
- Ability to assist supervisors, managers, and directors in the development, review, and revision of clinical policies and procedures
- Capacity to respond to requests for quality management intervention and provide troubleshooting assistance
- Ability to maintain strict confidentiality related to medical records and other data generated by departmental functions
- Ability to monitor patient concerns by overseeing complaints reported through clinical staff; ability to address, resolve, and follow up on complaints as needed
- Ability to develop a program for alleged violations of rules, regulations, policies, procedures, and standards of conduct

- Experience in conducting risk assessments on potential and actual litigations, and assisting insurers and counsel with defense issues
- Ability to identify trends and motivate workforce toward changes needed to adapt and remain competitive
- Ability to promote excellent customer service among all staff members, and work to ensure customer service measures are achieved
- Ability to identify opportunities for improvement and change
- Ability to utilize standard computer-related applications

COMPENSATION

Directors of utilization and case management can expect to earn between $90,000 and $115,000 per year. This salary will vary depending on the size, location, and medical specialty of the practice. Small practices will typically use the chief executive officer (CEO)/administrator to fill this role. Only mid- to large-size physician practices can afford to have their own director of utilization and case management.

EMPLOYMENT OUTLOOK

The U.S. Department of Labor projects strong, faster-than-average growth of directors of utilization and case management. A significant part of this growth is due to changes projected to occur as a result of healthcare reform that will shift the focus of care from the hospital to the physician clinic.

FOR FURTHER INFORMATION

- Medical Group Management Association (www.mgma.com)
- American Medical Group Association (www.amga.org)

35

JOB DESCRIPTION

The director of clinical operations directs, supervises, and coordinates all clinical operations and physician activities. This involves either direct or indirect responsibility for staffing, budgeting, fiscal planning, telecommunications and equipment purchases and maintenance, and facility development. This is carried out through daily interaction with physicians, managers, supervisors, and senior administrative personnel. The director also supervises a staff of supervisors, clinical coordinators, medical assistants, and other clinical support to provide for the healthcare needs of clinical patients and their families. The director works collaboratively with medical staff on patient care issues and departmental direction, and directs projects to improve departmental services and overall clinical goals.

EDUCATION AND EXPERIENCE

Directors of clinical operations typically possess a bachelor's degree and a current RN license. A master's degree in healthcare or business administration is the preferred educational preparation. Most persons in this role have a minimum of 3 years' experience in clinical operations.

CORE COMPETENCIES AND SKILLS

- Outstanding interpersonal skills, including the ability to effectively communicate with persons throughout the organization
- Excellent verbal and written communication skills
- Demonstrated track record developing and maintaining collaborative relationships among diverse groups, including board members, medical staff, and key external stakeholders
- Ability to build and maintain appropriate peer relationships to facilitate organizational objectives
- An in-depth working knowledge of regulatory licensing, certification, and accreditation applicable in clinical environments
- Experience balancing patient care priorities and departmental needs
- Ability to perform multiple tasks with multiple priorities
- Ability to lead the development and implementation of annual capital and operating budgets
- Skills to facilitate smooth clinical operations by supporting policies and acting as a mentor and resource for team members
- Ability to motivate staff and influence positive morale

■ Ability to utilize an electronic medical record and related computer applications

COMPENSATION

The director of clinical operations can expect to earn between $65,000 and $110,000 per year. This salary will vary depending on the size, location, and medical specialty of the practice. Small practices will typically use the chief executive officer (CEO)/administrator to fill this role. Only mid- to large-size physician practices can afford to have their own director of clinical operations.

EMPLOYMENT OUTLOOK

The U.S. Department of Labor projects strong, faster-than-average growth of directors of clinical operations. A significant part of this growth is due to changes projected to occur as a result of healthcare reform that shifts the focus of care from the hospital to the physician clinic.

FOR FURTHER INFORMATION

■ Medical Group Management Association (www.mgma.com)

 NAME: MARSHA CAMERON

Title: Director of Operations
Organization: C-Spine Institute

1. Briefly describe your job responsibilities.

I evaluate and recommend improvements for exemplary practice performance and direct and manage patient service units. My responsibilities
also consist of general oversight of clinical and administrative activities along with ensuring Occupational Safety and Health Administration
(OSHA), Health Insurance Portability and Accountability Act (HIPAA),
and other regulatory measures are complied with. I also engage in strategic planning and budgeting initiatives to maintain a systemic operational
framework.

2. What would you consider to be a "typical" day for you?

A "typical" day for me would begin with an interdepartmental morning
meeting to discuss the status of any pending issues that require immediate attention and cooperation. This would be followed by a review of any
reports pertaining to the daily operations of the practice that include, but
are not limited to, patient satisfaction, revenue cycle management, process enhancements, customer service, personnel, and adjustments to
staffing. I would then make any necessary adjustments or allocations to
any deficiencies that were identified by the reports. Taking time to read
and respond to e-mails and inquiries as well as meeting with any c-suite
executives who may request any information pertaining to the operations
and functions of each unit, also describe tasks that occur on a daily
basis. The remainder of the day would be spent implementing certain
components of a particular initiative for a predetermined campaign, service line, or accountability metric/benchmark.

3. What education or training do you have? Is it typical for your job?

My educational background is not typical for this job. I have a bachelor's degree in political science. However, I am currently in the process
of completing a master's degree in health administration at the George
Washington University. I have spent the last 10 years in the healthcare
administration field managing and supervising various aspects of a specialty
medical group that include, but are not limited to: managing and adhering
to the terms of managed care contracts; developing patient-centered care

Continued

protocols, medical privacy compliance, accounts receivable, insurance verification; and streamlining workflows to increase efficiency and reduce costs associated with delivering exceptional clinical care.

4. What is the most challenging part of your job?

The most challenging part of my job is to constantly adjust to the incessant changes in healthcare that dramatically impact and occasionally impede the deliverance of medical care. Our clinicians and administrative personnel strive to excel and relentlessly pursue avenues that afford them the opportunity to maximize the occurrence of the most favorable clinical outcomes. Amending policies, procedures, cycles, and protocols that accommodate the changes and ambiguities of some trends in healthcare while providing extraordinary care can be a perplexing and delicate balancing act.

5. What do you consider to be the best part of your job?

The best part of my job is participating and launching programs with researchers, consultants, clinicians, and personnel who share my visions of achieving the tenets of the Triple Aim of Healthcare. My work within the organization plays a role in ensuring efficient, adequate, and accessible medical care.

6. What path did you take to get to the job you are in today?

The path I took to get to my job today may be somewhat unconventional. I began my career with educational and professional experiences in political science, strategic lobbying, and campaign polling. I inadvertently began a career in health administration. I learned each aspect of managing and directing the operation of a medical specialty group by receiving hands-on training in each department, and I previously functioned as a staff member in each department I currently direct.

7. What advice do you have for someone who is interested in a job such as yours?

I would suggest that anyone who may be interested in a job such as mine acquire experience and knowledge of each division and unit he or she will direct. The best approach to directing the overall operations of an entity is to have a sound understanding and comprehension of the purpose and function of each department.

 NAME: DAMIEN COOK

Title: Vice President of Operations and Clinical Transformation
Organization: Premier HealthNet, Premier Health

1. Briefly describe your job responsibilities.

I am responsible for the strategic direction and operations for the employed primary group of Premier Health, Premier HealthNet. This includes overall operations, market strategies, recruitment and employment agreements, compensation model, as well patient and employee engagement. Employee engagement includes physician and practitioner engagement.

I also work with the Clinical Excellence department engaging our practices in practice transformation as a foundation for the broader clinical transformation efforts of Premier Health. These strategies recognize the need for change from the traditional practice model in order for the organization to be successful in the new healthcare landscape. The goal of this transformation effort, from a primary care perspective, enables a team model approach to meet the goals of the Triple Aim, while creating a practice of medicine that is engaging for the physicians, advanced practitioners, and the entire care team.

2. What would you consider to be a "typical" day for you?

A typical day includes a variety of meetings that range from strategic to operational in nature, including:

- Physician/Practitioner meetings as individuals or with the entire practice
- Recruitment interviews
- Collaborative meetings with
  - Physician enterprise senior leadership
  - Premier Health system leadership
  - Support departments and support leadership
- Meeting/rounding with direct reports

Continued

- Collaborating with physician leadership
- Preparation for governance meetings
- Allocated time to work on strategies and initiatives, also desk time for phone calls and e-mails

3. What education or training do you have? Is it typical for your job?

I received a Bachelor of Science from the University of Evansville. I also received a Master of Science degree from the Milwaukee School of Engineering, completing the didactic and practical requirements. I graduated in 2012 from Xavier University's Master of Health Services Administration (MHSA) program, including a residency experience at St. Elizabeth Physicians.

The current environment within primary care allowed me to gain valuable experience at St. Elizabeth Physicians to assist in the leadership of the physician group in a Centers for Medicare & Medicaid Services (CMS) pilot program, the Comprehensive Primary Care Initiative. My past roles allowed me to gain valuable experience working within a strong dyad model with physician leaders, as well as collaborating with physicians to implement programs and strategies. This experience provided the current opportunity of leading a primary care group that is looking to implement similar programs and infrastructure.

4. What is the most challenging part of your job?

The most challenging part of my job is not unique to my role. Many healthcare organizations are challenged to focus and prioritize vast amount of projects, initiatives, and agendas. Taking the time to evaluate current workload and understanding that in order to add something to the list, another project may need to be put on hold, is a unique skill set. It is challenging to say "no," or communicate that in order to accomplish a goal, another may need to be sacrificed. It is one that I have not mastered.

5. What do you consider to be the best part of your job?

So far in my healthcare career, I have found that those who work in healthcare are genuinely good people who have the best intent at heart. They want to deliver great care to patients, or to implement strategies or systems that support improved outcomes. In both organizations of which I have been part, there were great people with whom to work, including

Continued

NAME: DAMIEN COOK Continued

leadership, physicians, management teams, and clinical employees, who put in tremendous effort in taking care of patients. It is definitely the reason I always had an interest in healthcare. Especially at this time, primary care has the opportunity to be a leader of not just individual patient care, but in developing a coordinated healthcare operation—one that can manage large populations of patients and achieve outstanding clinical outcomes.

6. What path did you take to get to the job you are in today?

After my undergraduate education, I worked for a year in the health and wellness field while deciding my next steps. I took the Graduate Record Examinations (GRE) and had interest in a graduate program in the healthcare field. This led me to the Master of Science in Perfusion program at the Milwaukee School of Engineering. It is a great program and a wonderful field. However, I realized the career did not match my personality. I completed the degree and got back into the health and wellness field owning my own business. The convergence of learning business operations and my interest in healthcare was a match for me to enroll in the MHSA program at Xavier University. At Xavier, I had a great didactic and residency experience that initiated my healthcare career at St. Elizabeth Physicians.

7. What advice do you have for someone who is interested in a job such as yours?

Annually, I take the opportunity to go back to the Xavier MHSA program and talk with the current students about my residency and early career experience. One of my main talking points focuses on gaining a wide scope of experience early in your career. Experiencing a variety of projects develops a pool of skills that you can utilize in the future. You never know how a project may help you later in your career, no matter how small the project may seem while completing. Also, having a variety of experiences helps to shape a career path you may not have expected if you went into it with tunnel vision or a predetermined plan. I thought I knew what career path was best for me walking into my healthcare career. If I did not open myself up to a variety of experiences, I would not be on the current career path and may not have been able to achieve the same level of opportunities.

36 DIRECTOR OF FINANCE

JOB DESCRIPTION

The director of finance provides leadership and management of the organization's financial, business planning, and administrative activities. The director of finance is accountable for financial operating polices and internal controls, financial reporting, and budget preparation. In collaboration with the chief executive officer (CEO)/administrator and departmental staff, the director of finance develops plans and objectives regarding short- and long-range requirements in specific areas such as budgeting, capital equipment, space, profit and loss analysis, accounting systems, reporting, internal auditing, and corporate tax filing.

EDUCATION AND EXPERIENCE

Directors of finance typically hold a bachelor's degree in accounting, business administration, or related field. Ideally, this person will be master's prepared with more than 6 years of professional experience in accounting and finance as a supervisor, including 3 years in a medical practice group.

CORE COMPETENCIES AND SKILLS

- Outstanding interpersonal skills, including the ability to effectively communicate with persons throughout the organization
- Excellent verbal and written communication skills
- Demonstrated track record of developing and maintaining collaborative relationships among diverse groups, including board members, medical staff, as well as key external stakeholders
- Ability to build and maintain appropriate peer relationships to facilitate organizational objectives
- Skills in interpreting governmental regulations as required for billing and financial reporting
- Skills in analyzing financial, volume, and market data
- Ability to work with clinical leadership to develop financial statements, including balance sheets, profit and loss statements, and analysis of budget variances
- Experience presenting financial reports and other information to clinical physicians, administrative leaders, and board members
- Ability to lead the development and implementation of annual capital and operating budgets

- Ability to direct special projects in forecasting performance to budget and financial analysis, and service line expansion
- Ability to utilize standard computer-related applications

COMPENSATION

The director of finance can expect to earn between $60,000 and $100,000 per year. This salary will vary depending on the size, location, and medical specialty of the practice. Small practices will typically outsource their accounting and bookkeeping functions. Only mid- to large-size physician practices can afford to have their own finance director.

EMPLOYMENT OUTLOOK

The U.S. Department of Labor projects stable growth of finance directors. Persons in this role tend to stay in place unless offered opportunities at larger and more complex medical group practices.

FOR FURTHER INFORMATION

- Medical Group Management Association (www.mgma.com)
- Healthcare Financial Management Association (www.hfma.org)

JOB DESCRIPTION

The human resources (HR) specialist manages and conducts the employee relations functions within the practice. Responsibilities include advising managers on relationships, performance improvement, disciplinary procedures, and employee complaint procedures. The HR specialist counsels employees on issues including relationships, complaint procedure, and policy interpretation. The HR specialist maintains an advanced understanding of the clinic's pay program, and consults on appropriate pay decisions including employment-based salary changes. He or she also works effectively with other HR staff to resolve issues and complete projects. The HR specialist advises on performance, market, and internal equity. This person coordinates the recruiting function within assigned areas, consults on ad placement and development, identifies effective recruiting sources, and coordinates and attends job fairs. The HR specialist assures compliance with federal and state regulations, administers internal documentation process, and works effectively with the other HR staff to recruit and retain employees in the difficult-to-recruit areas. The HR specialist maintains an advanced understanding of the system benefit programs, and supports assigned departments through organizational development and training efforts.

EDUCATION AND EXPERIENCE

An undergraduate degree in business or health administration is required. Larger physician clinics typically ask for at least 3 years of experience in human resources with specific experience in physician practices preferred.

CORE COMPETENCIES AND SKILLS

- Outstanding interpersonal skills, including the ability to effectively communicate with persons throughout the organization
- Excellent verbal and written communication skills
- Demonstrated skill to make decisions independently through the use of analytical and critical thinking, as well as the ability to conduct research, utilize available data, and negotiate
- Demonstrated ability to effectively conduct and complete individual and group projects
- Proven ability to coach and mentor managers and employees, and be an effective team member as well as an individual contributor

■ Demonstrated ability to conduct training and presentations to groups of various organizational levels and sizes
■ Ability to identify opportunities for improvement and change
■ Ability to utilize standard computer-related applications

COMPENSATION

HR specialist compensation falls in a wide range of salaries. Entry-level HR specialists can expect an annual salary between $45,000 and $65,000, while more experienced HR specialists can earn as much as $100,000. As is the case in all physician practices, small practices of fewer than five physicians usually cannot justify supporting a separate HR department, so most, if not all, of the HR duties will fall on the practice administrator. Larger practices will typically have fully staffed HR departments.

EMPLOYMENT OUTLOOK

There exists an ongoing demand for persons skilled in HR management. The HR specialist is an excellent entry-level position for persons interested in healthcare management, and new positions open frequently as persons are either promoted within HR management or move to other parts of the organization.

FOR FURTHER INFORMATION

■ American Medical Group Association (www.amga.org)
■ Medical Group Management Association (www.mgma.com)
■ Society for Human Resource Management (www.shrm.org)

38 PHYSICIAN COMPLIANCE DIRECTOR

JOB DESCRIPTION

The physician compliance director is responsible for planning, designing, implementing and maintaining system-wide physician compliance programs and associated policies and procedures. This individual serves as the expert for compliance matters relating to employed, independent, and contracted physicians, as well as allied health providers, and as a compliance resource for quality-of-care compliance matters. The director is responsible for monitoring and disseminating pertinent new laws and regulations, and/or revisions to current laws and regulations as they pertain to physician compliance. Examples of these include, but are not limited to, the Federal Sentencing Guidelines and the Affordable Care Act.

EDUCATION AND EXPERIENCE

A graduate degree in health, law, or business administration is the required educational preparation. Typically, 5 years' experience in a medical care delivery organization is required. Most organizations hiring physician compliance directors require a minimum of 5 years of experience in healthcare operations, regulatory compliance, risk management, audit, law, or a similar field.

CORE COMPETENCIES AND SKILLS

- Outstanding interpersonal skills, including the ability to effectively communicate with persons throughout the organization
- Excellent verbal and written communication skills
- Demonstrated knowledge of the federal sentencing guidelines, healthcare laws/regulations, and fraud and abuse laws
- Relevant knowledge to serve as the compliance expert for the practice on matters involving physician compliance
- Ability to provide leadership for the development, implementation, maintenance, and evaluation of policies, procedures, tools, and templates to address changes in current laws and regulations and/or revisions to current laws and regulations related to physician compliance
- Ability to identify key areas for training and required policies and procedures related to physician compliance objectives
- Ability to analyze reports, data, and trends to keep management and governance informed of the current regulatory environment and the potential impact to the practice and to work with multiple stakeholder groups to develop and assess physician and clinical outlier risks through analysis of billing and quality data

- Experience in monitoring governmental recovery efforts for trends or patterns of noncompliance with billing, medical necessity, and coding issues affecting physician services
- Ability to provide consultation services, guidance, and ongoing education to various entities on new laws and regulations and/or revisions to current laws and regulations impacting physician relationships
- Ability to identify opportunities for improvement and change
- Ability to utilize standard computer-related applications

COMPENSATION

Physician compliance directors can expect to earn between $70,000 and $110,000 per year. Compliance directors with law degrees can expect to earn approximately $150,000 annually. This salary will vary depending on the size, location, and medical specialty of the practice. Small practices will typically use the chief executive officer (CEO)/administrator to fill this role. Only mid- to large-size physician practices can afford to have their own physician compliance director.

EMPLOYMENT OUTLOOK

There exists an ongoing demand for persons skilled in physician compliance. There are a multitude of new and existing laws for which physician practices are responsible for following, and it is unlikely that individual physicians have the time to keep up with these laws and regulations.

FOR FURTHER INFORMATION

- Medical Group Management Association (www.mgma.com)
- American Medical Group Association (www.amga.org)

39   QUALITY/RISK MANAGEMENT DIRECTOR

JOB DESCRIPTION

The quality/risk management director works closely with the medical legal consultant, practice operations director, medical director, and clinical administrator to ensure comprehensive program delivery and quality patient care. The quality/risk management director coordinates with all physicians and program and departmental directors to ensure high levels of quality performance. The director develops goals and objectives for the risk and quality management programs of the clinic, and explains quality, risk, and compliance management policies, procedures, systems, and objectives to all personnel employed by the clinic.

EDUCATION AND EXPERIENCE

A bachelor's degree in health or business administration is required, and a master's degree in one of these disciplines is the preferred educational preparation. Typically, 5 years' experience in a medical care delivery organization is required. Four years of experience in peer review with quality management responsibility is also required. Five years of nursing or patient care experience is preferred. Some clinics prefer nationally recognized certification as a risk/compliance officer.

CORE COMPETENCIES AND SKILLS

- Outstanding interpersonal skills, including the ability to effectively communicate with persons throughout the organization
- Excellent verbal and written communication skills
- Communication skills to maintain regular communication with physicians and providers regarding quality and risk management problems, issues, and potential resolutions
- Ability to assist supervisors, managers, and directors in the development, review, and revision of clinical policies and procedures
- Capacity to respond to requests for quality management intervention and provide troubleshooting assistance
- Ability to maintain strict confidentiality related to medical records and other data generated by departmental functions
- Ability to monitor patient concerns by overseeing complaints reported through clinical staff; address, resolve, and follow up as needed
- Ability to develop a program to address and follow up on alleged violations of rules, regulations, policies, procedures, and standards of conduct

■ Experience in conducting risk assessments on potential and actual litigations, and assisting insurers and counsel with defense issues
■ Ability to identify trends and motivate workforce toward changes needed to adapt and remain competitive
■ Ability to promote excellent customer service among all staff members, and work to ensure customer service measures are achieved
■ Ability to identify opportunities for improvement and change
■ Ability to utilize standard computer-related applications

COMPENSATION

Quality/risk management directors can expect to earn between $70,000 and $120,000 per year. This salary will vary depending on the size, location, and medical specialty of the practice. Small practices will typically use the chief executive officer (CEO)/administrator to fill this role. Only mid- to large-size physician practices can afford to have their own quality/risk management director.

EMPLOYMENT OUTLOOK

The U.S. Department of Labor projects strong, faster-than-average growth of quality/risk management directors. A significant part of this growth is due to changes projected to occur as a result of healthcare reform that will shift the focus of care from hospitals to physician clinics, coupled with the need to comply with rapidly changing federal and state laws.

FOR FURTHER INFORMATION

■ American Medical Group Association (www.amga.org)
■ American Society for Healthcare Risk Management (www.ashrm.org)
■ Medical Group Management Association (www.mgma.com)

CHAPTER 8
CAREERS IN LONG-TERM CARE

ADMINISTRATOR

JOB DESCRIPTION

Long-term care administrators can work in a variety of service organizations, such as nursing homes, assisted living or continuing care retirement communities, and home and hospice care. Administrators manage facilities that provide these types of personal care to elderly or incapacitated patients who can no longer care for themselves. Long-term care administrators oversee all of the various departments within the healthcare organization. Their primary job is to ensure effective operations through careful oversight of offered services and financial management. Administrators serve as the primary leadership position within a long-term care facility.

EDUCATION AND EXPERIENCE

In order to become an administrator, most organizations require a bachelor's degree in long-term care administration. A majority of organizations require considerable years of experience (10 years or more) in order to qualify. To direct the operations of a nursing home, administrators need to complete a 6-month administrator-in-training program, and successfully pass federal and state licensure examinations. Licensure is not required for other forms of long-term care administration roles.

CORE COMPETENCIES AND SKILLS

- Business management skills
- Extensive financial management knowledge
- Familiarity with applicable laws and regulations affecting long-term care
- Excellent written and verbal communication skills
- Analytical skills
- Thorough knowledge of healthcare industry
- Excellent intrapersonal skills
- Demonstrated ability to teach, mentor, and manage staff

COMPENSATION

The majority of long-term care administrators make between $100,000 and $150,000 annually; however, this number has increased significantly in recent years, and trends indicate that salaries will continue to increase. This number is also dependent on the size and geographic location of the organization and an individual's level of experience.

EMPLOYMENT OUTLOOK

There is a great need for long-term administrators. Given the large number of aging baby boomers, there will be a significant need for individuals with the appropriate skills to lead a long-term care organization. If anyone is considering a career in administration, long-term care would be an excellent choice.

FOR FURTHER INFORMATION

■ American College of Health Care Administrators (www.achca.org)
■ American Health Care Association (www.ahcancal.org)

NAME: BEN H. YOUNG

Title: Administrator
Organization: HCR ManorCare—Salmon Creek (120-bed skilled nursing facility [SNF])

1. Briefly describe your job responsibilities.

- Direct the location staff to provide high quality in daily care which meets/exceeds all internal/external standards within budget parameters, including, but not limited to, products, physical plant, and environment
- Listen to family questions and concerns, assist with resolving issues, and explain related company actions and decisions
- Complete rounds to assess resident climate and to address complaints or other issues; refer these issues to appropriate departmental head or other personnel
- Drive quality assurance program process in the center, and ensure the implementation of follow-up or corrective action
- Intervene as appropriate in potentially threatening situations and followup with staff after crisis has been resolved
- Oversee preparations for licensure certification surveys
- Scope renovation needs of the facility and gain appropriate support for renovations

2. What would you consider to be a "typical" day for you?

This is the trickiest question, as rarely are 2 days alike.

Wake and review e-mails and day's calendar from home. Arrive 7:30 a.m. to open office, review voice messages, and rounds. Staffing meeting at 8.30 a.m., where we review census and ensure appropriate staffing for nursing department. Interdisciplinary Team (IDT) meeting and 24-hour report meeting at 9 a.m. From here, each day has routine meetings unique to that day of the week or month. Often, the day is spent completing tasks/initiatives between response/management of

Continued

NAME: BEN H. YOUNG Continued

PRN issues. I am in contact with care partners and referring hospitals, as needed/scheduled. This includes bundle and Accountable Care Organizations (ACO) partnerships, which may include data reports. We have afternoon IDT, or "stand-down," at 3 p.m., to ensure closure to items discussed earlier in the day. From there, I work toward having tasks completed or in a good place to leave between 5:30/6:30 p.m.

3. What education or training do you have? Is it typical for your job?

A bachelor's degree is required. State and federal licensure requires a 6-month (minimum) training that is formatted uniquely to each state. This is completed under a licensed preceptor. Ongoing continuing education units (CEUs) are necessary to maintain state licensure.

4. What is the most challenging part of your job?

The punitive nature of the regulatory oversight.

5. What do you consider to be the best part of your job?

The people who choose to work in skilled nursing. They're most often very caring, purpose-oriented individuals who want to do something that improves the lives of others, which is inspiring to me.

6. What path did you take to get to the job you are in today?

In a nutshell, I entered the healthcare administration undergraduate program at Oregon State University (OSU) with an eye on both the acute/primary care and the long-term care tracks. I was president of the student chapters of American College of Healthcare Executives (ACHE) and American College of Health Care Administrators (ACHCA) at the same time, offering wonderful contacts in both fields. One day, I decided I wanted to volunteer in a healthcare setting, so I brought that to Dr. Friedman who connected me with the administrator of a local SNF. Dr. Friedman offered curriculum credits for that experience. As I completed those 8 weeks, the administrator and parent company of the SNF offered me an administrator-in-training (AIT) position, which I began during the summer prior to my senior year at OSU. We spread that over approximately 18 months, as I was still in school—working at the SNF evenings and weekends. I completed the AIT shortly after receiving my degree in

Continued

NAME: BEN H. YOUNG Continued

healthcare administration and was licensed 5 months after graduating. The rest is career movement and positioning.

7. What advice do you have for someone who is interested in a job such as yours?

Spend at least a year working in an SNF before beginning your journey toward licensure. Know first that your heart is in it. The rest, you can learn.

JOB DESCRIPTION

The director of nursing oversees and is responsible for the performance of an entire nursing staff in a hospital or other healthcare facility. He or she may also be responsible for helping to develop and implement patient care services. In addition to overseeing the nursing staff, the director also performs administrative duties. These include developing and implementing a budget for the nursing department and preparing reports for higher levels of management within the organization. The director is responsible for the recruitment, retention, and training of nurses. He or she makes sure that the work standards, legal procedures, and nursing laws are met in the healthcare facility. Directors will also inform nurses of any new nursing policies and procedures.

EDUCATION AND EXPERIENCE

This person who fills this position is an RN who is required to have a bachelor's degree in nursing, though most prefer a master's degree. In addition, the director must have 4 to 8 years of nursing experience, with at least 2 of those years in a supervising or leadership role such as a nurse supervisor or nurse manager. Depending on the state and nursing work environment, other certifications may also be needed.

CORE COMPETENCIES AND SKILLS

- Strong motivational skills
- Excellent interpersonal/human relations skills
- Ability to manage the work of other staff members
- Ability to pay attention to detail
- Ability to respond to emergency situations
- Ability to delegate responsibility and prioritize duties
- Proficiency in accounting and budgeting
- Strong management skills

COMPENSATION

The median salary for long-term care directors of nursing is $101,000, but that can go as high as $125,000 per year. Compensation for directors of nursing is often a function of the size of the organization and number of years of experience.

EMPLOYMENT OUTLOOK

The employment outcome is positive for nursing directors. Jobs for health services managers such as directors of nursing are expected to increase by 16% between 2016 and 2026 according to the Bureau of Labor Statistics (U.S. Department of Labor, 2015).

FOR FURTHER INFORMATION

- American Nurses Association (www.nursingworld.org)
- National Association of Directors of Nursing Administration in Long Term Care (www.nadona.org)

REFERENCE

Bureau of Labor Statistics, U.S. Department of Labor. (2015). Medical and Health Services Managers. In *Occupational Outlook Handbook*, 2016–17 Edition. Retrieved from https://www.bls.gov/ooh/management/medical-and-health-services-managers.htm

42

JOB DESCRIPTION

A home healthcare agency director administers day-to-day operations and activities of a home care agency, nursing home, assisted living facility, home health services, or other long-term care organizations. In some cases, the position is appointed by the board of directors. The position requires following the organization's mission, objectives, and values to ensure economical and efficient performance. Directors are responsible for creating and maintaining an operating budget, and overseeing the development of methods to measure agency activities. A home healthcare agency director must follow ethical, legal, and compliance guidelines. Another responsibility is to employ qualified personnel and provide continuous staff education and evaluations.

EDUCATION AND EXPERIENCE

The minimum educational requirement is a bachelor's degree in management or a related field. Prior experience in finance, healthcare management, or business administration is critical. Home healthcare agency director positions require at least 5 years' experience in home health or a related field. The organization might require a current RN license.

CORE COMPETENCIES AND SKILLS

- Ability to be an advocate for patients and employees
- Strong experience in finance
- Ability to solve financial and quality-related problems
- Independent thinker, who works unsupervised
- Ability to maintain numerous projects at one time
- Process working knowledge of federal and state regulations
- Strong written and verbal communication skills
- Creativity
- Excellent work ethic and work under stressful situations

COMPENSATION

Home healthcare agency directors median annual salary is $114,000. The salary range is wide, from $85,000 to $140,000 per year. Those working in an urban area stand to make more than those living in a rural area.

EMPLOYMENT OUTLOOK

The position of home healthcare agency director is an ongoing learning experience. With an aging population, home healthcare agencies will continue to expand and grow. The shortage of home healthcare agency directors allows for continuous growth for those already in the field.

FOR FURTHER INFORMATION

■ National Association for Home Care & Hospice (www.nahc.org)

43

JOB DESCRIPTION

This is a focused and specific role in which the individual will work in a supportive role to lead the assigned community sales team to successful sales results and occupancy. This position will interface with the company's regional marketing managers and vice presidents, as well as the communities they support, and other company departmental personnel. Additionally, this position will assist with other company marketing departmental functions as requested.

EDUCATION AND EXPERIENCE

A bachelor's degree in business or health administration, marketing, finance, or clinical field or equivalent experience is the minimum educational preparation required. Three to five years' experience in sales or marketing in the healthcare senior living industry. Experience in the skilled nursing environment strongly preferred.

CORE COMPETENCIES AND SKILLS

- Working knowledge of healthcare reimbursement models, such as Medicare, private insurance, and long-term care insurance
- Working knowledge of medical terminology
- Customer relationship management database and marketing analytic analysis abilities
- Competitive environment analysis and interpretation abilities
- Ability to participate with company's marketing team members to develop and produce marketing plans and marketing budgets for inclusion in development and expansion plans in accordance with project timelines
- Ability to consult on and understand marketing budget needs and allocations for assigned communities
- Ability to support tracking and implementation of the original marketing plan and subsequent "working" marketing plans
- Ability to participate in the oversight of community marketing communications through use of an advertising agency, public relations firm, or other related vendors
- Ability to monitor/review, as needed, results and activities; compare with the planned goals and objectives, using the sales expectation worksheet

■ Ability to provide sales support specializing in healthcare in a multiple-site environment; participate in review of hot leads and their "objections and delay reasons," and "next step" plans; discuss selling tactics for overcoming objections as needed

■ Ability to act professionally and honestly always in the representation of the community concept of senior living

■ Proficiency in Microsoft Word, PowerPoint, Excel, and Outlook

■ Ability to be a self-starter, attentive to detail; must possess excellent organizational and proofreading skills

■ Excellent interpersonal and leadership skills

■ Excellent oral and written communication and presentation skills

■ Ability to quickly learn and utilize healthcare-based referral management software programs

COMPENSATION

Marketing specialist's median annual salary is $65,000. The salary range is wide, from $45,000 to $82,000 per year. The level of salary is often a function of the size and scope of the long-term care company.

EMPLOYMENT OUTLOOK

The position of marketing specialist is critical for the success of multifacility long-term care companies. This is an entry-level position in long-term care and is the starting point for persons who wish to expand their career potential in the field. There is tremendous pressure to fill beds in skilled nursing and assisted living facilities, so talented marketing specialists are highly desired.

FOR FURTHER INFORMATION

■ American College of Health Care Administrators (www.achca.org)
■ American Health Care Association (www.ahcancal.org)

JOB DESCRIPTION

The regional director of operations monitors the overall operations of managed facilities, and promotes the successful implementation of the company's mission and strategic goals.

EDUCATION AND EXPERIENCE

Master's degree in business or health administration or equivalent; or 4 to 10 years' related experience and/or training; or equivalent combination of education and experience. Must possess Nursing Home Administrator license.

CORE COMPETENCIES AND SKILLS

- Ability to develop or expand corporate and facility programs
- Ability to monitor facility operations such as budget compliance, clinical services, and regulatory compliance
- Ability to consult on the hiring and training of personnel
- Ability to act as team leader to the operational team
- Ability to ensure that facilities comply with corporate directives and implement corporate programs
- Ability to direct activities of regional office support staff
- Ability to develop policies and procedures for facilities
- Ability to represent corporation and facilities at industry meetings, and promote programs through community involvement
- Outstanding interpersonal skills

COMPENSATION

Regional directors of operations' median annual salary is $198,000. The salary range is wide, from $145,000 to $275,000 per year. The level of salary is often a function of the size and scope of the long-term care company.

EMPLOYMENT OUTLOOK

The position of regional director of operations is critical for the success of multifacility long-term care companies. Persons in these roles tend to stay in place for long periods of time unless made offers by larger firms.

FOR FURTHER INFORMATION

- American College of Health Care Administrators (www.achca.org)
- American Health Care Association (www.ahcancal.org)

CHAPTER 9
CAREERS IN COMMERCIAL HEALTH INSURANCE

CLAIMS REPRESENTATIVE

JOB DESCRIPTION

A claims representative serves as the insurance companies' first line of contact to providers or individuals submitting claims. It is this position's responsibility to be knowledgeable about the insurance company's claims policies and procedures in order to answer any potential customer questions. The claims representative is often one of the first people to make initial assessments on a claim. This person will usually check for processing errors and missing information before moving the claim to a supervisor. If the claims representative deems a file incomplete or inaccurate, the representative will reach out to the client to resolve the matter.

EDUCATION AND EXPERIENCE

The claims representative position is an entry-level position within the claims department of an insurance company. Having an associate's degree or a bachelor's degree in a related field is strongly preferred. Any previous experience working with insurance claims is a bonus. As this position involves heavy customer interaction, previous customer service experience is often required.

CORE COMPETENCIES AND SKILLS

- Demonstrated quantitative and analytical ability in order to resolve daily claims problems in a swift, efficient manner
- Superior customer service experience and demonstrated ability to resolve customer issues
- Ability to work in a fast-paced work environment
- Excellent time-management skills
- Demonstrated ability to learn new information, such as medical terminology and ICD-9 coding systems
- Ability to work within a team

COMPENSATION

Claims representatives receive a fairly wide-ranging salary. Depending on geographic location, the insurance company, and experience, claims representatives should expect to earn between $41,000 and $67,000, with $54,000 being the approximate median.

EMPLOYMENT OUTLOOK

Claims representatives are the entry-level positions in claims divisions at insurance companies. There will continue to be positions available as long as coding and documentation systems remain as prevalent as they are today. Whereas these are entry-level positions, struggling insurance companies, however, may be more inclined to lay these positions off first.

FOR FURTHER INFORMATION

■ America's Health Insurance Plans (www.ahip.org)
■ American Health Care Association (www.ahcancal.org)

46

GROUP ENROLLMENT REPRESENTATIVE

JOB DESCRIPTION

The group enrollment representative is responsible for the service and retention of existing groups. This person provides employee benefit consultative services to prospective and existing clients; develops strategies for overcoming commercial competition; assists in developing marketing strategies for new product offerings with due consideration of potential problem areas; uses independent and creative thinking for planning and solving problems under the direction of the regional manager and within the plan's goals and objectives; and contributes to the development of planwide objectives and methods, including special project assignments.

EDUCATION AND EXPERIENCE

A bachelor's degree in business or health administration is preferred, or 3 years' prior sales experience required. One of either of the degree or previous sales experience is required.

CORE COMPETENCIES AND SKILLS

- Knowledge of public relations and human relation skills, and the understanding and motivating of people
- Excellent oral and written communication skills
- Ability to acquire a thorough knowledge of all product lines, contracts, related operating policies, rating practices of the corporation, and its subsidiaries
- Ability to acquire state insurance agent's license within 60 days
- Ability to establish, evaluate needs and wants of prospective customers, and to recognize and close sales opportunities
- High degree of persistence in a professional manner
- Required to sign a noncompete agreement
- Ability to acquire a thorough understanding of corporate goals and objectives, and the effect they have on the marketing division
- Ability to acquire the knowledge of federal mandated laws, alternate funding arrangements, rating practices, and retention formulas
- Ability to acquire an understanding of organizational procedures, structure, job practices, rating practices, operating policies, and benefit structures
- Ability to acquire approved sales techniques
- Ability to acquire a working knowledge of hospitals and physician practices
- Ability to travel a minimum of 75% travel throughout the state of employ

■ Completion of 120 on-site sales/retention calls a month

COMPENSATION

The annual compensation for group enrollment representatives ranges between $66,000 and $99,000. Total compensation is often dependent on the size of the insurance company and the number of years' experience held by the individual.

EMPLOYMENT OUTLOOK

There will be a continuing strong demand for group enrollment representatives. Health insurance companies are updating employer contracts on an annual basis necessitating skilled persons who can deal effectively with small, medium, and large employer groups.

FOR FURTHER INFORMATION

■ America's Health Insurance Plans (AHIP) (www.ahip.org)

NAME: KEN PROVENCHER

Title: President & Chief Executive Officer

Organization: PacificSource Health Plans

1. Briefly describe your job responsibilities.

I am chief executive officer (CEO) of a 300,000-member health plan with approximately $1.5 billion in revenues. We do business in Oregon, Idaho, Montana, and Washington, and offer a full range of commercial, Medicare, and Medicaid products. As CEO, it is my job to work with the board and our team to develop and execute our vision and strategy. I also have a significant role in setting the stage for our culture, values, and approach to our work.

2. What would you consider to be a "typical" day for you?

I think I don't really have a typical day, but some of the things that I do on a regular basis include the following:

1. *Board work:* I spend a fair amount of time planning, staffing, and participating in board and board committee meetings.
2. *Senior leadership and executive management meetings and retreats:* I chair and preside over our senior leadership and executive management group meetings. These groups are responsible for developing (in conjunction with board) and executing our strategic initiatives.
3. *Strategy development and execution:* I lead our strategic planning work, including work with the board and our executive team, coordination and supervision of strategic planning staff, and meeting with external stakeholders and experts to further the strategy.
4. *Management and supervision:* I have one-to-one meetings with my direct reports every 2 weeks.
5. *Culture and employee engagement:* I conduct monthly all-employee meetings, participate in meetings with all new

Continued

NAME: KEN PROVENCHER
Continued

employees, and hold employee roundtables. I travel frequently to our offices across our region.
6. *Key stakeholder relationships:* I regularly meet with provider, employer, broker, community, and political leaders.
7. *Industry and community leadership:* I serve on numerous community, state, and national committees.

3. What education or training do you have? Is it typical for your job?

I have a Master of Business Administration (MBA) with a focus on healthcare management. My training has been very helpful and many of my colleagues have MBA or Master of Health Administration (MHA) degrees, but I believe that leaders in our industry can come from many different backgrounds.

4. What is the most challenging part of your job?

Our industry has been through, and is still in, a highly volatile and disruptive environment. Keeping people focused and staying true to our mission and values can be challenging, but it is a challenge that we welcome.

5. What do you consider to be the best part of your job?

All of the work around vision, strategy, and culture.

6. What path did you take to get to the job you are in today?

I started out in provider contracting and eventually got immersed in all aspects of the business.

7. What advice do you have for someone who is interested in a job such as yours?

1. If possible, start out in a technical area: provider contracting, actuarial, finance, and so forth.
2. Be patient—don't jump to new opportunities too quickly—develop some deep experience.
3. Once you've established a track record, don't be afraid to broaden your background to learn other aspects of the business.
4. Find a mentor and develop your professional network.

47 PROVIDER CONTRACTOR

JOB DESCRIPTION

The provider contractor is responsible for helping to build and maintain a competitive network for current members. The provider contractor prioritizes network needs both quantitatively and qualitatively, strategically approaches physicians and ancillary provider communities, and negotiates contracts that are favorable to the business. Provider contractors also ensure that networks are competitive by helping to facilitate the sales force's ability to penetrate new business opportunities.

EDUCATION AND EXPERIENCE

Required: Bachelor's degree in business, finance, or a related field, or a minimum of 2 years' relevant provider contracting experience; prior demonstrated success in provider contracting with both large physician groups and ancillary providers required. A master's degree in business administration or a related field is preferred with experience in Accountable Care Organization (ACO)/risk contracting; working knowledge in the areas of group practice management, long-term acute care, home health, home infusion, behavioral health, ambulatory surgery, and the outpatient experience.

CORE COMPETENCIES AND SKILLS

- Interpersonal effectiveness: Understands oneself, effectively manages emotions, listens and communicates with respect, and builds trusting relationships
- Executes for results: Effectively leverages resources to create exceptional outcomes, embraces change, and constructively resolves barriers and constraints
- Accountability: Meets established expectations and takes responsibility for achieving results; encourages others to do the same
- Builds trust: Consistently models and inspires high levels of integrity, lives up to commitments, and takes responsibility for the impact of one's actions
- Proficiency in analyzing, understanding, and communicating financial trends
- Excellent written and verbal communication skills
- Experience presenting to varied audiences
- Ability to manage multiple priorities in a fast-paced environment
- Knowledge of Microsoft Office applications

COMPENSATION

The typical compensation for provider contractors is $53,600 to $74,700 per year. This amount can go higher depending on the size of the health insurance firm and the number of years' experience.

EMPLOYMENT OUTLOOK

There will be a continuing strong demand for provider contractors. Health insurance companies are updating provider contracts on an annual basis, necessitating skilled persons who can deal effectively with physicians, hospitals, and other healthcare providers.

FOR FURTHER INFORMATION

■ America's Health Insurance Plans (AHIP) (www.ahip.org)

Title: Chief Executive Officer
Organization: Samaritan Health Plans

1. Briefly describe your job responsibilities.

Vice president of corporate services responsibilities includes being responsible for various operational aspects of the integrated delivery network, including, but not limited to, the oversight of enterprise-wide credentialing, corporate planning, and involvement with data governance and health reform; serving as the chief executive officer for Samaritan Health Plans and InterCommunity Health Plans as subsequently described.

Samaritan Health Plans: Chief executive officer

Responsibilities include: being a strategic leader for a hospital-owned physician-driven insurance plan focusing on Medicare-managed care and commercial plans; being responsible for the design and implementation of the strategic plan that includes the research and development of new growth opportunities, development and monitoring of quality measures as they relate to National Committee for Quality Assurance (NCQA) standards, and the implementation of further expansion to all lines of business. Additional responsibilities include coordination with the owner physician hospital organizations (PHOs) to increase the effectiveness of the managed care delivery system within our community.

InterCommunity Health Plans: Chief executive officer

Responsibilities include being a strategic leader for a hospital-owned community/physician-driven Medicaid-managed care plan and being responsible for the design and implementation of the strategic plan. InterCommunity Health Plans is committed to improving the health of our communities while lowering or containing the cost of care. We accomplish this by coordinating health initiatives, seeking efficiencies through blending of services and infrastructure, and engaging all stakeholders to increase quality, reliability, and availability of care.

Continued

NAME: KELLEY C. KAISER Continued

2. What would you consider to be a "typical" day for you?

Usually half of my day is spent in strategic meetings at the system level, and the other half focusing on the plans. Depending on the day, I may be at meetings at the Capital discussing the Medicaid plan and where it is going, or dealing with Centers for Medicare & Medicaid Services (CMS) about our Medicare plan, or working with the state on specifics to our commercial plans. I meet with my direct reports weekly to ensure I have visibility into what is happening operationally.

3. What education or training do you have? Is it typical for your job?

Oregon State University
Corvallis, Oregon
Bachelor of Science in Health Care Administration

Oregon State University
Corvallis, Oregon
Master of Public Health (MPH) in Health Policy and Management

Yes, most in my field have an MPH, Master of Business Administration (MBA), or Master of Public Policy (MPP)

4. What is the most challenging part of your job?

For me, the most challenging and rewarding part of my job is working toward the balance of the triple aim: How do we as a delivery system ensure cost, quality, and access while maintaining the services and delivery system that is needed? Getting to work on this through the lens of an integrated delivery system with my focus on being on the payer side is very rewarding. I believe that we are set up very well to navigate through the changes in reform, and the opportunity to work on this daily is challenging and rewarding.

5. What do you consider to be the best part of your job?

The people with whom I work and the mission we have to take care of those we serve.

6. What path did you take to get to the job you are in today?

I started out on the provider side, so I have a passion for making sure that we create a delivery system that allows the providers and the patients

Continued

to connect in the easiest way possible. Coming to the health plan side allowed me to see the delivery of care across the whole spectrum of a member's life, which allows a more holistic approach and one that should create better outcomes.

7. What advice do you have for someone who is interested in a job such as yours?

Be open minded and ready for change. The healthcare environment is not only complicated, but very complex. Be prepared for the regulatory oversight and the community scrutiny that comes with providing such an important service to the members you serve.

 NAME: MATT KLOSTERMAN

Title: Senior Data Analyst
Organization: BlueCross BlueShield of New Mexico

1. Briefly describe your job responsibilities.

I have overall accountability for the BCBSNM Medicaid Manage Care Plan's databases, infrastructure for data processing, validation and integrity, and a variety of operational and mandated reporting. I frequently serve as a subject matter expert for Medicaid reporting across the organization.

2. What would you consider to be a "typical" day for you?

A typical day blends development on long-term projects, answering questions/providing guidance, and daily operational reporting needs. I frequently help management understand and utilize data.

3. What education or training do you have? Is it typical for your job?

I have a Master of Health Administration (MHA) from the University of Alabama at Birmingham. This is not typical for my job. Most analysts come from more of a coding background, which means that typically they lack an understanding of healthcare organizations and how patients interact with the healthcare system. My background gives me a critical advantage in that I have a deep understanding of the healthcare system and how organizations can affect outcomes. This allows me to take the lead in developing reports and approaching management with ideas. Analysts with knowledge and skills that intersect programming, healthcare policy, and hard knowledge about how organizations can improve care are powerful and can drive positive change. Because of this, I am highly appreciated in my organization.

4. What is the most challenging part of your job?

Three things.
First, analysts typically have a significant "data literacy" advantage over their peers in any given organization, so a primary challenge is figuring out how to explain the nuts and bolts of report programming, what numbers mean, and the strengths/weaknesses of data in terms that others can understand.

Continued

NAME: MATT KLOSTERMAN
Continued

Second, senior analysts are typically the "bottom line" when it comes to figuring out business challenges. When faced with a tough problem to solve, I typically have no one to turn to because I am the top expert. This is challenging because in these situations, the analyst needs to be self-motivated and a bulldog. Analysts with the confidence and tenacity to stick with and ultimately solve difficult programming challenges are highly valuable to organizations.

Third, analysts need to be tough. Not uncommonly business owners and management will challenge numbers and analysts need to have the ability to thoughtfully and confidently articulate how they produce their work.

5. What do you consider to be the best part of your job?

One of the main things I love about my job is my job security. To borrow the language of business management, my job involves hard technical skills that are not readily reproduced. This gives me a competitive advantage vis-à-vis my peers who lack technical skills. There are simply things I can do that they cannot do. My generation had our formative job market experiences in the depths of the 2008 recession and I am a huge proponent of job security, and I would encourage the next generation to acquire real, technical skills that are needed regardless of the economy's health.

Especially given the proliferation of online and in-person Master of Business Administration (MBA) or MHA programs, these degrees are not conferring the advantages they used to. In my experience, these degrees are useful for checking a box for human resources (i.e., "meets minimum requirements"), but I am not seeing the differentiation and job security advantages that these degrees used to confer—there are simply too many people with MBAs these days.

I would encourage the future generations to consider nontraditional paths in addition to their MBA or MHA. Certifications in programming languages give you a hard technical skill set (that organizations sorely need) and something to show for it during the job application process. Same with the Certified Public Accountant (CPA), Juris Doctor (JD), RN, and so forth. These degrees and licenses give you credibility and real skills.

Job security and the paths to attaining job security should never be discounted and should be part of everyone's career plan. Healthcare will always be changing and, as a result, lay-offs and other forms of "downsizing" are a fixture in this industry. The people who have serious technical skills that add value to organizations will be less vulnerable to catastrophic career disruption.

Continued

NAME: MATT KLOSTERMAN
Continued

6. What path did you take to get to the job you are in today?

My path ultimately boils down personality/skills match with the management track. I got my MHA thinking I wanted to be a hospital chief executive officer (CEO), but quickly realized that I find little joy in the day-to-day activities of management. I should have figured this out before going to graduate school, but sometimes you figure these things out along the way, but the journey sure has been fun.

I was at a crossroads reflecting on where I wanted to take my career, and figured out that where I was happiest was when I was essentially functioning as an analyst in my previous management roles. The path forward become pretty clear after that.

I was lucky in that my current role opened up when I came to this realization and was looking to change my career path. I was also fortunate that in my previous roles I had done enough "analyst" type stuff that I was credible on my resume and in my interviews for my current role.

7. What advice do you have for someone who is interested in a job such as yours?

My first piece of advice is to reflect long and hard on your creative skills and self-motivation. It doesn't matter how good of a programmer you are, ultimately successful analysts are tenacious and creative enough to figure out whatever challenge is in front of them. I say this because no two business problems are alike and analysts are pretty consistently challenged (tenacity/don't quit) to solve problems (creativity).

Related to the above point, be ready to get frustrated. All I have to say here is that learning programming is hard, but you will learn if you stick with it!

If you are interested in pursuing an analyst path, the good news is that you can take training courses that provide tangible certifications that employers will view positively. Learn the Microsoft products cold, and become an expert in both Microsoft and Oracle SQL (Structured Query Language).

I would also highly encourage budding analysts to learn project management skills. Being the technical experts, analysts often find themselves with primary responsibility for managing their deliverables. Analysts need to understand lag and lead time, dependencies, and project planning to be successful and to be able to communicate project status to management.

48

JOB DESCRIPTION

Risk managers are in charge of anticipating and reducing the number of accidental incidents at hospitals. This position is responsible for implementing a risk management system that incorporates policies, procedures, and guidelines that hospitals use to avoid accident claims. Education is a key component of risk management system because hospital employees must learn new, safer, more efficient procedures. The risk manager often supervises risk management teams to spearhead these educational programs. It is not uncommon for the risk manager to work closely with a hospital's legal staff when dealing with accidents that lead to lawsuits.

EDUCATION AND EXPERIENCE

Individuals interested in healthcare risk management should have a bachelor's degree in business, mathematics, nursing, or another health-related field. An Associate in Risk Management (ARM) or a master's degree would also be beneficial. Providers hiring risk managers typically expect to see 3 to 7 years of previous experience in business or healthcare.

CORE COMPETENCIES AND SKILLS

- Demonstrated quantitative skills required for departmental data analysis
- Superior management ability to lead a team in developing and implementing a risk management system throughout the provider
- Ability to communicate with a wide range of healthcare workers, such as doctors, nurses, case managers, and other administrative managers
- Strong time management skills, as this position requires the individual to balance numerous tasks at once
- Excellent problem-solving skills
- Proven ability to work with a team to achieve a task under general direction
- Superior organizational skills

COMPENSATION

A risk manager's salary is dependent upon the position's responsibilities. This position stands to make anywhere from $72,000 to $141,000, while directors of risk management often make well over $180,000. Other contributing factors to a risk manager's salary include the firm's geographic location and the individual's previous experience.

EMPLOYMENT OUTLOOK

While risk management does not experience the level of growth that other healthcare departments receive, this function is critical to payer's success. Commercial health insurance companies will continue to utilize healthcare risk managers in the future to ensure that they are providing the safest and highest quality care available.

FOR FURTHER INFORMATION

■ Health Care Compliance Association (www.hcca-info.org)
■ American Society for Healthcare Risk Management (www.ashrm.org)

 NAME: JOE SCHOMER

Title: Director, Managed Care
Economics & Analysis
Organization: Centura Health

1. Briefly describe your job responsibilities.

Manage and lead commercial and Medicare Advantage strategic initiatives for 17 hospitals and 1,000 physicians, with emphasis in payer revenue, charges, employer solutions, transparency initiatives, and value-based reimbursement.

2. What would you consider to be a "typical" day for you?

Drive and influence priorities, projects, workgroups, and staff to ensure products and deliverables are on time, accurate, and enlightening. Interact and coordinate with department, finance, sales, hospital service line directors, brokers, insurance companies, and provider affiliates. I work in a typical corporate environment, attending meetings and managing e-mail, with some travel to individual hospitals.

3. What education or training do you have? Is it typical for your job?

I have an undergraduate degree in healthcare administration, advanced skills on Microsoft products, strong proficiency with tools/systems, federal reform and Centers for Medicare & Medicaid Services (CMS) initiatives and leadership training/coaching. Skills and experience are typical for my role; however, rare to find an actuarial-analytical-geek mind with excellent communication and strong leadership and influence.

4. What is the most challenging part of your job?

Employee behavior, from C-suite to frontline. Technology is also a challenge, from desktop applications to billing/payment systems to integrated electronic medical records.

5. What do you consider to be the best part of your job?

Responsible for the largest book of business for the entire organization, and all effort, leadership, and competencies relate to a patient's

Continued

experience. Being on the provider healing side and focusing on mission, ministry, values, and integrity.

6. What path did you take to get to the job you are in today?

Corporate ladder—titles include—junior analyst, senior analyst, actuarial analysts, lead actuarial analyst, regional manager of healthcare economics, manager of total medical costs, and director of managed care economics and analysis; totaling 22 years of healthcare work experience with four different organizations.

7. What advice do you have for someone who is interested in a job such as yours?

Get your base credentials and skills and then focus on human behavior and emotional intelligence. People are the biggest barrier, and teamwork is critical to success.

CHAPTER 10
CAREERS IN PUBLIC HEALTH ORGANIZATIONS

49

COUNTY HEALTH DEPARTMENT ADMINISTRATOR

JOB DESCRIPTION

The county health department administrator directs operations of the local county health department through developing policies, setting and developing goals, managing resources, obtaining funding through various state and federal grants and not-for-profit foundations, and selecting key personnel. The administrator directs and provides the basic "core public health functions" and the essential services of public health, including community health assessments and evaluations to determine the county's public health needs and public health preparedness requirements. The administrator obtains and utilizes resources to meet programs and services through developing policies and procedures, establishing budgets, hiring qualified employees, evaluating programs and employees, overseeing revenues and expenditures, maintaining facility and equipment, and assuring staff remain current in their public health training, educational requirements, and required continuing education programs.

EDUCATION AND EXPERIENCE

Depending on the size of the county health department, a bachelor's degree in nursing, social work, or other clinical area is typically required. Many county health departments give preference to persons with a master's degree in health administration. Most county health department administrator positions require a minimum of 3 years of experience in public health administration.

CORE COMPETENCIES AND SKILLS

- Outstanding interpersonal skills including the ability to effectively communicate with persons throughout the organization
- Excellent verbal and written communication skills
- Demonstrated track record of developing and maintaining collaborative relationships among diverse groups, including elected officials, medical staff, as well as key external stakeholders
- Experience in facilitating the prioritization of community health needs and identification and initiation of responsible solutions
- Skill in coordinating departmental services with various other healthcare providers and community agencies
- Ability to direct operations according to regulatory agencies and county commission requirements

- Thorough knowledge of the principles, practices, and objectives of public health administration
- Demonstrated understanding and practice of ethical and legal issues associated with public health administration
- Experience with the principles and practices of financial and managerial accounting including budgets and/or grants
- Ability to utilize standard computer-related applications

COMPENSATION

County health department administrators can earn between $101,000 and $150,000 per year. This wide variation is due to the size and overall budget of the particular county. The vast majority of these positions report to an elected group of local officials (usually county commissioners or supervisors) and, hence, the compensation is frequently a function of competing budget priorities within the county.

EMPLOYMENT OUTLOOK

The employment outlook for county health department administrators is expected to be stable. There is a growing need for persons in this role to have training in management, given the complexity of managing personnel and budget, planning, and meeting the diverse needs of communities in an era of shrinking budgets for county health departments.

FOR FURTHER INFORMATION

- American Public Health Association (www.apha.org)
- National Association of County and City Health Officials (www.naccho.org)

Title: Commissioner of Health and Commissioner of Hospitals
Organization: Rockland County Department of Health

1. Briefly describe your job responsibilities.

Chief executive and chief medical officer for Rockland County Department of Health, employing more than 170 full-time employees with annual expenditures of $73 million; commissioner of health (designated official and senior local health authority for Rockland County), with regulatory powers to license, inspect, establish standards, and monitor compliance under Section 352 of Public Health Law, and statutory responsibility for core public health services to 340,000 county residents of a large, full-service, public health department with responsibility for regulation and enforcement of the State and County Sanitary Code provisions; commissioner of hospitals as per the county charter, overseeing the county hospital, long-term acute care, and subacute care facilities.

2. What would you consider to be a "typical" day for you?

Every day is different from the one before. I could be called to the county executive's office for a cabinet meeting, drive to Albany for meetings with legislators or other county health officials, lead my own management meeting with senior health department officials, visit one or more of my public health clinics, or have a conference call with the state commissioner of health.

3. What education or training do you have? Is it typical for your job?

I am a board-certified family physician with a Doctor of Osteopathic Medicine degree. I also have a Master of Public Health (MPH) in Health Policy and Management from the Mailman School of Public Health of Columbia University, and have also attained the advanced credential as a Certified Physician Executive (CPE) of the Certifying Commission in Medical Management.

Continued

My position requires a medical degree, board certification, and an MPH degree. I have attained the additional CPE credential owing to my personal quest for additional leadership education and skills in order to become a more successful physician leader.

4. What is the most challenging part of your job?

My challenge is to balance "putting out fires" with the need for strategic leadership of my department. I do enjoy the ability to utilize my leadership skills as I live by my leadership philosophy. This includes my values of honesty, integrity, and competence along with my overarching goals of the development of others along with successful outcomes. My leadership style is one of approachability in a team atmosphere.

5. What do you consider to be the best part of your job?

I have always felt honored that patients would trust me with their most personal concerns in their most vulnerable situations and look to me for treatment and guidance. On a population health level, I consider that each person in our county is my own patient, as his or her needs are paramount in each decision that I make. I am a "people person," a family doctor always, and I enjoy patient and staff interactions along with the confidence to lead my department with a strategic approach, keeping our mission, vision, values, and my leadership philosophy in the forefront.

6. What path did you take to get to the job you are in today?

Upon completion of my residency in family medicine, I became board certified and worked in a faculty practice while teaching family medicine residents. I then joined an internal medicine private practice for over a decade where I had the privilege of treating multiple generations of family members. Along the way, I was a physician reviewer for an independent peer-review organization and worked as a house officer; I then joined the staff as a hospitalist at a renowned rehabilitation hospital where I became the medical director of employee health, the physician liaison to admissions, president of the medical staff, and chairperson of the medical executive and credentialing committees. I was then appointed by the previous county executive to the position of commissioner of health and reappointed by the present county executive, who later additionally appointed me as commissioner of hospitals. I was confirmed to both positions by the legislature.

Continued

7. What advice do you have for someone who is interested in a job such as yours?

I'd advise that person to stay current in the area of expertise, remaining board certified, but to include business and leadership courses in one's curriculum. I would also recommend the pursuit of an MPH degree, preferably in health policy and management. A management degree and leadership skills are essential for a sitting health and or hospital commissioner.

DEPUTY HEALTH SYSTEM ADMINISTRATOR–INDIAN HEALTH SERVICE

50

JOB DESCRIPTION

The deputy health system administrator serves as the primary assistant to the chief executive officer (CEO) of the designated health system within the Indian Health Service. Deputy health system administrators have day-to-day operational authority and responsibility for the activities of their health system. In consultation and coordination with the CEO, the deputy recommends and initiates program improvements and modifications to meet the changing needs of the beneficiary population in order to achieve Indian Health Service goals and objectives, while making the best possible use of all available resources. The deputy plans and assigns work to be accomplished, either directly or in general terms to supervisors, and reviews work product/evaluations made by supervisors of work accomplishments. The position will have direct responsibility and supervision over the procurement/property and supply, information technology, compliance program, facilities management, housekeeping departments.

EDUCATION AND EXPERIENCE

The minimum educational required for this position is a Master of Health Administration degree from a program accredited by the Commission for Accreditation of Healthcare Management Education (CAHME). The position requires that the candidate possess at least 1 year of specialized management experience equivalent to at least the General Schedule (GS)-13 level.

CORE COMPETENCIES AND SKILLS

- Outstanding interpersonal skills including the ability to effectively communicate with persons throughout the organization
- Excellent verbal and written communication skills
- Demonstrated experience in overall management duties with planning, organizing, directing, and evaluating clinical and environmental support services
- Experience in evaluating and adjusting organizational structure to ensure most effective and efficient delivery of healthcare and healthcare programs
- Significant experience in leading quality improvement teams
- Experience in facilitating the prioritization of community health needs and identification and initiation of responsible solutions

■ Skill in ensuring customer service to Tribal Health Programs, Urban Health Programs, Alcohol Treatment Programs, Behavioral Health Programs and Federal Service Units

■ Knowledge of planning, coordination, and execution of business functions, resource allocation, and production

■ Ability to influence, motivate, and challenge others; adapt leadership styles to a variety of situations

■ Demonstrated ability to make sound, well-informed, and objective decisions; perceive the impact and implications of decisions; commit to action, even in uncertain situations, to accomplish organizational goals; cause change

■ Demonstrated understanding and practice of ethical and legal issues associated with health administration

■ Experience with the principles and practices of financial and managerial accounting including budgets and/or grants

■ Ability to utilize standard computer-related applications

COMPENSATION

Deputy health services administrators in the Indian Health Service can earn between $97,000 and $126,000 per year. These are positions funded by the U.S. government, and persons in these roles receive all the benefits available to federal employees.

EMPLOYMENT OUTLOOK

The employment outlook for health services administration in the Indian Health Service will be strong into the foreseeable future. Preference is given to veterans and members of the U.S. Public Health Service commissioned corps for these jobs.

FOR FURTHER INFORMATION

■ American Public Health Association (www.apha.org)
■ Indian Health Service (www.ihs.gov)

51

JOB DESCRIPTION

The emergency management coordinator will work as part of the leadership team in city, county, or state governmental agencies. The coordinator's role is to plan and coordinate comprehensive emergency management program activities. The person in this position will be responsible for developing, implementing, and maintaining emergency management programs, plans, policies, and procedures with the goal of reducing injury and loss of life, property, or environment in the city/county/state as a result of an emergency or disaster. This person will work in all aspects of emergency management programs including mitigation, preparedness, response, and recovery. In addition, this person will perform a role during emergency operations center (EOC) activations.

EDUCATION AND EXPERIENCE

Emergency management coordinators generally possess a bachelor's degree in communication, business administration, education, emergency management, healthcare management, or public administration along with a minimum of 2 years' experience in emergency management. In addition, emergency management coordinators must have completed a series of courses (either in person or online) in the areas of incident command and National Incident Management System (NIMS). Finally, experience in emergency and disaster plans development is highly desirable.

CORE COMPETENCIES AND SKILLS

- Outstanding interpersonal skills including the ability to effectively communicate with current and potential customers, along with persons throughout the organization
- Excellent verbal and written communication skills
- Knowledge of natural and human-caused hazards, with particular attention paid to those common to the area in which the person will work
- Knowledge of the functions of emergency management including mitigation, preparedness, response, and recovery
- Knowledge of incident command systems and emergency/recovery support functions
- Knowledge of federal and state emergency management planning requirements
- Facilitation skills in working with multidisciplinary and multiagency groups

- Ability to work in an environment where changing priorities are the norm and flexibility is a must; demonstrated skills in managing multiple tasks
- Ability to conduct research and present recommendations, both orally and in writing
- Ability to use standard computer office software
- Experience conducting risk analysis using software such as HAZUS, or other loss estimation tools

COMPENSATION

Emergency management coordinators typically earn $60,000 to $120,000 per year depending upon the level of experience and the size of the governmental entity.

EMPLOYMENT OUTLOOK

The employment outlook for emergency management coordinators is generally good. City, county, and state governments are required to actively work at being prepared for emergencies and disasters, so there is a continuing need for skilled persons in these roles.

FOR FURTHER INFORMATION

- National Emergency Management Association (www.nemaweb.org)

JOB DESCRIPTION

The health systems specialist provides a wide variety of specialized management services including healthcare management and statistical analysis, financial management, program analysis, long-range policy and planning, and general administrative support to the clinical director/director of the various health service lines within the Veterans Administration Health System.

EDUCATION AND EXPERIENCE

As a federal agency, the Veterans Administration Health System employs the General Schedule (GS) developed by the Office of Personnel Management to determine the education and experience required for each job, as classified by where it is placed in the GS rating system. Program analysts are ranked as either a GS-12 or GS-13. This position requires a master's degree, preferably in business administration or health administration. Necessary experience includes at least 1 year at a GS-11 for appointment as a GS-12, and 1 year of experience at a GS-12 for appointment as a GS-13.

CORE COMPETENCIES AND SKILLS

- Outstanding interpersonal skills including the ability to effectively communicate with current and potential customers, along with persons throughout the organization
- Excellent verbal and written communication skills
- Product planning skills including documenting and maintaining product strategies and roadmaps
- Ability to recommend changes for improvement, implement/initiate approved processes, and monitor the improvements
- Ability to be responsible for the tactical, business, and strategic plans within the service line
- Ability to develop and formulate budget requests for coming fiscal year and multiple years
- Ability to establish guidelines and performance expectations for subordinates that are clearly communicated through the formal employee performance management system
- Ability to work in an environment where changing priorities are the norm and flexibility is a must; demonstrated skills in managing multiple tasks

- Ability to conduct research and present recommendations, both orally and in writing
- Ability to use standard computer office software
- Ability to develop performance standards and write position description and observe performance; resolve informal complaints and grievances

COMPENSATION

Veterans Administration Health Systems specialists earn $68,800 to $105,900 per year.

EMPLOYMENT OUTLOOK

The employment outlook for VA Health Systems specialists is generally good. The Veterans Administration Health System is growing to respond to the need created by veterans who served in Korea and Vietnam, but most recently from those who served in the Iraq and Afghanistan conflicts. The large number of injured young veterans will require health services over multiple decades and the Veterans Administration must be able to respond in kind.

FOR FURTHER INFORMATION

- Veterans Administration Careers (www.vacareers.va.gov)

JOB DESCRIPTION

The program analyst works within the Veterans Administration (VA) Point of Service (VPS) office in the chief business office (CBO). The program analyst is responsible for assisting the deputy program director with product planning, communication, and execution throughout the product life cycle. The program analyst works to determine product needs and customer requirements, and collaborates closely with internal teams and external contractors to ensure development according to project vision and agency strategy and goals. In this position, the program analyst will implement business plans and maintain project schedules and budget.

EDUCATION AND EXPERIENCE

As a federal agency, the VA Health System employs the General Schedule (GS) developed by the Office of Personnel Management to determine the education and experience required for each job as classified by where it is placed in the GS rating system. Program analysts are ranked as either a GS-12 or GS-13. This position requires a master's degree, preferably in business administration or health administration. Necessary experience includes at least 1 year at a GS-11 appointment.

CORE COMPETENCIES AND SKILLS

- Outstanding interpersonal skills including the ability to effectively communicate with current and potential customers, along with persons throughout the organization
- Excellent verbal and written communication skills
- Product planning skills including documenting and maintaining product strategies and roadmaps
- Ability to manage activities associated with systems engineering and modeling systems
- Ability to test and implement healthcare software in medical centers at a nation-wide level
- Ability to provide guidance on patient and clinical processes in a medical center to support healthcare program development and healthcare-tracking software improvement
- Facilitation skills in working with multidisciplinary and multiagency groups
- Ability to work in an environment where changing priorities are the norm and flexibility is a must; demonstrated skills in managing multiple tasks

- Ability to conduct research and present recommendations, both orally and in writing
- Ability to use standard computer office software
- Knowledge of Veterans Health Information Systems and Technology Architecture (VistA) program in a healthcare setting

COMPENSATION
VA program analysts earn $68,800 to $105,900 per year.

EMPLOYMENT OUTLOOK
The employment outlook for VA program analysts is generally good. The VA Health System is growing to respond to the need created by veterans who served in Korea and Vietnam, but most recently from those who served in the Iraq and Afghanistan conflicts. The large number of injured young veterans will require health services over multiple decades and the VA must be able to respond in kind.

FOR FURTHER INFORMATION
- Veterans Administration Careers (www.vacareers.va.gov)

CHAPTER 11
CAREERS IN CONSULTING FIRMS

BUSINESS SOLUTIONS ADVISOR

JOB DESCRIPTION

Business solution advisors work closely on projects with physician groups, hospitals, health systems, and other customers to drive system changes. Business solution advisors are experts in their respective project fields, which include health IT, supply chain management, operations, and finance. This position analyzes the customer's needs and develops strategic metrics for measuring improvement. The business solution advisor serves as a project expert throughout the project's transition period, coaching key institutional employees.

EDUCATION AND EXPERIENCE

Whereas the business solutions advisor is considered an expert on each project, significant relatable experience and education is required. A master's degree in a field that is associated with the projects on which the individual will work is often expected. A minimum of 5 to 7 years of demonstrated experience working in healthcare or business is required.

CORE COMPETENCIES AND SKILLS

- Demonstrated success working with operational projects during previous employment
- Ability to analyze system inefficiencies and develop strategic metrics
- Superior quantitative skills and comfort working with data reports
- Proven ability to communicate with a broad range of people that includes physicians, nurses, and administrative staff
- Outstanding leadership skills, as this position requires mentoring customers during project implementation
- Excellent problem-solving skills

COMPENSATION

Salaries for business solutions advisors vary owing to a range of issues, such as the position's field of expertise, the individual's background experience, and the position's level of responsibility. Business solution advisors should expect to make anywhere from $75,000 to $140,000 per year.

EMPLOYMENT OUTLOOK

Consulting, in general, is a stable field that health systems and individual providers will continue to utilize. External expert opinions will continue to be a primary source of improving healthcare systems. Significant experience is required to become business solutions advisors because their expertise is highly regarded by hospitals around the country.

FOR FURTHER INFORMATION

- National Society of Certified Healthcare Business Consultants (www .nschbc.org)
- Healthcare Financial Management Association (www.hfma.org)

NAME: GILLIAN V. JAEGER

Title: Vice President, Healthcare and Biosciences
Organization: The Spectrum Group

1. Briefly describe your job responsibilities.

I lead the healthcare team at The Spectrum Group, a Washington DC–based consulting and governmental relations firm. I have over 30 years' experience in Department of Defense (DoD)/Veteran Affairs (VA) and in the private sector, focused primarily in the U.S. healthcare federal markets. As a consultant and lobbyist, I lead and manage a diverse client portfolio that includes medical research organizations, medical devices, biotechnology, pharmaceutical, and health information technology companies focused on developing new programs, fixing problems, and growing existing programs within the federal government and commercial markets. I advise clients on issues affecting business goals, develop solutions, and lead large-scale program development, U.S. Food and Drug Administration (FDA) regulatory services, and program implementation and evaluation. In addition, I assist clients in navigating the intricacies of federal governmental agencies and organizations, both in Congress and within the Executive Branch while developing and executing business development and legislative solutions. I provide due diligence support to private equity firms focused on middle market debt and equity investments for healthcare companies providing services or products in the DoD/VA federal healthcare.

2. What would you consider to be a "typical" day for you?

The work is varied. A typical day could involve an early morning meeting with the firm's president, followed by: a meeting with existing clients to brief them on our progress and to discuss the path forward to solve the issues; a review of our practice financials; a lunch with a prospective client; afternoon meeting with our business development team to discuss our responses to requests for proposals (RFPs); returning phone calls to

Continued

NAME: GILLIAN V. JAEGER Continued

companies that may be interested in our firm's services; accompanying a client to a meeting on Capitol Hill and later attending an evening event positioning the firm for new business, or participating in a panel event.

3. What education or training do you have? Is it typical for your job?

A master's degree in healthcare administration from the George Washington University; master's certificate in organizational effectiveness and program management from Villanova University; bachelor's degree in healthcare management, Southern Illinois University; associate degree—liberal arts, University of Maryland. I'm adjunct professor at Albany State University, Albany, Georgia, and the George Washington University, Washington DC.

Most consultants I have encountered have achieved graduate degrees. Consultants with graduate degrees and extensive experience in their respective fields or healthcare discipline are generally much more regarded and tend to have an extensive network and a tremendous breadth of experience.

4. What is the most challenging part of your job?

I find my leadership role to be the most challenging. Though I have clients whom I support, I must find time to avoid being consumed by the daily grind, think strategically, and constantly reassess my internal and external business environment to not only keep clients apprised, but to pursue new business opportunities—making early morning time to read and stay abreast of relevant policy and federal budgetary changes and opportunities for clients; reexamining our company's strategy, customers, competition, and industry trends are always at the forefront of my thoughts and actions. My role also requires that I work with our team to analyze our internal challenges, develop and execute solutions. For example, our firm plans to expand our FDA regulatory services—I must lead the growth strategy and ensure that all facets are aligned and executed to achieve the desired results; this can keep me up at night.

Another challenge is my ability to constantly prioritize and balance my day to ensure that our team is working toward providing our clients with on-time deliverables, marketing and positioning for new business, as well as supporting our growth strategy. In addition, the job often requires long commutes, long hours that include international conference calls, and working away from home across the globe, and being responsive to clients in different time zones. I am currently working with

Continued

NAME: GILLIAN V. JAEGER Continued

clients in South Korea and Algeria; learning cultural norms can also be a challenge. Consulting is a very rewarding career, but it is not easy and requires you to be a highly effective functioning professional who can deliver results/solutions to existing clients as they are our greatest source of generating new leads for new business.

5. What do you consider to be the best part of your job?

I enjoy working with my colleagues to help clients solve large-scale problems. When a client comes back to us because of the previous work performed, it is very gratifying and rewarding, that is the best part of my job! When I get an e-mail or a phone call that states because of our experience with your firm I need your help, or I have referred someone to you—that makes my day!! Many of our projects involve companies selling services, products, or solutions to the DoD/VA; having the opportunity to work on projects that impact the quality of life of military service members, their families, and veterans is one of my greatest reward—that is worth the hard days and long nights. Another satisfying aspect I enjoy is working with companies to get a drug or device an FDA approval or clearance. For example, we are currently working with a client to get a medical diagnostic device for the Zika virus approved by the FDA; I enjoy being a part of something that will make the lives of others better.

6. What path did you take to get to the job you are in today?

I was a former Medical Service Corps Officer and veteran leader and manager in healthcare management and policy addressing the Navy's most significant programs such as force health protection, quality of life, and resources (e.g. TRICARE, suicide prevention, anthrax, secretarial designee, and research/clinical trials) that impact Navy personnel and their families. During a 27-year Navy career, I worked in tertiary care and community care hospitals as a healthcare leader with oversight and responsibilities for contracting, strategic planning, compliance and regulatory programs, program management and evaluation, organizational analysis, medical research, and health policy. Upon receiving my graduate degree in healthcare administration, my assignments included deputy director at the Office of Assistant Secretary of the Navy for Manpower and Reserve Affairs, and congressional liaison for Navy Medicine at the Office of the Assistant Secretary for Legislative Affairs; deputy director of patient administration, National Naval Medical Center, Bethesda; and director of plans, programs and analysis, Naval Hospital, Camp Pendleton.

Continued

NAME: GILLIAN V. JAEGER Continued

Following retirement from the military, I worked as director of governmental relations for a large defense healthcare payer delivering health insurance in 21 states to military beneficiaries. Representing this client, I worked with both the executive and legislative branches of government focused on improving the delivery of healthcare services to military beneficiaries in 21 states. Later I became a consultant and lobbyist working at a large defense consulting firm, managing a diverse client portfolio—medical research organizations, universities, hospitals, biotechnology, biopharmaceutical, and health information technology companies, developing new programs and growing existing programs within the federal government.

Principal and founder, Capitol Consulting Group, LLC, Alexandria, VA, I have extensive experience assisting clients in navigating the intricacies of federal governmental agencies and organizations both in Congress and within the Executive Branch while developing and executing business development and legislative solutions. Over the years, aside from my primary duties, I became involved as much as possible serving on committees and volunteering to broaden my knowledge and expand my network.

7. What advice do you have for someone who is interested in a job such as yours?

As you know, the healthcare environment is dynamic and change is constant, so you must keep abreast and be informed of the changes and their impact. If you like people and like solving problems and are interested in becoming a consultant, I recommend the following:

Field experience: Learn your craft from the bottom up—you will have credibility! Diversify your experience; a broader experience and knowledge will serve you well; get involved as much as you can. You must be knowledgeable about your field—and this is where your networking will begin, but must not end; it is a continuous process.

Relationships: As a consultant, relationships are key; as you progress through your career, maintain good relationships, building a solid network. As a consultant, your network is important. To keep your existing clients and to generate new business, much of that comes down to building and maintaining relationships. People work with people whom they like and trust, and a consultant's ability to influence and build trust comes down to having strong relationships with clients and potential clients

Listening: To get new business and to keep your clients, you must develop your ability to be a good listener; it is not only about what

Continued

services you have to sell but also what solutions you can provide to help a particular client solve a problem; understand why it is critical to his or her business.

Strategic thinking: Clients come to you to help them solve problems that impact their business. People who think strategically constantly assess the environment that includes programs, policies, requirements, trends, and budgets, and are more likely to offer a client a better course of action or help them think through choices to balance short- and long-term concerns.

Knowledge and experience: Continually work to broaden your knowledge and experience. Doing so will help you to see connections and patterns across seemingly unrelated fields of knowledge. Join professional organizations, such as National Defense Industrial Association (NDIA) and Women in International Trade, to stay current in your field and enhance your network.

JOB DESCRIPTION

The position of senior health analytics consultant requires a person with an entrepreneurial way of thinking and can shape analytics solutions for today's and future health challenges, as well as deliver business intelligence and analytics initiatives to improve health outcomes. This role is for someone who: is interested in both thought leadership and hands-on analysis; has a health business background, analytical methodology experience, and knowledge of health data in order to understand and communicate with clinicians, operations, finance and IT clients; can develop analyses that lead to actionable insights from health data; and can drive business growth for both the clients and the consulting firm. The senior health analytics consultant will work with other health and analytics experts as well as others to provide clients with information and tools for reporting and advanced analytics.

EDUCATION AND EXPERIENCE

Minimum education is a bachelor's degree in business or health administration; a master's degree would be preferred. In addition, it is preferred that persons seeking these positions should have 5 or more years of experience with health clinical, financial, and operational data, and/or experience in business intelligence and analytics.

CORE COMPETENCIES AND SKILLS

- Interest in applying critical thinking, problem solving, and understanding of issues from both business and technical perspectives
- Experience designing and delivering analytical studies on the basis of disease and treatment trends, quality of care, expenses, and income
- Ability to present and explain the value of analytics to clients and drive business opportunities
- Proficiency with analytic tools and methods such as R, SAS, Tableau, and other statistical software
- Experience working with clinical information systems such as EPIC, Cerner, and so forth
- Ability to convey complex technical specification into language easily digestible by nontechnical business stakeholders and vice versa
- Experience with health interoperability standards including clinical terminologies, health messaging standards, health information, and data model standards

- Proficiency in the use of computers and programs that specialize in data collection and data management
- Proven ability to extract/source data from multiple data sources and integrate them into a single source view/report/dataset
- Ability to work independently on projects with minimal direction
- Strong interpersonal skills and effective team player
- Strong verbal/written communication skills
- Business intelligence, predictive and prescriptive analysis of clinical, financial, and operational data to improve healthcare utilization, costs, population health, and clinical outcomes; to solve data and informatics needs; and support emerging technologies

COMPENSATION

Compensation for senior health analytics consultants ranges between $53,000 and $165,000 per year. This amount will vary depending on the size of the consulting firm and often on possible year-end bonuses.

EMPLOYMENT OUTLOOK

The expected employment outlook for senior health analytics consultants is expected to be faster than average. Healthcare organizations are continuously hiring healthcare consultants from large, nationally known firms and smaller local firms and individual consultants to help them identify and solve problems for which they do not have the internal capacity to address.

FOR FURTHER INFORMATION

- American College of Healthcare Executives (www.ache.org)
- National Society of Healthcare Business Consultants (www.nschbc.org)

 NAME: DAVID J. KERRIGAN

Title: Founder, Principal and Managing Director
Organization: Sante Nasc, LLC
Previous Organization: Conduent (formerly Xerox HR Services)

1. Briefly describe your job responsibilities.

In January of 2017, I started my own healthcare consulting and advisory firm named Sante Nasc, LLC. This is in addition to my volunteer work at TiE Boston's ScaleUp program where I act as an advisor to the healthcare organizations in the cohort, as well as facilitate the chief executive officer (CEO) roundtable discussions that are part of the program.

In that same month, I was downsized from my full-time job at Conduent, where I was responsible for solution partner (vendor) strategy, integration, and performance. This included expansion of our portfolio of solutions partners, evaluation of solution partners, contracting, recontracting, and integration of solutions within the exchange. I served on the leadership team of the RightOpt Health Solutions Exchange Practice.

2. What would you consider to be a "typical" day for you?

I work from home 100% of the time which allows a flexible schedule. Typically, I had spent a good portion of my day on calls related to each of the solution partners, with health insurance carriers being the bulk of these calls owing to the important nature of their work with our exchange. Now, I am networking for a new position, while continuing my volunteer work with TiE Boston's ScaleUp program. I am also working with a number of healthcare startups on project-related work through my company, Sante Nasc, LLC.

3. What education or training do you have? Is it typical for your job?

I graduated with an undergraduate degree in healthcare administration from Stonehill College. With the exception of one company, every role I've held in my career has been with a healthcare company. I would say that my education is typical for this sort of field. I will say that my work in the healthcare startup space has augmented my own education and has helped me grow as a professional.

Continued

NAME: DAVID J. KERRIGAN Continued

4. What is the most challenging part of your job?

Ambiguity can be challenging, as exchanges are still somewhat of a new phenomenon, but the largest challenge is resources. There are only limited resources to use/share and a lot more work to do.

5. What do you consider to be the best part of your job?

While with Conduent, I had a hand in our product strategy that helped shape the future of our exchange and assure that we delivered to our employers and employees the promise of our exchange—to improve overall health, lower cost, engage our members, and arm them with the tools needed to make better decisions about their health.

With my work at Sante Nasc, I am energized to see the work that healthcare startups are doing in this field, and am thrilled to bring my many years of experience to help these firms make an impact in health care.

6. What path did you take to get to the job you are in today?

I have followed a rather unconventional path, I would say. My curiosity and passion for the field of healthcare has led me to experience a number of aspects of the healthcare field including payer, provider, insurance brokerage, patient advocacy, health informatics, and private, as well as public, exchanges. In addition, I've historically volunteered time with healthcare startups.

7. What advice do you have for someone who is interested in a job such as yours?

I'm not sure I would advise people to do it the way I've done it, but I would advise someone interested in this field and this job to stay curious and be passionate. Ask questions, attend events, network with people in this field and adjacent fields, offer your time to help others, and always keep the patient at the center of whatever you do.

 NAME: KIMBRA WELLS METZ

Title: Partner
Organization: The Advisory Board
Company

1. Briefly describe your job responsibilities.

- Serve as a thought partner to C-suite leaders across healthcare.
- Oversight for a portfolio of accounts made up of health systems currently partnered with Advisory Board across research, technology, and consulting services.
- Lead delivery teams in service to our members, while ensuring our healthcare partners are receiving value from their investment in the form of improved quality, reduced cost, and increased revenues.
- Supporting development of new relationships and business needs that grow account responsibilities while fostering existing relationships.

2. What would you consider to be a "typical" day for you?

A typical day consists of a combination of in-person and/or virtual meetings with healthcare leaders at health systems, hospitals, and ambulatory care facilities to discuss status of current partnership, drive steering of critical decisions, and identify or address issues and opportunities while fostering strong relationships. Additionally, there are recurring internal meetings with Advisory Board colleagues and delivery teams across research, technology, and consulting to ensure we are optimally and effectively serving our members, while driving value.

3. What education or training do you have? Is it typical for your job?

My education consists of a Master of Health Administration (MHA) and a bachelor's in psychology; my training and experience have spanned healthcare: from hospital operations to ambulatory care, health plan to healthcare technology and consulting. Many of my colleagues pursue organizations like the Advisory Board Company right after completing undergraduate education. There is opportunity for learning and growth in a variety of roles at different stages of a career. The key is to bring "talent" to the firm, with the ability to be flexible and an eagerness to learn and grow, while driving value for our members.

Continued

NAME: KIMBRA WELLS METZ
Continued

4. What is the most challenging part of your job?

The challenges in healthcare are immensely complicated, and yet, so important. It is a great responsibility, for which I am humbled, to serve as thought partner with healthcare leaders, while attempting to solve for these challenges. Our firm has a breadth and depth of data-driven insight, and best practices delivered by very talented teams, which makes addressing these challenges very rewarding at the same time.

5. What do you consider to be the best part of your job?

There are many aspects I love about my job: leveraging all of the insights that the Advisory Board has to offer to help healthcare leaders solve some of their most challenging "up at night" issues; working with smart, talented, and hardworking people who also appreciate a healthy, fun, and rewarding quality of life; and mentoring early careerists in the process.

6. What path did you take to get to the job you are in today?

There are several paths to this type of job. There are many early careerists who start right out of college and move up in the organization; some have a little experience in healthcare, technology, and/or consulting and apply at a midlevel, while my path was one of a pretty extensive background working in many capacities across the continuum of healthcare, and discovering that I can be most effective ensuring healthcare organizations are positioned well for improved quality, reduced costs, and revenue growth as a senior leader and thought partner, representing all that the Advisory Board has to offer.

7. What advice do you have for someone who is interested in a job such as yours?

It's important to gain an awareness of the type of culture in which you want to work and what your strengths and interests might be. Reach out to someone already working at the firm, to gain a better understanding of appropriate positions. There are many opportunities for learning and growth in a variety of roles at different stages of a career. The key is to bring "talent" to the firm, with the ability to be flexible and an eagerness to learn and grow, while driving value for our members (clients). Be open to entry positions if you are an early careerist; upward movement happens pretty quickly at that level and it gets your foot in the door.

HEALTHCARE CONSULTANT

56

JOB DESCRIPTION

Consultants conduct much of an engagement's quantitative and qualitative analysis, draft written reports, and prepare a wide range of materials required for client presentations and meetings. They will direct other staff in these activities as well. Consultants work in a deadline-oriented, fast-paced environment, and are typically part of a growing team consisting of consulting and operations staff. Consultants frequently gain experience in more than one product line while developing sophisticated consulting skills and abilities that will lead them to broader and deeper roles. They must demonstrate success in working with multiple managers/senior staff. Experienced consultants will be given the opportunity to manage projects to develop broader management skills.

EDUCATION AND EXPERIENCE

- Bachelor's degree from an accredited college or university
- Master's degree (preferred)
- Project Management Professional (PMP), Change Management Advanced Practitioner (CMAP), and/or Lean Six Sigma Green or Black Belts (preferred) qualifications
- At least 5 years' experience in consulting and/or program management for federal clients
- Expertise in at least one of these capabilities: program/project management, project management office (PMO) operations, change management, strategic communications, business process improvement, planning/programming/budgeting/execution (PPBE) implementation, end-to-end requirements management (E2ERM), acquisition project management framework (APMF), performance measurement/monitoring

CORE COMPETENCIES AND SKILLS

- Creative problem-solving ability and a consultancy mindset
- Commitment to exceptional client service and ability to lead confidently
- Dedication to accomplishing goals and challenges presented by clients and management
- Ability to interact with various levels of management and clients
- Flexibility, self-starter possessing intellectual curiosity
- Ability to move multiple projects forward within a specific timeline and budget while working at a detailed level

- Strong analytical and financial data analysis skills
- Ability to pay attention to detail, and work with large data sets while ensuring accurate results
- Ability to follow, critically evaluate, and improve upon current processes
- Ability to recognize issues and identify solutions
- Excellent oral presentation and written communication skills
- Solid organizational and time management skills
- Research and project management capabilities
- Expertise in all MS Office products

COMPENSATION

The compensation for healthcare consultants ranges from $55,000 to $170,000 per year. Experienced consultants at large firms can earn significantly more than the national norm.

EMPLOYMENT OUTLOOK

The expected employment outlook for healthcare consultants is expected to be faster than average. Healthcare organizations are continuously hiring healthcare consultants from large nationally known firms and smaller local firms and individual consultants to help them identify and solve problems for which they do not have the internal capacity to address.

FOR FURTHER INFORMATION

- American College of Healthcare Executives (www.ache.org)
- National Society of Certified Healthcare Business Consultants (www .nschbc.org)

 NAME: RICKY D. ALLEN

Title: Managing Partner
Organization: Spirit Media Group, LLC

1. Briefly describe your job responsibilities.

As managing partner of Spirit Media Group, I am responsible for developing the strategic direction of the company and growing our client base. Having a career experience heavily rooted in military service, health administration, leadership, and customer service, my position has many tentacles, some of which take me outside my company's realm of responsibilities. For example, I am also an adjunct professor teaching leadership and ethics in the Executive Master of Health Administration program in the Department of Health Policy and Management at Milken Institute School of Public Health at the George Washington University.

2. What would you consider to be a "typical" day for you?

Meeting with clients and reviewing business opportunities and proposals take up most of my day. However, because of the many hats I wear, it is important to keep abreast of current trends in management, health administration, leadership, and customer service. Therefore, a portion of my day is devoted to reading on those subjects.

3. What education or training do you have? Is it typical for your job?

Having started my career in the Navy by enlisting just after high school, I have all types of training. Military service schools, on-the-job, traditional and online university education are among my suite of training and educational experiences. Nevertheless, I ended up with two hard-earned and very useful postgraduate degrees: a Master of Health Administration and a Master of Divinity. I believe the two combined perfectly and positioned me for my three favorite career focuses—helping, leading, and serving people. Anyone seeking a career in health administration should seek a degree focus in health administration, finance, economics, law, or other field closely related to the provision of health services, policies, and products.

Continued

NAME: RICKY D. ALLEN Continued

4. What is the most challenging part of your job?

A very challenging part of my job is translating the messages, directions, and intentions from top leadership to the language of the followers. I apply this thought from a leader and manager perspective. As a leader, it's important to understand that the primary reason for your existence is to accomplish the mission and vision of the organization. The challenge is to do it in a fashion where there is a win-win in the end. The organization wins because it achieves its mission and vision, and then each member of the team wins when they feel like they too are achieving their own personal mission and vision.

5. What do you consider to be the best part of your job?

Helping people is by far the best part of my job. From the parking lot to the executive offices, there are ample opportunities to help people every day. In my formal roles, I use policies and procedures as the structures to achieve the outcomes, but paired with my own leading and service style. I get to predetermine whether that outcome is going to be average or phenomenal. I'll seek phenomenal every time.

6. What path did you take to get to the job you are in today?

After completing my military career in health and dental services as an enlisted officer, I intended to go directly into business ownership in management and services consulting and customer service training, but had several unexpected but very rewarding detours. I volunteered at a community outreach center in a full-time capacity in an underserved area, became a governmental contractor on the staffs of the Air Force Surgeon General and the Navy's Surgeon General, and served as an associate director at the Veterans Health Administration—all of which has culminated in my serving as an adjunct professor teaching leadership and ethics to future leaders in health administration and other fields.

7. What advice do you have for someone who is interested in a job such as yours?

Figure out what you love doing and strive to become the best at it. Nothing can stop you except you. However, I am not the result of a planned career. I just made the best of wherever I landed. Yes, that's right, I bloomed where I was planted. However, from there I began to see where I wanted to go, figured out what was needed or required, got

Continued

the training, experience, or education needed, developed the faith and confidence to pursue my goals, and persevered, and achieved them. My advice to you is to do the same. It doesn't matter where you start, or the limitations you perceive you have; history is filled with success stories from anyone's place in life and ensuing journey.

NAME: LAUREN FISHKIN KIES

Title: Healthcare Consulting Manager
Organization: PricewaterhouseCoopers
Public Sector

1. Briefly describe your job responsibilities.

As a strategy consultant, my main responsibility is to lead teams to solve our clients' most pressing challenges. For each of my projects, I work with the client to define the needs and goals of the engagement. I then guide the team to create a detailed project plan, complete the work steps, and measure and assess outcomes. I provide industry knowledge about healthcare operations, and, importantly, monitor quality and openly communicate with the client throughout. I am responsible for mentoring and developing my PwC staff. Additionally, I build relationships in the market, write white papers, present on panels and at industry events, and pursue new client opportunities.

2. What would you consider to be a "typical" day for you?

Every day is different for me. Some days begin on a plane to see a client; others begin at my PwC office, a local client site, or telecommuting from home. I spend about 70% of my day performing advisory services for clients. This involves strategy discussions, research and analysis, review of work products my team creates, writing reports, and meetings. A fifth of my time is spent on business development activities, such as writing responses to requests for proposals (RFPs) and attending healthcare events. The remainder of my time is dedicated to internal firm activities such as continuing education courses and developing staff.

3. What education or training do you have? Is it typical for your job?

I earned a Bachelor of Science in Brain and Cognitive Sciences with a minor in psychology and concentration in foreign languages from

Continued

NAME: LAUREN FISHKIN KIES
Continued

Massachusetts Institute of Technology (MIT) and a Master of Science in Health Systems Administration from Georgetown University. While I would not call my background typical for a consultant, I do have many colleagues with Science, Technology, Engineering, and Medicine (STEM) and healthcare administration training. People often think careers in consulting are available only for Master of Business Administration (MBA) graduates; the reality is consultants come from various backgrounds, and having a specialized background such as healthcare can really differentiate you.

4. What is the most challenging part of your job?

The most challenging part of my job is planning how to allocate my time across client service, sales, mentoring, and personal development priorities. My natural tendency is to be "all in, all the time" on everything I do, so I need to consciously plan where my effort is most valuable and be diligent about adhering to the plan. For example, I am talented in writing RFP responses. If I let these responses consume my entire day, I would run out of time to focus on my main priority: client work. I have a great team, and being able to delegate work is the only way I am able to keep things balanced and still get everything completed on time. The team also likes this approach because they get exposure to many types of projects and tasks.

5. What do you consider to be the best part of your job?

The best part of my job is getting to constantly be on the cutting edge of healthcare. My job is to solve clients' current challenges, and those are constantly changing. For example, when a new legislation passes, my clients look to me to determine what practical steps they need to be compliant, and what strategic moves they can make to benefit from the change. I enjoy that my job is ever changing; I get to continuously learn, and I need to use all my skills—from technical to communications—every day. Other great parts of my job are my boss and mentors in the firm, and the flexibility to work where and how is most effective.

6. What path did you take to get to the job you are in today?

My path to a career in healthcare consulting was not direct. In high school and college, my internships were technical and frequently

Continued

NAME: LAUREN FISHKIN KIES
Continued

laboratory based. Following undergraduate studies, I planned to pursue a PhD in neuroscience and have a career in spinal cord injury research. Before beginning a PhD program, I decided to work in a neuroscience lab. I quickly learned that while I love bench research, the lifestyle was not for me and I could impact many lives at once through the management/administration side of healthcare. I went back to school and earned my MHSA to round out my understanding of the healthcare system, and then I began my formal career in healthcare consulting.

7. What advice do you have for someone who is interested in a job such as yours?

Reflect on why you want to be a consultant and what unique skills, understanding, and talents you will bring to clients. Know that you will not have a standard 9 to 5 job, and be prepared for weekly travel if you work in the commercial sector. If you are in school, build your resume through industry or consulting internships, and take advantage of on-campus career services and recruiting events. Remember that everything you do is a reflection of yourself, so complete tasks with quality, have a great attitude, and raise your hand for new challenges.

JOB DESCRIPTION

Research analysts are responsible for the coordinating, designing, and implementing research for healthcare clients. They collect and analyze data on market trends and business opportunities using a variety of methods such as literature reviews, focus groups, site visits, and surveys. The research analyst needs to be skilled in writing for various types of audiences. Oftentimes, research analysts publish their research and present it at conferences. They are experts in the healthcare industry and as such help to provide status reports and create business strategies for their clients. Healthcare analysts also seek to create and maintain relationships with healthcare organizations.

EDUCATION AND EXPERIENCE

A bachelor's degree is the minimum educational requirement for most research analyst positions; most positions prefer applicants have a graduate degree with a focus in business administration, healthcare administration, or public health. Prior research experience is critical as is experience in the use of statistical programming. Most organizations require 2 years of work experience as a research analyst.

CORE COMPETENCIES AND SKILLS

- Knowledge of how to use statistical databases such as SPSS, SAS, STATA, NVivo, Excel, and so on
- Excellent quantitative, analytical, and critical thinking abilities
- Strong English-writing ability
- Ability to work in a team environment
- Experience with communication and presentation of concepts and results
- Ability to work in a high-intensity environment

COMPENSATION

The mean wage of research analysts is around $59,000. They can make as little as $38,000, or as much as $86,000. Research analysts with more experience or those working at larger firms will likely earn a higher salary. Similarly, those working in a busier, urban area, stand to make more than someone living in a rural setting.

EMPLOYMENT OUTLOOK

This position will be in high demand as healthcare providers try to navigate through healthcare reform and the changing characteristics of the population. As healthcare providers seek strategies to gain market share and maximize reimbursements, they will need to use the expertise of consulting firms and their healthcare research analysts.

FOR FURTHER INFORMATION

- National Society of Healthcare Business Consultants (https://nschbc.org/)
- American College of Healthcare Executives (www.ache.org)

CHAPTER 12
CAREERS IN HEALTH INFORMATION TECHNOLOGY AND HEALTH INFORMATICS

DIRECTOR OF HEALTH INFORMATION TECHNOLOGY PLANNING AND OPERATIONS

JOB DESCRIPTION

The director of health information technology (IT) planning and operations is accountable for IT strategic planning, IT governance, portfolio operations, and ensuring all IT priorities are aligned with the organization's strategic priorities and goals. The director must have extensive understanding of healthcare, future trends in the areas of technology portfolio management, and the role of IT in advancing the organization's capabilities. The director keeps abreast of new developments and forecasts future trends in the areas of technology portfolio management. The director maintains a strong understanding of IT technologies and the technologies to deliver services to the organization, and works closely with all other IT management personnel in identifying, evaluating, and selecting specific IT that supports the business plans and IT strategic direction.

EDUCATION AND EXPERIENCE

A bachelor's degree in business administration or information technology is the minimum academic qualification, although a master's degree in either business or information technology is becoming the standard level of education for IT directors. Most healthcare organizations require a minimum of 7 to 10 years of senior IT experience within healthcare.

CORE COMPETENCIES AND SKILLS

- Outstanding interpersonal skills including the ability to effectively communicate with persons throughout the organization
- Excellent verbal and written communication skills
- Deep understanding and proven track record over several years in IT strategy delivery, and excellent awareness of the strategic goals and ability to define and influence those goals
- Strong process improvement orientation, with experience in establishing portfolio management and IT governance frameworks
- Ability to lead effectively and utilize social influence to achieve organizational objectives
- Ability to coach and mentor a wide variety of staff
- Strong analytic skills
- Substantial knowledge of technology solutions in a healthcare provider environment

COMPENSATION

Directors of health IT planning and operations earn in the range of $132,000 to $231,000, although the total salary will vary depending on the size and location of the healthcare organization.

EMPLOYMENT OUTLOOK

The employment outlook for directors of health IT is particularly strong. Each and every hospital in the nation is working to develop their IT infrastructure in response to demands by the federal government and the need to provide ever-higher levels of quality care. Possessing an IT background is an important requirement, but the applicant must also be familiar with the unique requirements of healthcare delivery.

FOR FURTHER INFORMATION

■ Healthcare Information and Management Systems Society (www.himss.org)

59

DIRECTOR OF EDUCATION AND TRAINING

JOB DESCRIPTION

The director functions under the senior director of information systems and provides direct supervision of the corporate training development team, which is responsible for developing training materials necessary for health information systems (HIS) and technology education and support. The director is responsible for building and providing direction to the overall information technology (IT) training program. The training materials and delivery media are designed to facilitate the train-the-trainer sessions, and facilitate independent interactive learning for IT system implementations and enhancements. This position oversees the collaboration with content and IT system experts in developing the materials in cooperation with the care site training and support personnel. The director oversees contract fulfillment and service levels of an outsourced training function; assigns personnel to the various training tasks and directs their activities; reviews and evaluates work and prepares performance reports related to training programs. This position will be responsible for directing multiple concurrent projects, and will provide guidance to multiple teams on issues that range from prioritizing, operational issues, and conflict management that may be associated with multiple projects.

EDUCATION AND EXPERIENCE

The director of education and training requires a minimum of a bachelor's degree in computer science or a related area. Preferred education includes a master's degree in business administration or health administration. Experience in instructional design is highly preferred. A minimum of 2 years of database development and design, web design, and technical assistance is required.

CORE COMPETENCIES AND SKILLS

- Outstanding interpersonal skills including the ability to effectively communicate with persons throughout the organization
- Excellent verbal and written communication skills
- Advanced-level computer skills, including Microsoft Office platforms such as Word, Excel, PowerPoint, Access, Visio, and web design
- Familiarity working in a data warehouse environment
- Outstanding customer service skills
- Experience with negotiations and contract development
- Demonstrated ability to develop creative solutions to complex problems

- Ability to utilize creative and analytical problem-solving techniques to extremely varied situations
- Substantial knowledge of technology solutions in a healthcare provider environment

COMPENSATION

Directors of education and training earn in the range of $40,000 to $86,000, although the total salary will vary depending on the size and location of the healthcare organization.

EMPLOYMENT OUTLOOK

The employment outlook for directors of education and training is particularly strong. Each and every hospital in the nation is working to develop their IT infrastructure in response to demands by the federal government and the need to provide ever-higher levels of quality care. Possessing an IT background is an important requirement, but the applicant must also be familiar with the unique requirements of healthcare delivery.

FOR FURTHER INFORMATION

- Health Information Management Systems Society (www.himss.org)
- Association for Talent Development (www.td.org)

NAME: JENNIFER LEE

Title: Senior Program Coordinator
Organization: McGaw Medical Center
of Northwestern University

1. Briefly describe your job responsibilities.

My organization, McGaw Medical Center of Northwestern University, hired me to pilot the transition to global utilization of web-based residency management software which will allow the organization to provide effective institutional oversight for more than 200 accredited and nonaccredited residency and fellowship training programs. As such, I manage various projects within the residency management software related to finance, human resources, training, education, and accreditation.

2. What would you consider to be a "typical" day for you?

A typical day involves simultaneously working on projects, running reports as needed for my leadership team, providing technical assistance for our software's end users (house staff, faculty, and administrators), and training new program coordinators and administrators.

3. What education or training do you have? Is it typical for your job?

I received my Bachelor of Arts from the University of Illinois at Chicago (UIC), with a major in criminal justice. I'm currently a candidate for an Executive Masters of Health Administration from the George Washington University. While it is ideal to receive graduate-level training to meet the demands of my job, it is not a requirement.

4. What is the most challenging part of your job?

McGaw has over 200 training programs comprising approximately 1200 house staff. Because the needs of and educational training for the programs vary greatly from program to program, it can be challenging to find or offer universal solutions or best practices for the software. Another continual challenge is the number of turnovers in departmental and programmatic staff.

Continued

NAME: JENNIFER LEE Continued

5. What do you consider to be the best part of your job?

The best part of my job is that those challenges exist. I enjoy planning, researching, testing, and deploying best practices and solutions for my organization and the software's end users. The complexity and depth of understanding required to formulate best practices and solutions for such diverse programs and personnel needs makes my job interesting and stimulates my growth in knowledge in my field.

6. What path did you take to get to the job you are in today?

While I was pursing my undergraduate degree from UIC, I was a student administrative assistant in UIC's Office of Graduate Medical Education (GME). Upon graduation, I decided to stay in UIC GME and continue to build my knowledge about many different administrative and educational aspects of graduate medical education. Through networking with my counterparts at nearby academic medical centers and universities, I was offered a similar, but more senior-level position at McGaw Medical Center of Northwestern University.

7. What advice do you have for someone who is interested in a job such as yours?

Do not be put off by the simplicity of the job responsibilities of a program coordinator in graduate medical education. Instead, embrace the challenges of the knowledge base and experience you'll gain as it will help you understand how essential and important excellence in graduate medical educational training of physicians is to the future of healthcare.

60 ELECTRONIC MEDICAL RECORDS DIRECTOR

JOB DESCRIPTION

The electronic medical records (EMR) director oversees the EMR information system that supports the integration of the organization's business entities. The director works with senior and middle management to develop strategic plans and priorities for the EMR system, and ensures implementation of agreed-upon objectives. The director will utilize creative and analytical skills to solve new and complex problems. The EMR director directs a staff of information systems and training professionals consulting with and assisting all levels of management and staff throughout the organization. Technical currency is maintained by ongoing education tempered and supplemented by applicable work experience.

EDUCATION AND EXPERIENCE

EMR directors typically possess a master's degree in computer sciences, business administration, or health administration, along with 5 years' increasingly responsible information system management experience, preferably in a healthcare computer environment.

CORE COMPETENCIES AND SKILLS

- Outstanding interpersonal skills including the ability to effectively communicate with persons throughout the organization
- Excellent verbal and written communication skills
- Ability to recommend goals and objectives for the EMR automated information system to senior management; establish plans and recommend policies and procedures for the EMR system within the information systems department to meet the organization's mission
- Ability to oversee large-scale development efforts, implementations of commercial software packages, and modifications to the EMR system; maintain quality of information systems, implementing corrective action and identifying needs for new or improved information services; direct information systems activities relative to the EMR system for the entire organization
- Ability to work independently and in a complex team environment
- Ability to work independently and make decisions consistent with overall corporate and departmental objectives
- Ability to maintain confidentiality and integrity of data, materials, and user information within the program

- Ability to utilize creative and analytical problem-solving techniques to extremely varied situations
- Substantial knowledge of technology solutions in a healthcare provider environment
- Ability to effectively manage activities and personnel

COMPENSATION

EMR directors earn in the range of $137,000 to $226,000, although the total salary will vary depending on the size and location of the hospital.

EMPLOYMENT OUTLOOK

The employment outlook for EMR directors is particularly strong. Each and every hospital in the nation is working to develop their IT infrastructure in response to demands by the federal government and the need to provide ever-higher levels of quality care. Mid-size to large physician practices are also hiring EMR directors. Possessing an IT background is an important requirement, but the applicant must also be familiar with the unique requirements of healthcare delivery.

FOR FURTHER INFORMATION

- Healthcare Information Management Systems Society (www.himss.org)

61 HEALTH INFORMATION MANAGEMENT CODER

JOB DESCRIPTION

Health information management (HIM) coders are responsible for coding clinical procedures properly for providers to be reimbursed the correct amount of money. HIM coders identify, review, and interpret highly complex/high acuity codes such as ICD-9-CM, ICD-10-CM, current procedural terminology (CPT), product composer systems (PCS), power of attorney (POA), and patient safety indicators (PSI) indicators; abstract highly complex clinical information from high acuity inpatient, surgical outpatients, and observations for the purpose of reimbursements, research, and compliance with federal regulations and other agencies utilizing established coding principles and protocols.

EDUCATION AND EXPERIENCE

A high school diploma is required for work as an HIM coder. A minimum of 3 years of experience abstracting, identifying, reviewing, and assigning highly complex/high acuity ICD-9-CM, ICD-10-CM, CPT, PCS, POA and PSI indicators for inpatient, surgical outpatient, and observations is required. Finally, licensure as a Registered Health Information Administrator (RHIA), Registered Health Information Technician (RHIT), or Certified Coding Specialist (CCS) is required and must be maintained.

CORE COMPETENCIES AND SKILLS

- Critical thinking skills, decisive judgment, and the ability to work with minimal supervision; ability to work in a stressful environment and take appropriate action
- Ability to clarify highly complex discrepancies in documentation and coding; to assure accuracy and timeliness of highly complex/high acuity coding/abstracting assignments to expedite the billing process; and to facilitate data retrieval for physician access and ongoing patient care
- Ability to identify, review, and interpret highly complex/high acuity codes
- Ability to abstract highly complex clinical information from high acuity inpatient, surgical outpatients, and observations for the purpose of reimbursements, research, and compliance with federal regulations and other agencies utilizing established coding principles and protocols
- Advanced analytical coding skills to accurately code high complexity/high acuity cases

■ Ability to extract pertinent highly complex information from clinical notes, operative notes, radiology reports, laboratory reports, specialty forms, and so on, using ICD-9-CM/ ICD-10-CM / PCS codes, POA indicators, and PSI indicators

■ Ability to determine code assignments pertinent to diagnostic workups for accurate Medicare Severity Diagnosis Related Group (MS-DRG)/All Patients Refined Diagnosis Related Group (APR-DRG) assignment

■ Ability to perform follow-up of highly complex/high acuity coding of medical records as a result of internal or external reviews that have identified Coding, APC, or DRG discrepancies

■ Ability to support special studies in relation to coding and abstracting information according to policies and procedures

■ Ability to maintain knowledge and skills; read current coding resources clinical information, videos, and so on

■ Ability to meet or exceed productivity and quality standards and established departmental benchmarks; other duties as assigned

COMPENSATION

HIM coders typically earn between $46,000 and $65,000 per year. Salary levels are frequently a function of years of experience and location of the job.

EMPLOYMENT OUTLOOK

The employment outlook for HIM coders is much faster than average. There is projected to be a continuing need for skilled and experienced coders.

FOR FURTHER INFORMATION

■ American Health Information Management Association (www.ahima.org)

62 HEALTH INFORMATION MANAGEMENT EXCHANGE SPECIALIST

JOB DESCRIPTION

A health information management exchange specialist manages health information exchange planning and implementation projects. The position collaborates with vendors to ensure success of technological implementations. The exchange specialist must assist in the review and evaluation process of proposals. It is the responsibility of the health information management exchange specialist to monitor the health exchange project for timeliness and accuracy to achieve compliance and project goals. The position requires directing and delegating staff members by overseeing execution and problem solving. Finally, it is critical that the exchange specialist keeps projects under budget.

EDUCATION AND EXPERIENCE

Health information management exchange specialists require a bachelor's degree in business, health administration, economics, information technology, or a related field. A master's degree is preferred. The position requires at least 5 years of experience in implementation and management of information technology (IT) projects.

CORE COMPETENCIES AND SKILLS

- Strong background working with health information exchange operations
- Strong familiarity with healthcare environment and health information exchange services and products
- Ability to follow federal and state guidelines and regulations
- Experience in managing numerous projects effectively
- Ability to communicate across industries and political lines for the good of the organization
- Excellent listening skills
- Excellent verbal and written communication and presentation skills

COMPENSATION

The salary range for health information management exchange specialists is $64,000 to $90,000. Organizations that require broad responsibilities will pay higher than those with narrow responsibilities. Those in urban, fasted-paced areas will stand to make a higher salary than those in rural areas.

EMPLOYMENT OUTLOOK

Over the next 5 years, the health information management exchange specialist will experience a 50,000 shortfall in personnel. Health information exchanges are the way of the future in healthcare information. Organizations nationwide will require individuals knowledgeable in information exchanges.

FOR FURTHER INFORMATION

■ Healthcare Information and Management Systems Society (www.himss.org)

63

JOB DESCRIPTION

In more organizations, the information technology auditor position is a three-level position. The job title can end with either a I, II, or III depending on the experience and knowledge of the individual. Information technology auditor I is considered an entry-level position, while information technology auditor III is the most advanced position. All levels have the same job description; however, salary, independence, and responsibility are greater as the levels increase. The position requires auditing of information systems and procedures to accord with the organization's guidelines for efficiency, accuracy, and security. The information technology auditor evaluates the information technology (IT) infrastructure to determine risk to the organization, while providing improvements for current risk issues.

EDUCATION AND EXPERIENCE

All technology auditor levels require a bachelor's degree in information technology or a related field. Information technology auditor I is an entry-level position that requires at least 1 year's experience in the field. Information technology auditors II and III are more advanced and require 2 to 5 years of experience in the field.

CORE COMPETENCIES AND SKILLS

- Knowledge of concepts, practices, and procedures within the field
- Ability to conduct audit interviews to identify key control activities
- Ability to prepare vulnerability assessments of technology and support business and IT processes
- Ability to identify control issues and assess the adequacy of controls
- Ability to complete all audit program steps
- Ability to communicate and validate findings
- Ability to participate in special projects and perform other duties as assigned
- Excellent written and verbal communication

COMPENSATION

The median salary range for an information technology auditor is $45,000 to $90,000. Depending on the level of auditor, the individual's position determines the salary range of the position. On average, auditor I makes $50,000, auditor II makes $65,000, and auditor III makes $80,000.

EMPLOYMENT OUTLOOK

The growing use of information technology in healthcare requires individuals to maintain systems with organizations. Promotion within information technology is endless even within one organization. IT systems need positions to validate security and make crucial improvements.

FOR FURTHER INFORMATION

■ Healthcare Information and Management Systems Society (www.himss.org)

64

JOB DESCRIPTION

The knowledge management specialist supports the hospital's mission, vision, strategic initiatives, program priorities, and organizational goals. They achieve this by using clinical and business systems and technical expertise along with designing, creating, and developing automated business intelligence solutions. The knowledge management specialist also provides internal consultation and project management expertise. This person provides knowledge in business/clinical processes and analytical expertise, knowledge, and strong leadership skills to work with key stakeholders, end users, and project team members. The specialist identifies and resolves issues throughout the project phases of assessment, design build, testing, training, and implementation; accountable for identifying opportunities for continuous improvement in workflow processes in the implementation of technology solutions. The knowledge management specialist is responsible for frequently taking a formal or an informal lead on project tasks.

EDUCATION AND EXPERIENCE

Knowledge management specialists typically possess a bachelor's degree in health science, computer science, math, business, or related field, or an equivalent technical training/certification; work experience that demonstrates technical competency may be substituted for formal education along with at least 8 years of experience in progressively more responsible work as a data analyst and consultant or equivalent.

CORE COMPETENCIES AND SKILLS

- Outstanding interpersonal skills including the ability to effectively communicate with persons throughout the organization
- Excellent verbal and written communication skills
- Ability to create, read, understand, and interpret data models
- Familiarity working in a data warehouse environment
- Ability to work independently and in a complex team environment
- Strong experience with massively parallel processing (MPP), specifically Netezza
- Strong Structured Query Language (SQL) skills
- Ability to utilize creative and analytical problem-solving techniques in extremely varied situations

■ Substantial knowledge of technology solutions in a healthcare provider environment

COMPENSATION

Knowledge management specialists earn in the range of $46,000 to $110,000, although the total salary will vary depending on the size and location of the hospital.

EMPLOYMENT OUTLOOK

The employment outlook for knowledge management specialists is particularly strong. Every hospital in the nation is working to develop their IT infrastructure in response to demands by the federal government and the need to provide ever-higher levels of quality care. Possessing an IT background is an important requirement, but the applicant must also be familiar with the unique requirements of healthcare delivery.

FOR FURTHER INFORMATION

■ Healthcare Information Management Systems Society (www.himss.org)

65 PROJECT MANAGER

JOB DESCRIPTION

The project manager is responsible for the clinical informatics project process, including requests, reviews, approvals, scoping, feasibility studies, and project delivery. He or she leads multidisciplinary teams of stakeholders to ensure projects are evaluated, triaged, initiated, and completed in a timely manner, within projected scope and budget. The project manager consults for all clinical information technology initiatives at the organization requiring project management expertise; leads business process analyses, needs assessment and cost–benefit analyses in an effort to align informatics solutions with business initiatives; organizes, directs, and develops project team resources in order to effectively meet project commitments and business objectives.

EDUCATION AND EXPERIENCE

The project manager requires a minimum of a bachelor's degree in computer science, business administration, or health administration. Preferred education includes a master's degree in business administration or health administration. Experience in instructional design is highly preferred. A minimum of 2 years of database development and design, web design, and technical assistance is required.

CORE COMPETENCIES AND SKILLS

- Outstanding interpersonal skills including the ability to effectively communicate with persons throughout the organization
- Excellent verbal and written communication skills
- Advanced-level computer skills including Microsoft Office platforms such as Word, Excel, PowerPoint, Access, Visio, and project management software
- Outstanding customer service skills
- Experience with conflict resolution
- Demonstrated ability to work effectively in team-oriented environments
- Ability to utilize creative and analytical problem-solving techniques in extremely varied situations
- Substantial knowledge of technology solutions in a healthcare provider environment

COMPENSATION

Project managers earn in the range of $70,000 to $175,000, although the total salary will vary depending on the size and location of the hospital and the scope of responsibility. The national average for information technology (IT) project managers is $102,000.

EMPLOYMENT OUTLOOK

Industry experts anticipate a growth in the number of healthcare IT project managers, as healthcare providers comply with federal mandates to transition to electronic records. This requires providers to install and manage new software systems. Project managers with expertise in health informatics are needed to not only handle the implementation of these new systems, but the ongoing process of managing records.

FOR FURTHER INFORMATION

■ Healthcare Information Management Systems Society (www.himss.org)

 NAME: **LARRY T. JESSUP**

Title: Deputy Division Director
Organization: U.S. Department of
Health and Human Services, Office
of the National Coordinator for
Health IT (ONC)

1. Briefly describe your job responsibilities.

As the deputy division director of the Health IT Exchange and Transformation Division, I am currently responsible for programmatic oversight and monitoring of two Health Information Exchange Cooperative Agreements and one supplemental cooperative agreement that have awarded $33.1 million dollars to 26 communities and states to advance the interoperable exchange of health information across the United States. I currently ensure the alignment of all three programs with the priorities of the secretary, the Federal Health IT Strategic Plan, and the ONC-Shared Interoperability Roadmap as each program provides technical assistance support to target populations across the care continuum including, but not limited to, emergency medical services (EMS), long-term and postacute care (LTPAC) facilities, behavioral health (BH) settings, individuals (consumers/caregivers), public health immunization registry, poison control centers, critical access hospitals, home health, and skilled nursing facilities. I serve as the primary lead and subject matter expert directly responsible for establishing all standard operating procedures for the comprehensive tracking of awardee progress across all three programs. I also supervise three public health analysts. These analysts serve as project officers for the ONC grant programs, as well as provide the oversight and subject matter expertise required for three highly functioning communities of practices (CoP): the LTPAC CoP which is focused on improving exchange between LTPAC facilities and other providers across the care continuum; the BH CoP which is focused on integrating BH providers into community and state exchange efforts; and the consumer engagement CoP which is focused on increasing consumers' access, contribution, and exchange of their own digital health information.

Continued

NAME: LARRY T. JESSUP Continued

2. What would you consider to be a "typical" day for you?

The "typical day" is very fast-paced as this is a very exciting time to be involved in the implementation of health IT and all of the accompanying delivery system reform efforts. Given that these are cooperative agreements, there is constant interaction with all of our awardees, which includes, but is not limited to, the following:

- Programmatic monitoring and program oversight via our biweekly project officer calls
- Helping awardees mitigate constantly emerging issues and challenges
- Partnering with our technical assistance support contractors to develop scalable and replicable tools, resources, educational material bright spots for the awardees
- Coordinating with the different divisions across ONC to ensure alignment with the secretary's priorities of high-quality care, low costs, healthy populations, and engaged people
- Responding to the numerous requests from our federal and non-federal stakeholders to learn more about what is going on with our program as the goals are tied closely to the ONC Interoperability Roadmap
- Constantly thinking of different ways that our program may support the agency's larger delivery system reform efforts
- Multiple conversations with the Office of Procurement and Grants to ensure diligent and responsible stewardship of federal funding
- There are also wider policy considerations as we must constantly assess the national health IT landscape and incorporate feedback from the field of how states are evolving in relation to the landscape

Fortunately, I work with a team of exceptional project officers who do a wonderful job of managing their individual portfolios, leading their respective CoPs, and conducting site visits that really drive the direction of everything we do.

3. What education or training do you have? Is it typical for your job?

I have been blessed to have exposure to multiple facets of the healthcare system throughout my professional career. I began studying sports medicine in the clinical setting; served as an emergency medical technician (EMT) in the emergency department of a Level II trauma center

Continued

NAME: LARRY T. JESSUP Continued

throughout college; worked for the Laboratory Corporation of America in the private sector as a key account executive; and studied hospital administration and public health in graduate school. I have been very fortunate to bring all of these different experiences and perspectives to my federal position here at the Department of Health & Human Services (HHS). I'm not sure if my specific experience and background is typical, but it's not atypical to find individuals who are remarkably unique in the perspectives they bring to this job, given the significance and magnitude of what we have undertaken as we transform the way care is delivered in the United States. One must have a clear understanding of what is at stake and what needs to be done to improve patient care despite the many barriers that exist.

4. What is the most challenging part of your job?

The most challenging part of the job is the relentless, unpredictable pace and the demands of the work itself. This is a massive undertaking and federal dollars don't go nearly as far as anyone would like. It's difficult at times to really stop and appreciate how far we have come on this remarkable journey. For example, as of 2014 nearly all hospitals (Charles, Gabriel, & Searcy, 2015) and nearly 80% of physician practices (Office of the National Coordinator for Health Information Technology, 2016) reported using certified electronic health records (EHRs). The Regional Extension Center technical assistance program assisted over 120,000 healthcare providers with adopting and meaningfully using certified EHRs. This is significant considering that in 2008, only 8% of hospitals (Jha, DesRoches, Kralovec, & Joshi, 2010) and 13% of physicians practicing in ambulatory settings had adopted at least a basic EHR (DesRoches et al., 2008).

5. What do you consider to be the best part of your job?

The best part of my job is, without a doubt, being at the forefront of this healthcare journey from the very beginning. I was part of one of the largest technical assistance programs ever in the United States and am able to witness the progress of the nation, state by state, as we transform the way healthcare is delivered. There is an intrinsic sense of passion, belief, and energy that accompanies this work as you commit to changing the lives of millions of Americans. A colleague put it best recently when describing our professional journey as she said, "You are lucky in this world if your work is part of a moment in time once. Twice would be a miracle." Healthcare remains the issue of the day and has been

Continued

NAME: LARRY T. JESSUP Continued

since I started my career at HHS. It has been a critical issue and central focus throughout the current presidential administration. My job has allowed me to travel the country and interact with providers, patients, state and community leaders, and federal and nonfederal stakeholders. It's amazing to see the many innovative ways that states are supporting their communities and how our current and former awardees continue to be resilient and work together to make the vision of using health IT for better patient care a reality.

6. What path did you take to get to the job you are in today?

The path I took to get to the job I have today is an unconventional path, given that many of my peers from my graduate program went on to wonderful careers in the hospital setting. I was blessed to have an opportunity to do my residency here at ONC at the very time the health IT conversation was reaching its peak and there was the influx of federal funding to advance adoption. It was my graduate school residency and the resourceful guidance from the academic faculty at the George Washington University School of Public Health that guided me on this path.

7. What advice do you have for someone who is interested in a job such as yours?

My advice would be to get as much exposure as possible to the many different parts of our healthcare system. The U.S. healthcare system is extremely vast and complex and there are various moving pieces, all contributing to the care of the patient. One must possess some type of perspective of how these all fit together in order to contribute to policy discussions about the healthcare system at the federal level.

REFERENCES

Charles, D., Gabriel, M., & Searcy, T. (2015, April). Adoption of electronic health record systems among U.S. non-federal acute care hospitals: 2008–2014 (ONC Data Brief No. 23). Retrieved from https://www.healthit.gov/sites/default/files/data-brief/2014HospitalAdoptionDataBrief.pdf

DesRoches, C. M., Campbell, E. G., Rao, S. R., Donelan, K., Ferris, T. G., Jha, A., . . . Blumenthal, D. (2008). Electronic health records in ambulatory care—A national survey of physicians. *New England Journal of Medicine, 359*(1), 50–56.

Jha, A. K., DesRoches, C. M., Kralovec, P. D., Joshi, M. S. (2010). A progress report on electronic health records in U.S. hospitals. *Health Affairs, 29*(10), 1951–1957. doi:10.1377/hlthaff.2010.0502

Office of the National Coordinator for Health Information Technology. (2016). Office-based physician electronic health record adoption (Health IT Quick-Stat #50). Retrieved from http://dashboard.healthit.gov/quickstats/pages/physician-ehr-adoption-trends.php

CHAPTER 13
CAREERS IN DURABLE MEDICAL EQUIPMENT

CUSTOMER SERVICE MANAGER

JOB DESCRIPTION

The customer service manager's primary responsibility will be to manage a team of customer service representatives, shipping/warehouse staff, and supply chain analysts. The primary goal is to assure that customers receive the service and support needed for the optimal functioning of medical devices.

EDUCATION AND EXPERIENCE

A bachelor's degree in business or healthcare administration is preferred. A minimum of 5 years of customer service experience where customer is serviced from order entry to postdelivery. Customer service managers typically have experience in managing a diverse group of customer service staff.

CORE COMPETENCIES AND SKILLS

- Ability to handle all aspects of customer service, including entering, tracking, and invoicing orders and releasing material for shipment
- Ability to effectively manage customer service staff
- Ability to handle heavy communication (via email and telephone) with customer base for all orders, enquiries, and follow-up in a prompt and professional manner
- Ability to assist in reviewing and controlling the finished goods inventory level
- Ability to complete invoices
- Ability to coordinate movement of raw material from fabrication to finished product
- Ability to interact with internal departments and outside processors, as needed
- Ability to maintain office services by organizing office operations and procedures; prepare payroll; control correspondence; design filing systems; review and approve supply requisitions; assign and monitor clerical functions
- Ability to develop and maintain affirmative action program; prepare EEO-1 report annually; maintain other records, reports, and logs to conform to equal employment opportunity (EEO) regulations
- Ability to ensure compliance with federal, state, and local regulations pertaining to environmental, health, and safety, and to maintain company regulatory compliance records

- Ability to manage environmental health services (EHS) policies and procedures in compliance with local, state, and federal Occupational Safety and Health Administration (OSHA) and environmental protection agency (EPA) rules and regulations
- Ability to support timely submittal, acquisition, and maintenance of all environmental permits and reports to maintain compliance with state and federal requirements
- Ability to assist in monitoring the skills and capabilities of those assisting with, or leading, EHS programs, recommend training, and provide day-to-day coaching, feedback, and functional direction

COMPENSATION

The typical compensation for a customer service manager is between $76,000 and $94,000 per year.

EMPLOYMENT OUTLOOK

This field is incredibly competitive for experienced customer service managers. It may take an individual several years to develop an expert understanding of the industry and specific information about products supported by the organization. Those individuals who are successful will be well received by providers who look for ways to continuously improve quality of care.

FOR FURTHER INFORMATION

- Medical Device Manufacturers Association (www.medicaldevices.org)
- Society for Healthcare Strategy & Market Development (www.shsmd.org)

67

ACCOUNT MANAGER

JOB DESCRIPTION

The job of the account manager is to lead and manage the sales and support of the given medical device in a particular geographic region, or to a given sector of the healthcare industry (e.g., hospitals or physician offices). The account manager is responsible for supervising the activities of the sales representatives in his or her particular area. The account manager plans and executes sales activities, including development of key account strategies, their implementation, and the required coordination of resources. The account manager develops proposals and price quotations for a variety of healthcare professionals including physicians, nurses, biomedical engineers, and administrators. Finally, the account manager completes quarterly business reviews, detailing all account activity and strategies employed to assure the attainment of sales goals.

EDUCATION AND EXPERIENCE

The account manager requires a minimum of a bachelor's degree in health administration, business administration, or science. Account managers typically possess at least 5 to 7 years of medical device sales experience.

CORE COMPETENCIES AND SKILLS

- Outstanding interpersonal skills including the ability to effectively communicate with current and potential customers, along with persons throughout their organization
- Excellent verbal and written communication skills
- Direct selling experience of medical devices in a competitive strategy-intensive market
- Experience in negotiations with executive administration levels, that is, chief financial officer (CFO), chief information officer (CIO), chief executive officer (CEO), chief medical officer (CMO)
- Strong data analysis, evaluation, and problem-solving skills
- Demonstrated creative coaching for field personnel recognizing different styles and types of motivation
- Demonstrated ability to achieve sales plans
- Ability to provide evaluation of performance after sales calls, presentations, and so on, in order to improve technical and selling skills of sales people
- Relationship management, strategy development, problem-solving, and change management skills

■ Demonstrated ability to use standard computer software programs including Microsoft Office applications such as Word, Excel, Access, and PowerPoint

COMPENSATION

Account managers generally earn a base salary and then a commission based on the total sales of the team. A base salary of $100,000 is typical for medical device account managers, with additional commission pushing the total package as high as $220,000, depending on the geographic area and type of device sold. The nature of the work requires significant travel and, in most cases, sales representatives receive compensation for the use of their personal vehicle.

EMPLOYMENT OUTLOOK

The employment outlook for account managers is good. This represents the first supervisory managerial position available in the domain of medical device sales. There is regular turnover in these positions particularly for well-known medical device manufacturers. Medical devices represent an important technology for every healthcare organization and there are a number of start-up firms every year that require experienced account managers.

FOR FURTHER INFORMATION

■ Medical Device Manufacturers Association (www.medicaldevices.org)

68 REGIONAL SALES MANAGER

JOB DESCRIPTION

The job of the regional sales manager is to lead and manage a large geographic region in the sales of one or several medical device products. The regional manager will lead a group of corporate and national account managers and achieve and exceed sales plans within specified budget. The regional manager will also recruit, hire, develop, and retain regional sales personnel. The regional manager provides input to the national director of sales regarding sales and negotiation strategies and plans. The regional manager develops sales goals and objectives for each territory on a fiscal and quarterly basis to achieve the organizational sales annual operating plan as well as ensures all field personnel are meeting or exceeding all objectives set including both revenue/cost-saving–based objectives and market development objectives.

EDUCATION AND EXPERIENCE

The regional sales manager requires a minimum of a bachelor's degree in health administration, business administration, or science. Regional managers typically possess 7 to 10 years of medical device sales experience.

CORE COMPETENCIES AND SKILLS

- Outstanding interpersonal skills including the ability to effectively communicate with current and potential customers, along with persons throughout their organization
- Excellent verbal and written communication skills
- Experience and success in negotiating contracts, selling to medical directors of health plans, and working collaboratively with field sales personnel to achieve goals
- Demonstrated skills in business planning, consulting, and territory financial analysis
- Strong data analysis, evaluation, and problem-solving skills
- Demonstrated creative coaching for field personnel recognizing different styles and types of motivation
- Ability to interpret and explain business/marketing policies and programs to employees in order to maintain consistency and responsiveness to customer needs, ensuring that market and territory strategies are fully executed
- Ability to provide evaluation of performance after sales calls, presentations, and so on, in order to improve technical and selling skills of sales people

COMPENSATION

Regional sales managers generally earn a base salary and then a commission based on the total sales of the team. A base salary of $150,000 is typical for medical device regional sales managers with additional commission pushing the total package as high as $250,000, depending on the geographic area and type of device sold. The nature of the work requires significant travel and, in most cases, regional sales managers receive compensation for the use of their personal vehicle.

EMPLOYMENT OUTLOOK

The employment outlook for regional sales managers is stable. This is one of the highest level positions available in the domain of medical device sales. There is limited turnover in these positions particularly for well-known medical device manufacturers. That said, medical devices represent an important technology for every healthcare organization and there are a number of start-up firms every year.

FOR FURTHER INFORMATION

■ Medical Device Manufacturers Association (www.medicaldevices.org)

 NAME: JULIE VIOLA

Title: Senior Field Marketing Manager,
Healthcare Informatics Solutions
Organization: Philips Healthcare

1. Briefly describe your job responsibilities.

To create and execute a marketing plan to meet the needs of the company and customers it serves. This plan has an objective to grow the business and corresponding strategies and activities to meet or exceed that set objective. All activities are measured with time commitments, owners, budget, and expected results.

2. What would you consider to be a "typical" day for you?

A typical day would entail meeting with key stakeholders who are a part of executing my marketing plan. This would mean getting together with product managers who are working on building out the solutions I am marketing, and ensuring their timelines for delivery match to my timelines to sell and promote in the market. I always set aside time every day to read up on what the market is doing through either Twitter or industry thought leader publications. The key things I look for are: Are there any new products out from competition? Are there any recalls or policy changes? Are any customers asking for something that we have in our pipeline that we should try and meet with? Are there things customers are asking for that aren't in our pipeline? From this market research, I typically write up an email and share a market update with my peers and leadership in a concise format. Lastly, I connect with my downstream teams who are close to the customer to ensure they have the tools and resources they need to stay relevant and efficient. This means connecting on our digital presence, sales tools, elevator pitches on our products, and anything else they need to prove our products' value in the market.

3. What education or training do you have? Is it typical for your job?

I have my undergraduate degree in fine arts. This is not typical. However, I am currently pursuing my Master of Health Administration, and have received a number of certifications in business to be more proficient

Continued

NAME: JULIE VIOLA Continued

in my job. I will say that my diverse background has served me well in marketing. The ability to think outside the box has been critical in times that my product has been an underdog and we needed to find a way to get ahead.

4. What is the most challenging part of your job?

The most challenging part of my job is bringing together all the different teams with which I work to meet the same timeline and goal. In marketing, you have to work with everyone—engineering, product management, sales, communications, public relations, and all the different leadership teams. Making my priority their priority can sometimes be very challenging, especially in a global business. The needs I have in North America may not be the same in Australia, South America, or Asia. I have to build out a business case and prove that what I need takes precedence and get everyone on board to start working toward the timeline I have targeted.

5. What do you consider to be the best part of your job?

The best part of the job is meeting with customers. I have the opportunity to go into a number of hospitals and health systems each year and hear what they need, what they want, what pains them, and what excites them. It is incredibly rewarding to go back to a customer from whom we solicited that feedback and say, "Yes, we completed what you asked for," and then keep on building on that foundation. There are days I get the negative feedback, but the opportunity to turn it into a positive is incredibly rewarding, especially when it improves care delivery or outcomes.

6. What path did you take to get to the job you are in today?

I am a learner and connector through and through. I am constantly digging into what is next. I read market updates, healthcare books, and utilize social media platforms to know what is next. That knowledge has served me well because it has allowed me to be not just horizontally knowledgeable, but 360 degrees. I know what the history is, I know what is next, and I know what is happening now all around me. Peers and leaders alike have gravitated to that, I believe. Additionally, and most importantly, I have had fantastic mentors and guidance from peers. I have a network that I lean on for advice, coaching, and I always try to stay humble and open to feedback. So, my path has been one of hard work,

Continued

constant research, and trying my hardest not to burn bridges. When I first started at Philips, I was in the call center. When they asked me to take 40 to 50 calls a day, I tried to take 60. When they asked me to upsell $10,000 a month, I tried to get $20,000. That mentality moved me into marketing. I have tried to maintain that sense of competition and thirst to always do better for my company and the customers we serve. My first job in healthcare was actually at a local cancer hospital working with children and their families. I have not lost sight of who is on the other end of the work my company does. If you don't have a strong work ethic in healthcare, you are probably in the wrong business.

7. What advice do you have for someone who is interested in a job such as yours?

I would say there are three key components. First, you need to be collaborative and open. Marketing requires cross-functional leadership to meet goals and objectives. Second, we are in a world of big data and analytics. You have to be able to interpret data and find the clues to make your company and solution stand out. You have to know what segment you are going after, why you are going after them, what makes you unique in that segment, and how much business you can obtain in that segment. Lastly, you have to be a learner. Marketing is changing and you need to constantly be in tune with changes in policy, customer needs, and what your competition is doing.

JOB DESCRIPTION

The job of the sales representative is to conduct sales calls to physicians and hospitals to promote, sell, and service the particular products manufactured and sold by the firm. The sales representative will make regular calls on clients to assist in all aspects of product training and evaluation. It is expected that the sales representative will possess a high level of technical expertise about the particular products being sold.

EDUCATION AND EXPERIENCE

The sales representative requires a minimum of a bachelor's degree in health administration, business administration, or science. Experience in a high-pressure sales environment is strongly desired along with experience selling medical devices.

CORE COMPETENCIES AND SKILLS

- Outstanding interpersonal skills including the ability to effectively communicate with current and potential customers
- Excellent verbal and written communication skills
- Experience in making multiple referral calls on a daily basis
- Outstanding selling and negotiation skills
- Ability to successfully plan and manage accounts
- Demonstrated ability to work effectively in team-oriented environments
- Ability to develop and successfully follow through with a strategic plan
- Substantial knowledge of technology solutions in a healthcare provider environment

COMPENSATION

The average compensation for a medical device sales representative is $147,000 per year, although the total salary will vary depending on the type of product being sold and the number of years of experience in the field. In many cases, sales representatives are compensated on the basis of the number of sales made in a given time period. The nature of the work requires significant travel and, in most cases, sales representatives receive compensation for the use of their personal vehicle.

EMPLOYMENT OUTLOOK

The employment outlook for sales representatives is robust. This is frequently used as the entry-level position for persons interested in medical devices and durable medical equipment; therefore, there is a great deal of turnover as persons are either promoted to supervisory roles or leave the field entirely.

FOR FURTHER INFORMATION

■ Medical Device Manufacturers Association (www.medicaldevices.org)

CHAPTER 14
CAREERS IN PHARMACEUTICAL AND BIOTECHNOLOGY FIRMS

ACCOUNT MANAGER

JOB DESCRIPTION

A pharmaceutical company account manager is in charge of the budgets, performance evaluations, and development of sales accounts. The area of responsibility could represent a small or large sales area with a varying number of sales teams being managed. The account manager stays in contact with customers, acts as a liaison between the pharmacy and the buyers, and implements programs that will increase sales and service activities. The account manager is a professional, a problem solver, and a data analyzer, interacting with clients and working within the organizational structure to build new relationships for sales opportunities. Account managers are the face of the company.

EDUCATION AND EXPERIENCE

A bachelor's degree is a minimum expectation for most account manager positions. Many qualification listings desire a background in medicine of some sort, from pharmacy, nursing, or health education. Work experience in a leadership role is a benefit.

CORE COMPETENCIES AND SKILLS

- Outstanding presentation skills for internal and external customers
- Exceptional verbal and written communication skills
- Ability to work with standard computer software programs
- Proven analytical skills and ability to solve complex customer problems
- Ability to interact with a wide range of diverse groups
- Demonstrated ability to manage the work of sales representatives
- Demonstrated organizational abilities and ability to deal effectively with multiple demands
- Knowledge of pharmaceuticals for which the account manager is responsible, and the healthcare industry as a whole

COMPENSATION

The average salary of account managers is approximately $100,000 annually. They can make as little as $60,000, or as much as $150,000. Account managers at larger firms with a greater client base and more bonuses will likely earn a higher salary. Similarly, those traveling more and having the ability to reach out to larger users of pharmaceuticals will have a greater chance at increasing their income.

EMPLOYMENT OUTLOOK

With the ever-changing healthcare environment, it is hard to tell what the future holds for care. In the pharmaceutical area, there has historically been gap coverage for prescription medication. Changes in this payscale along with healthcare reform will allow more people access to healthcare and medications that they need. Skilled account managers who can deal with large healthcare firms along with smaller offices to gain a client base will have a great opportunity in the future of our healthcare market. An increasing elderly population and the possibility of "universal" coverage means more demand for pharmaceuticals. People have also started to become more active in their purchasing of pharmaceuticals, and marketing to individuals is becoming more important to pharmaceutical companies.

FOR FURTHER INFORMATION

- National Association of Pharmaceutical Sales Representatives (www .napsronline.org)

71

JOB DESCRIPTION

The associate program manager is an entry-level position and plays an important role in a client-focused program management team. Associate program managers will be responsible for coordinating with the director of client engagement and program manager for key meetings/presentation execution, and being an internal and external resource for timelines/project status and providing overall program support.

EDUCATION AND EXPERIENCE

Bachelor's degree in statistics, biostatistics, or a related scientific program is required; an advanced degree is preferred.

Seven years of industry clinical trial experience along with knowledge of the drug/devices development process and U.S. Food and Drug Administration (FDA) and International Council for Harmonisation of Technical Requirements for Pharmaceuticals for Human Use (ICH) guidelines.

CORE COMPETENCIES AND SKILLS

- Ability to thrive in a fast-paced, detail-oriented, very hands-on organization
- Ability to assist in the management of timelines, internal/external operational steps for business managed by its team
- Knowledge of basic and advanced statistical designs and analytical methods
- Knowledge of SAS programming techniques
- Strong written and verbal communication skills
- Effective oral and written communication of statistical concepts and results
- Detail-oriented and demonstrated leadership skills
- Ability to assist in the routing of materials, including proofing and client review team revisions
- Ability to coordinate and implement successful projects from start to finish
- Ability to prioritize and monitor the completion of tasks on a daily and weekly basis
- Ability to assist in the coordination of outside contractors and partners

COMPENSATION

Average compensation for associate program managers is approximately \$65,000. This salary varies depending on the size of the biotechnology firm and geographic location. Many biotechnology firms are located outside of the United States.

EMPLOYMENT OUTLOOK

It is expected that the growth for associate program managers in biotechnology firms will grow at a steady pace. While there is going to be continued consolidation in the biotechnology industry, the need for entry-level staff will continue.

FOR FURTHER INFORMATION

■ Biotechnology Industry Association (www.bio.org)

72

COMPLIANCE SPECIALIST

JOB DESCRIPTION
The compliance and quality systems department is responsible for maintaining a positive relationship with customers by completing annual product reviews, responding to necessary field actions including recalls, and assuring compliance with established quality agreements. The compliance specialist serves as a compliance resource for the company and provides compliance support with regulatory matters and customer-filing strategies; this person manages the routine renewal of regulatory licenses as well as regulatory updates to the applicable regulatory authorities.

EDUCATION AND EXPERIENCE
A bachelor's degree in the sciences and 2 to 3 years in quality assurance and/or compliance/regulatory experience within the pharmaceutical industry; or 5 to 10 years' relevant experience, of which 1 to 2 years is in the pharmaceutical industry.

CORE COMPETENCIES AND SKILLS
- Knowledge of technical writing and technical terminology including technical writing skills
- Ability to assess and communicate regulatory risks
- Knowledge of aseptic processing and regulatory and industry guidelines and requirements
- Ability to train and counsel quality professionals and production personnel
- Knowledge of general conference on weights and measures (cGMPs), current good documentation practice (cGDPs), as well as sound quality and regulatory principles consistent with "best practices"
- Leadership qualities; ability to be attentive to detail; ability to read, understand, interpret, and apply technical writing and instructions; good verbal and written communication skills
- Ability to support operations and quality by rendering advice/opinions on compliance with regulatory matters, including compliance/regulatory evaluation of proposed changes through the change control program, to the facilities or processes, and evaluation of compliance implications of new product entry into the facility
- Ability to facilitate updates to the site quality risk management process (QRMP), and participate with team members to develop product specific QRMPs

- ■ Ability to support customer filings for marketing authorizations by generating portions of the chemistry, manufacturing, and controls (CMC) sections of new drug applications, and also generate supplements to marketing authorizations as required
- ■ Ability to generate position papers or formal communications that may serve as customer notifications, to address facility modifications, media fills, shutdown activities (pre/post), and new product introduction (Part 1 and Part 2)
- ■ Ability to generate and file various kinds of drug master files (e.g., drug master files (DMF), biologics master files (BBMF), veterinary master files (VMF), and site master files (SMF) with FDA and foreign agencies (e.g., SRF)
- ■ Ability to file documentation for state, local, and national licenses, permits, establishment registrations, and so forth, as required to keep the facility in compliance with applicable laws and regulations
- ■ Ability to establish quality agreements with customers, including negotiation of terms/responsibilities, and manage revisions to existing quality agreements; monitor compliance with the terms of the customer-specific quality agreement
- ■ Ability to provide oversight for the Controlled Substance Program to assure Drug Enforcement Administration (DEA) and New Mexico Board of Pharmacy requirements are met
- ■ Ability to provide compliance/regulatory approval for new/revised printed components

COMPENSATION

Average compensation for compliance specialists is approximately $60,000. This salary varies depending on the size of the biotechnology firm and geographic location. Many biotechnology firms are located outside of the United States.

EMPLOYMENT OUTLOOK

It is expected that the growth for compliance specialists in biotechnology firms will slightly decrease. While there is going to be continued consolidation in the biotechnology industry, the need for quality control managers will hold steady or slightly decrease.

FOR FURTHER INFORMATION

- ■ Biotechnology Industry Association (www.bio.org)

73

MANAGER, QUALITY CONTROL

JOB DESCRIPTION

The manager is responsible for administration of analytical quality control and microbiological quality control to assure timely delivery of results to manage the company objectives and production, as well as new product introduction on time. He or she ensures compliance to procedures of quality systems, validation, change control, general conference on weights and measures (cGMP), and Good Laboratory Practice (GLP), and administers programs for product stability.

EDUCATION AND EXPERIENCE

Bachelor of Science degree with a minimum of 5 years' related work experience including a minimum of 3 years of supervisory experience is required. Advanced degree is strongly preferred. Position requires advanced training or experience in cGMPs and GLPs.

CORE COMPETENCIES AND SKILLS

- Ability to be responsible for the operation of the chemical and microbiology laboratories
- Ability to identify and recommend testing equipment
- Strong working knowledge of regulatory requirements and ISO requirements in the pharmaceutical industry, as well as other legal requirements for business operations
- Advanced computer skills
- Ability to ensure appropriate equipment installation, validation, and operation
- Ability to ensure timely test completion and result reporting
- Ability to implement projects related to computer system control of the laboratory
- Ability to undertake stability test program as required by standard operating procedures (SOP)
- Ability to ensure appropriate staff appointment and training
- Ability to manage staff performance and address issues in a timely and sensitive manner
- Ability to maintain an updated knowledge of quality control (QC) and good manufacturing practices (GMP) trends
- Ability to implement improvement projects to drive increased flexibility and reduce costs

COMPENSATION

Average compensation for quality control managers is approximately $75,000. This salary varies depending on the size of the biotechnology firm and geographic location. Many biotechnology firms are located outside of the United States.

EMPLOYMENT OUTLOOK

It is expected that the growth for quality control managers in biotechnology firms will slightly decrease. While there is going to be continued consolidation in the biotechnology industry, the need for quality control managers will hold steady or slightly decrease.

FOR FURTHER INFORMATION

■ Biotechnology Industry Association (www.bio.org)

74

JOB DESCRIPTION

A pharmaceutical company sales representative is a salesman. Sales representatives directly market to the customer and follow the plan set forth by the account manager on their areas and sales goals. The market for sales representatives is competitive and they must continually build their client base and gain new customers for the company. It is their job to interact and establish new connections for the company.

EDUCATION AND EXPERIENCE

A bachelor's degree is a minimum expectation for most sales representative jobs. Most have a business- or healthcare-focused background or education. Sales experience or other healthcare/pharmacy experience can sometimes be substituted for educational experience.

CORE COMPETENCIES AND SKILLS

- Outstanding presentation skills for internal and external customers
- In-depth knowledge of specific pharmaceutical products
- Exceptional verbal and written communication skills
- Ability to work with standard computer software programs
- Proven analytical skills and ability to solve complex customer problems
- Ability to interact with a wide range of diverse groups
- Demonstrated organizational abilities and ability to deal effectively with multiple demands
- Knowledge of pharmaceuticals for which the account manager is responsible and the healthcare industry as a whole

COMPENSATION

The average pharmaceutical sales representative makes $122,000 annually. There are different levels of sales representatives, such as sales specialist and manager. These increased titles also come with increasing salaries and can earn upward of $160,000 when managing sales of large areas and receiving bonuses.

EMPLOYMENT OUTLOOK

Pharmaceuticals are a growing business. With an increase in coverage for Americans with Medicare Part D, there will be more people with the ability to access doctors and needed pharmaceuticals. The sales representative is a key player in making sure that the doctors and hospitals have the required drugs in their pharmacies that their patients desire. The representative will also network to help doctors better understand the specific brand of drug that is prescribed in order to increase use and get it added to the formulary.

FOR FURTHER INFORMATION

■ National Association of Pharmaceutical Sales Representatives (www .napsronline.org)

JOB DESCRIPTION

Program officers are responsible for managing a discrete grant portfolio and/or providing research and analysis work in support of grant making, strategy development, coordination, communications, and advocacy.

EDUCATION AND EXPERIENCE

Education and experience vary in the global market. Most firms desire a minimum of a bachelor's degree, with most wanting some sort of further education, such as a master's, or significant work experience. Educational focus should be representative of business quality methodology, business degree, healthcare degree, or engineering. Experience for global positions is significant with many wanting at minimum 5 years' relevant work experience in the healthcare field and knowledge of the country where the person is to be placed. Experience in grant writing and program evaluation is essential.

CORE COMPETENCIES AND SKILLS

- Ability to plan, manage, and execute a wide range of activities in support of strategic planning, as well as to prospect and develop complex investment opportunities, grant management, and external relationship management
- Ability to review letters of enquiry and grant proposals; provide clear, concise, and insightful written analyses and recommendations for funding, including drafting and editing proposal summaries and progress reports for existing grants for review by foundation leadership
- Ability to consult with grantees to achieve desired impact of grants; conduct site visits when appropriate; provide technical guidance; convene meetings; and apply and evaluate milestone-based performance objectives
- Ability to manage internal processes and portfolio progress while ensuring appropriate documentation, grant budgeting, and reporting; improve operational efficiency and effectiveness
- Ability to prepare and write briefs and synthesize existing literature; provide written analysis of key topics for foundation management; fulfill data requests from leadership
- Strong knowledge across relevant technical area/expertise
- Leadership abilities to work with multiple stakeholders, including government, other donors, grantees to create a common vision and visualize simple and effective, but implementable, solutions to complex problems

- Ability to be comfortable in a wide range of cultural, geographic, and operational situations, demonstrating culturally sensitive behavior with a diverse range of people
- Strong understanding of shaping and managing sustainable and scalable ventures
- Understanding of strategies for automating the process of data collection in a variety of settings and sites
- Experience with research methodologies and deployment of data strategies
- Strong analytical, writing, and verbal skills for communicating with a broad and diverse audience
- Effectiveness as a collaborator in complex internal and external organizations
- Extensive project contribution and management experience
- Ability to work with efficiency and diplomacy

COMPENSATION

The compensation for program officers varies greatly. Depending on the location of the project and the size of the organization, program officers can earn from $145,000 to $200,000, or more. It is very dependent on previous experience and the type of work being done.

EMPLOYMENT OUTLOOK

Governmental and nongovernmental health organizations depend on having a steady flow of qualified program officers to fulfill their missions in countries around the world. There is a high demand for program officers willing to relocate to countries in which important health-related work is being done.

FOR FURTHER INFORMATION

- The American International Health Alliance (www.aiha.com)
- American Public Health Association (www.apha.org)

76

JOB DESCRIPTION

The project coordinator's role in an international healthcare organization is to support key project activities including project scope, timeline, resources, risk, and partner and internal communications. The project coordinator will draw on the experience of staff members working across the portfolio for mentorship and alignment. The coordinator will work closely with the managerial, scientific, technical, and other project staff. They will be responsible for making critical connections among staff and partners on clinical, manufacturing, and other issues related to the specific project.

EDUCATION AND EXPERIENCE

The project coordinator should have a bachelor's degree in global health management, or equivalent education and experience. A minimum of 3 years of experience coordinating and integrating multiple projects for international clients and agencies is required. A high-level understanding of the project management processes is preferred.

CORE COMPETENCIES AND SKILLS

- Superior organizational skills demonstrated in managing scientific development work
- Proficiency in project management tools, such as Microsoft Project and Excel
- Experience using web-based information-sharing tools, such as SharePoint and Skype for Business
- Good analytical skills and global vision
- Excellent verbal and written communication skills
- Demonstrated ability to work effectively in a multisite/multicultural organization and as part of a team
- Willingness to travel internationally and domestically up to 50%

COMPENSATION

The compensation for project coordinators varies greatly. Depending on the location of the project and the size of the organization, salaries can be larger or smaller. The size of the project and scope of responsibility also play a role. This career has a starting salary of what appears to be about $50,000, and increases greatly when doing large-scale work.

EMPLOYMENT OUTLOOK

Increased need in other countries for people who are trained in project coordination will continue. Healthcare is a growing market worldwide, and being able to borrow competencies from other countries is an emerging competitive advantage on which other countries, as well as the United States, are trying to capitalize.

FOR FURTHER INFORMATION

■ The American International Health Alliance (www.aiha.com)
■ Medical Tourism Association (www.medicaltourismassociation.com/en/index.html)

GLOBAL SERVICES QUALITY MANAGER

JOB DESCRIPTION

Global services quality managers (GSQM) have many different titles. They can work all over the globe or in the United States and oversee large projects abroad. They apply quality improvement principles, such as Six Sigma, Lean management, and other continuous quality improvement methodologies, to hospitals and healthcare systems across the globe. Quality managers must also adhere to legal guidelines and regulations in each country and understand social norms and values. Monitoring and process review are part of their job and they analyze data, such as customer feedback, financial information, and demographic health needs, to better use change management theory to put in place the right processes using the right quality improvement principles.

EDUCATION AND EXPERIENCE

Education and experience vary in the global market. Most firms desire a minimum of a bachelor's degree, with most wanting some sort of further education, such as a master's, or significant work experience. Educational focus should be representative of business quality methodology, business degree, healthcare degree, or engineering. Experience for global positions is significant with many wanting upward of 7 years' relevant work experience in the healthcare field and knowledge of the country where the person is to be placed.

CORE COMPETENCIES AND SKILLS

- Exceptional verbal and written communication skills
- Outstanding analytical ability and skill at solving complex problems
- Exceptional interpersonal skills with diverse groups of customers
- Significant skill and ability in Six Sigma and Lean methods
- Knowledge and understanding of human factors engineering
- Skill and demonstrated experience in change management
- Proven ability to work independently in rapidly changing environments
- Significant experience working overseas with many different cultures
- Knowledge of global marketplace and regulations
- The ability to speak, write, and understand languages other than English
- Presentation ability and ability to speak with diverse groups

COMPENSATION

The compensation for GSQMs varies greatly. Depending on the location of the project and the size of the organization, GSQMs can earn anywhere from $45,000 to $200,000, or more. It is very dependent on previous experience and the type of work being done. Larger companies have top C-Suite positions for global quality managers who oversee multiple sites and have increased salaries due to their increased responsibilities.

EMPLOYMENT OUTLOOK

Due to increases in medical tourism and doctors being trained in the United States and other countries, there is an increased demand for GSQMs who have been trained in the Western style of continuous quality improvement. They can take these skills to developing or established countries in order to improve their processes. There is also opportunity to learn from these healthcare facilities overseas. As travel continues to improve, people will begin to desire healthcare options that are on par with some of the top performing hospitals and care facilities.

FOR FURTHER INFORMATION

- The American International Health Alliance (www.aiha.com)
- Medical Tourism Association (www.medicaltourismassociation.com/en/index.html)

CHAPTER 16
CAREERS IN HEALTH SECTOR ASSOCIATION MANAGEMENT

DIRECTOR OF GOVERNMENT AFFAIRS

JOB DESCRIPTION

The director of government affairs is a member of the executive team of the association and is responsible primarily for acting as the liaison between the association and local-, state-, and federal government–elected officials and governmental agencies. The director is expected to critically analyze current and proposed governmental legislation for its effects on the association. The director is also called on to monitor legislative and regulatory activity and to develop positions that should be taken by the association in response to that activity.

EDUCATION AND EXPERIENCE

The director of government affairs typically requires a bachelor's degree in business administration, health administration, public administration or political science, although a master's degree is frequently the preferred educational preparation. Most directors of government affairs have 5 to 7 years of experience in governmental affairs.

CORE COMPETENCIES AND SKILLS

- Outstanding interpersonal skills including the ability to effectively communicate with current and potential members and other stakeholders, along with persons throughout their organization
- Excellent verbal and written communication skills
- Relationship management, strategy development, problem-solving, and change management skills
- Ability to motivate volunteers to further the mission of the association
- Outstanding motivation and organizational skills
- Ability to stay calm and composed even under difficult circumstances
- Experience with lobbying and influencing elected officials
- Demonstrated ability to work with staff members of elected officials
- Ability to quickly learn and understand the field in which the association members work
- Demonstrated ability to use standard computer software programs including Microsoft Office applications such as Word, Excel, Access, and PowerPoint

COMPENSATION

Health management association directors of government affairs typically earn between $75,000 and $200,000 per year depending on the size of the association. This salary does not include annual performance bonuses.

EMPLOYMENT OUTLOOK

Effective directors of government affairs are highly valued members of the association and, while turnover in these positions is relatively low, they are frequently in a position that is promoted into senior management roles in the association.

FOR FURTHER INFORMATION

■ American Society of Association Executives (www.asaecenter.org)

79

DIRECTOR, MARKETING AND COMMUNICATIONS

JOB DESCRIPTION

The director, marketing and communications will be responsible for development of the overall marketing and communications strategy and execution to drive revenue for all initiatives, products, services, and events. This includes marketing and communications planning, audience-building campaigns, social media presence, advertising, direct mail, web presence, and collateral development. Additional responsibilities include managing the marketing automation platform, measurement and continual analysis of marketing and communications activities, as well as oversight for media and public relations activities.

EDUCATION AND EXPERIENCE

- Bachelor's degree in marketing, public relations, communications, or journalism; advanced degree preferred
- A minimum of 10 years of experience preferred in relevant field with at least 3 of those years in a management role; experience with new product/segment support; experience in managing external agencies
- Experience using marketing automation platforms (Marketo, Eloqua, etc.)

CORE COMPETENCIES AND SKILLS

- Ability to guide staff and content expert volunteers with strategic messaging and communications initiatives; build and maintain the association's leadership position; articulate the contributions of personal technologies to improve the quality, safety, access, and cost effectiveness of individual care
- Ability to establish annual social media strategic messaging and engagement, and direct execution by social media staff; coordinate with company's social media team
- Ability to develop marketing strategies based on business unit objectives and strategies using data-driven market research including client/market needs assessment, competitive understanding, and product segmentation/positioning
- Ability to take on primary responsibility for design, implementation, and coordination of annual marketing plan against defined business unit strategies focused on audience development, new client acquisition, existing client up/cross-sell, client retention, and brand awareness
- Ability to direct internal and external marketing resources for creative input, graphic design, content creation, collateral development, and so on

- Ability to seek, evaluate, and manage public relations efforts; oversee annual public relations plans for specific initiatives and constituencies; execute conflict resolution; execute contractual agreements; convene stakeholders for specific initiatives beyond weekly updates; direct implementation of projects and related deliverables (including key initiatives, activities at the annual conference and other events), related collateral, and overall tools and resources for selected constituencies
- Ability to oversee and support the association's outreach to and interaction with national, trade, and online media
- Ability to identify appropriate vendors, negotiate and approve contracts, guide scope of work within budgetary guidelines including financial management of services including photography, speechwriting, copywriting, media distribution and tracking, and other related needs
- Ability to develop and manage annual marketing and communications budgets
- Ability to manage strategic marketing, corporate communications, and public relations programs, including budget development, program development, and program evaluation that support the overall corporate goals of the organization
- Understanding of and ability to meet multiple deadlines on various projects and initiatives
- Strong analytical skills
- Proficient communicator with excellent written and verbal communication skills including experience with public speaking, and ability to work effectively in both independent and team-based situations with coworkers, volunteers, and other organizations
- Ability to think and act strategically
- Ability to work independently
- Project management skills
- Adept at identifying and understanding client/market needs

COMPENSATION

Health management association marketing and communications directors typically earn between $104,962 and $138,515 per year. Some larger associations provide year-end bonuses.

EMPLOYMENT OUTLOOK

Effective directors of marketing and communications are highly valued members of the association, and they are frequently in a position that is promoted into senior management roles in the association. As a result of these promotions, there is an estimated 9% growth opportunity.

FOR FURTHER INFORMATION

- American Society of Association Executives (www.asaecenter.org)

80

PRESIDENT AND CHIEF EXECUTIVE OFFICER

JOB DESCRIPTION
Health management associations represent individuals who practice healthcare management or organizations that are otherwise related to the field. The role of the association is to provide a venue for members to pursue professional development, create best practices, and speak with one voice for issues of concern to their constituency. Additionally, health management associations help to define the field of healthcare management by working to link members with the practice-based organizations in healthcare delivery, finance, manufacturing, consulting, and others. The role of the president and chief executive officer (CEO) is to lead the association and represent the membership before a wide variety of external stakeholders. The president and CEO has the responsibility for all strategic, operational, and financial activities of the association.

EDUCATION AND EXPERIENCE
The association president and CEO typically requires a minimum of a master's degree in business administration or health administration, along with at least 10 years of progressively responsible experience in association management. The Certified Association Executive (CAE) credential is highly preferred.

CORE COMPETENCIES AND SKILLS
- Outstanding interpersonal skills including the ability to effectively communicate with current and potential members and other stakeholders, along with persons throughout their organizations
- Excellent verbal and written communication skills
- Demonstrated ability to work effectively with members of the association's board of directors
- Experience in strategic planning
- Relationship management, strategy development, problem-solving, and change-management skills
- Skill in directly managing staff members
- Ability to motivate volunteers to further the mission of the association
- Demonstrated experience in developing partnerships and coalitions with other organizations and stakeholder groups
- Ability to read and understand standard financial documents
- Experience with lobbying and influencing elected officials

- Ability to quickly learn and understand the field in which the association members work
- Demonstrated ability to use standard computer software programs including Microsoft Office applications such as Word, Excel, Access, and PowerPoint

COMPENSATION

Health management association presidents and CEOs typically earn between $150,000 and $500,000 per year not including annual bonuses based on performance. Base salary is frequently a function of the size of the association.

EMPLOYMENT OUTLOOK

While there are many opportunities in health association management, there is very limited turnover of presidents and CEOs. The typical president and CEO stays in the job a decade or more and when these jobs open up, there is usually very intense competition.

FOR FURTHER INFORMATION

- American Society of Association Executives (www.asaecenter.org)

 NAME: ANTHONY C. STANOWSKI

Title: President and CEO
Organization: Commission on
Accreditation of Healthcare
Management Education

1. Briefly describe your job responsibilities.

The Commission on Accreditation of Healthcare Management Education's (CAHME) mission is to serve the public purpose by enhancing the quality of graduate healthcare management education. CAHME is fortunate to have many practitioners, academics, and healthcare organizations committed to this mission. I am honored to serve these volunteers, and I work to ensure that our staff and volunteers have the resources and processes to meet our mission. I am humbled and thankful for the ability to work with faculty in the great universities in the United States and Canada (and soon globally) to create the curricula and processes that ensure that the next generation of healthcare leaders will be more likely to succeed.

2. What would you consider to be a "typical" day for you?

There really is not a typical day for a chief executive officer (CEO). However, there is a rhythm in the months, quarters, and years of an organization. A CEO needs to identify and work within that rhythm.

Budget planning, strategic planning, information technology, marketing, operational functions, accounting, finance, legal, and human resources are among my concerns. On a daily basis, I may be meeting with program directors, working with corporate members who help sponsor us, or our staff to get the work done. I could be revising policies, or making sure we have enough money to pay our bills. I could be on a plane, a train, or a car to visit our programs or a sponsor, or at a conference where I am discussing our value. I could be working with my board and key stakeholders on new initiatives like enhancing our benchmarking process, or developing new approaches to recognize excellence in our programs. The tricky part is knowing how to balance the detail with the strategy.

Continued

NAME: ANTHONY C. STANOWSKI
Continued

3. What education or training do you have? Is it typical for your job?

I earned a doctorate in healthcare administration, a Master of Science in Marketing, and a Master of Business Administration (MBA) degree in healthcare administration. My undergraduate majors were communications and psychology. I earned these degrees in different schools, which enabled me to learn from faculty that brought different perspectives. My advanced degrees were attained while I was working. In fact, my doctorate studies occurred while I was an executive at a Fortune 200 company. This required a sacrifice of personal time and resources, but I viewed that as an investment in myself. I use my educational background continuously.

4. What is the most challenging part of your job?

Being the CEO of a relatively small company, you have to be the jack of all trades. There are things in which I do not have expertise, nor the time to invest in learning them. I have to depend on the advice and recommendations of my team including our business partners. My challenges include knowing the right questions to ask, determining the right areas in which to concentrate limited time and resources, and confronting unequivocally the demands on our organization.

5. What do you consider to be the best part of your job?

CAHME is all about the students, and the best part for me is meeting the students. These are the people who will be leading our healthcare system. I am amazed at the energy that our program's students bring to their studies, and I am in awe of the skills that they have. Many in this generation have a genuine commitment to public service, intuitive technological skills, and a broad connection to their peers whom they readily ask for advice. When these students advance to leadership roles, they will change the world.

6. What path did you take to get to the job you are in today?

When they occurred, I did not realize the moments in my life that directed my career choices. Hindsight illuminates the impact of the path taken.

When I was 5 years old, I battled childhood cancer, which was a far different battle than exists today. I was scared, as any kid would be, but

Continued

the people in the hospital were kind and comforting. Much later, when I was an undergraduate, I met with the physician who cured me. He was not just happy talking to me, he was quite proud. He told me about research he conducted about my community that showed it had a far higher than expected cancer rate. That conversation was a turning point for me.

Upon graduation, I taught fifth grade in the same school I attended as a child, committed to make a difference in the education and life of these children, and, in particular, with lifestyle choices related to cancer. I included in my curriculum antismoking and drug/alcohol-abuse education. While teaching, I began my master's in healthcare management, and learned about preventive health and long-term impacts of environmental factors. I left my teaching role after receiving a fellowship at a hospital in that same community; one of the projects that I worked on and implemented was a cancer prevention center.

I became a director of planning and market research at Jefferson Health System, which coincidentally included Thomas Jefferson University Hospital, the hospital that treated me as a child. Following that role, I was fortunate to travel across the nation with the Thomson Reuters Healthcare division (now IBM Watson Healthcare). We were doing exceptional work in predictive analytics, planning, marketing informatics, and clinical and operational benchmarking. I worked with some of the best health systems and healthcare organizations across the country.

I landed an executive role at Aramark based on the networks that I developed and my knowledge of healthcare. During my time there, I led the creation of an innovative fellowship program in partnership with the American Hospital Association (AHA's) Institute for Diversity and Aramark's partner hospitals. That reintroduced me to CAHME, which had accredited my graduate MBA program. I was asked to be on the board at CAHME, and my passion for CAHME's mission eventually earned me a slot on the executive committee, and I was slated to be the board chair.

When the CAHME CEO told me that she was going to retire, I asked her to stay. I was then working at Applied Medical Software and implementing a physician gainsharing program in several states. I worried that I would not have the time to be the chair of CAHME, recruit a CEO, and bring a new CEO along—as well as be a success for my employer. Several board members suggested that I consider the CAHME CEO role. After a nationwide search conducted by an independent search firm, I was given the honor of leading CAHME as its president and CEO.

I am thankful to be part of an organization that seeks to foster the success of the next generation of healthcare leaders. We do this by

Continued

establishing standards, promoting excellence, and ensuring that the students in our great universities are prepared to lead upon graduation.

7. What advice do you have for someone who is interested in a job such as yours?

Education has to complement your passion. One of the big mistakes that young people make is to choose their major and degree on the basis of a published list of starting salaries of graduates with a specific major or degree. Love what you do! And work to become the best in what you love.

Education is an essential way to show your commitment to your profession. Through it, you learn what processes and approaches are successful, and how to be more likely to avoid failures. Education allows you to advance more quickly in your career, but like all investments, you have to invest in the right education. Buying letters after your name through diploma mills is not the answer. For example, if you want to succeed in healthcare management, choosing a degree program from a CAHME-accredited program will take you longer, and require you to work harder. But you will graduate with a skill set that will more likely contribute to your success.

The completion of your degree is not the end of your journey, it is the beginning. I highly recommend joining a professional society to continue your education and participation in the profession. I am a Fellow in the American College of Healthcare Executives. Your responsibility as a professional is to continue to learn, to read, to participate, to write, and to present. Your responsibility is to make healthcare better.

I have two pieces of advice.

1. It is not all about being smart. The world is full of smart people. My father gave me the best advice many years ago: "Be the best. People always want to hire the best." You have to work hard to be the best; it is not just talent or your GPA. Hard work means completing your projects, exceeding goals, and not being a 9 to 5 employee.
2. Care deeply and passionately about the people you meet, your customers, and your stakeholders. When you put others ahead of yourself, you will be recognized as someone who is interested in making other people successful. When you lead, you have to let people know that you are interested in helping them reach their goals.

If you do these two things, you will be more likely to succeed. And the world will be a lot better place.

81

JOB DESCRIPTION

The membership manager supports the activities of the membership and corporate relations team. Duties include tracking membership statistics; responding to member requests; light website maintenance; supporting of key relationships; and proposal development and project management. The membership manager will be responsible for supporting all membership activities: recruitment and retention, member services and engagement; oversight of all membership database activities, data collection and reporting; and assistance with other department activities, including the board of directors and other projects.

EDUCATION AND EXPERIENCE

Bachelor's degree in business or health administration is the minimum education required. Five to seven years of membership experience with a proven track record of achieving outreach and recruitment goals; prior nonprofit health experience is a plus.

CORE COMPETENCIES AND SKILLS

- Exceptional written, oral, interpersonal, and organizational skills
- High level proficiency in Microsoft Office—MS Word, Excel, Access, and PowerPoint; familiarity with membership database software preferred
- Ability to contribute to a strong team-based environment
- Results-oriented with a high attention to detail, ability to multitask, and meet deadlines in a demanding, fast-paced environment
- Ability to relate effectively to multiple stakeholder groups

COMPENSATION

Health management association membership managers typically earn between $46,000 and $95,000 per year. The salary is a function of the size of the association and number of years of experience. Some larger associations provide year-end bonuses.

EMPLOYMENT OUTLOOK

Effective membership managers are highly valued members of the association and they are frequently in a position that is promoted into more responsible management roles in the association. As a result of these promotions, there is an estimated 9% growth opportunity.

FOR FURTHER INFORMATION

■ American Society of Association Executives (www.asaecenter.org)

CHAPTER 17
CAREERS IN FEDERAL, STATE, AND LOCAL GOVERNMENT HEALTHCARE ORGANIZATIONS

AREA DIRECTOR, INDIAN HEALTH SERVICE

JOB DESCRIPTION

The area director provides executive leadership, guidance, and senior management support to area office staff organizations, service units (SUs), and their personnel; delivers high-quality, comprehensive health services suited to the needs of the identified American Indian/Alaska native (AI/AN) population; oversees medical facilities that meet quality of care requirements and Medicare quality standards to which all hospitals are surveyed by accrediting organizations and the Center for Medicare & Medicaid Services (CMS); directs and supervises an executive, professional, and administrative staff in planning, developing, coordinating, and managing health programs of preventive, curative, and environmental and traditional health services for AI/ANs; leads the development and demonstration of alternative means and techniques of health services management and delivery to provide Tribes, Tribal health care programs, Urban Indian Health programs and AI/AN community groups with optimal ways of participating in Indian health programs; enables leaders, tribal members, and AI/AN community groups to participate in devising, identifying, and developing alternative means and techniques that could increase the effectiveness of health service delivery.

EDUCATION AND EXPERIENCE

A master's degree in public health, business or public administration, behavioral or social sciences, finance, political science or any degree demonstrating the capacity for the knowledge and skills required for this position. Persons must provide evidence that they possess a record of progressive experience that includes knowledge of Indian health policy–related issues, regulations, and policies; and demonstrated experience that evidences the ability to work with Tribal governments and Tribal organizations in planning, directing, and evaluating comprehensive public health programs or other healthcare delivery systems.

CORE COMPETENCIES AND SKILLS

- Knowledge of legislation relating to the provision of healthcare to American Indians and knowledge of federal healthcare delivery systems
- Demonstrated experience in the oversight of a medical facility or department, and knowledge of quality care requirements, accreditation standards, and healthcare management processes

- Demonstrated experience and ability in formulating, implementing, and evaluating high-impact policies, programs, and projects, and advising senior executives of a large organization on options or resolving problems caused by existing or proposed policies or conditions
- Demonstrated experience and working knowledge of disseminating information to customers and the general public, including, but not limited to, Tribal governments, Tribal organizations, Indian community organizations, and other stakeholders
- Demonstrated progressive experience in effectively managing a comprehensive and complex interdisciplinary health program targeted to serve American Indians and Alaska Natives or serving another specified target group of stakeholders
- Ability to review and evaluate area health program progress with measurable outcomes, resource utilization, and control of professional services to assure that high-quality, effective, and cost-efficient health services are provided
- Outstanding verbal and written communication skills

COMPENSATION

The compensation for Indian Health Service (IHS) area directors ranges from $123,000 to $185,000 per year. This is a federal, public trust, Level IV position. The salary is dependent on the number of years in service and merit increases.

EMPLOYMENT OUTLOOK

IHS area directors are senior-level leaders within the IHS. There is comparatively little turnover in these jobs and they infrequently become open—typically as a result of retirement.

FOR FURTHER INFORMATION

- Public Health Jobs (publichealthjobs.org)
- USA Jobs (www.usajobs.gov)

83 DATA ANALYST

JOB DESCRIPTION

The data analyst's primary function is to perform data quality analysis and data entry work contributing to the improvement of public health programs through evidence-based practices. The incumbent of this position serves as a data analyst and is responsible for: developing procedures to enhance data entry and query capabilities to improve efficiency and accuracy; utilizing immunization information system to create program reports; assuring integrity of data; and using software programs for retrieval of historical data, requests for information, summary reports, and ad hoc analyses.

EDUCATION AND EXPERIENCE

- Bachelor's degree in statistics, data analytics, health informatics, mathematics, or other related field, is strongly preferred.
- Applicants must have at least 1 year of specialized experience that has equipped them with the knowledge, skills, and abilities to successfully perform the duties of the position. Specialized experience is: work with Structured Query Language (SQL) queries; experience collecting and compiling data; experience using statistical analysis software; manipulating and analyzing data; or performing similar work experience.

CORE COMPETENCIES AND SKILLS

- Ability to assist in the implementation of data-sharing agreements with stakeholders, internal and external, to the department of health (DOH)
- Ability to ensure the quality of deliverables related to technical design, implementation, testing, and adherence to reporting standards
- Ability to capture, develop, and document data definitions, rules, data quality requirements, and logical and physical data models based on program requirements
- Ability to give project or task data requirements, determine the most efficient approach to data entry, data collection, and validation, and work independently to obtain needed data
- Ability to determine the most informative approaches to summarizing data and communicating analytical results
- Ability to develop, as required, innovative or customized templates and formats

- Ability to devise qualitative and quantitative techniques for analyzing and measuring the effectiveness, efficiency, and productivity of the program
- Ability to conduct studies, analyze findings, and make recommendations to enhance program operations
- Ability to demonstrate proficiency in communicating program goals, objectives, and strategies to professionals, paraprofessionals, and the general public
- Ability to communicate effectively, both orally and in writing, with varied audiences
- Data entry and data quality assurance skills, with the ability to interpret complex immunization document sets
- Ability to develop complex and detailed plans and procedures
- Experience of automatic data entry techniques, equipment, and software, including the demonstrated ability to appropriately use immunization information systems
- Experience preparing forms, maps, tables, and other data tools in the applications that capture, report, and consolidate data

COMPENSATION

The compensation for a public sector data analyst ranges between $51,000 and $66,000 per year. The salary is dependent on the number of years in service and merit increases.

EMPLOYMENT OUTLOOK

It is expected that the demand for data analysts will grow faster than average over the next 5 years. These are entry-level positions for which there is a significant amount of turnover as people move into positions with greater amounts of salary and responsibility.

FOR FURTHER INFORMATION

- USA Jobs (www.usajobs.gov)

84

DEPUTY DIRECTOR OF PUBLIC HEALTH SERVICES

JOB DESCRIPTION

The deputy director of public health services plans, organizes, and directs the activities, functions, and budgets of one or more major sections and/or programs of the County Health Department. The deputy director assists with the development and implementation of quality control and quality improvement programs and initiatives. The incumbent analyzes and monitors performance indicators and ensures that assigned operations meet established standards; recommends process improvements to ensure operational effectiveness and superior customer service; analyzes and summarizes complex narrative information and statistical data; prepares or supervises the preparation of reports and correspondence for county management as well as federal, state, or other external agencies; prepares board of supervisors' reports and related documents; and makes presentations to groups and individuals, including boards and commissions. The deputy director analyzes and interprets existing and proposed federal, state, and local legislation, policies, procedures, and other directives to determine impact on assigned operations.

EDUCATION AND EXPERIENCE

- A master's degree in public health, business or public administration, behavioral or social sciences, finance, political science, or any degree demonstrating the capacity for the knowledge and skills required for this position
- Minimum of 5 years of managerial experience in public health organizations

CORE COMPETENCIES AND SKILLS

- Demonstrated leader with the proven ability to effectively manage and build consensus among staff, collaborate with local, state, and federal agencies on public health–related issues that affect the community
- Innovative and strategic thinker on improving and maximizing public health programs
- Excellent written and verbal communication skills
- Well-versed on public health–related federal and state laws and regulations and community trends
- "Big picture" understanding of complex programs and funding measurements to effectively lead and provide strategic guidance to professional staff
- Proven track record of identifying employee talent and developing it
- High level of integrity and strong sense of ethics
- Strong analytical skills, sound judgment, and a positive attitude

COMPENSATION

The compensation for deputy directors of public health services ranges between $107,000 and $130,000 per year. The salary is dependent on the number of years in service and merit increases.

EMPLOYMENT OUTLOOK

It is expected that the demand for deputy directors of public health services will grow at an average pace over the next 5 years. These are senior management positions for which there is a low amount of turnover, as people retire or move into positions with greater amounts of salary and responsibility.

FOR FURTHER INFORMATION

■ Public Health Jobs (publichealthjobs.org)
■ American Public Health Association (www.apha.org)

85

HEALTH PROGRAM DIRECTOR

JOB DESCRIPTION

The health program director will oversee the Bureau of Managed Long-Term Care (MLTC) and will be responsible for the following duties: overseeing of the planning, implementation, evaluation, and reporting of the MLTC programs; overseeing of the Bureau of MLTC systems' policy, financial, surveillance, and technical assistance center (TAC); supporting the goals and objectives of the long-term care initiatives and Medicaid global spending cap; serving as liaison between senior-level executive staff and program staff to advance long-term care system reform, including the review and approval of policy and program reports for external dissemination; providing policy recommendations to upper-level management and responding to critical and high-profile issues and requests for information; and representing the agency as a liaison with other governmental entities on a state or federal level, and managing relationships with diverse stakeholders, including stakeholder outreach, education, and engagement.

EDUCATION AND EXPERIENCE

- A bachelor's degree in management is the minimum educational preparation required. A master's degree in an appropriate field may be substituted for an additional 1 year of that experience.
- Nine years of professional-level work experience, 3 of which must have included managerial, decision-making, and/or oversight of a major health-related program, or in the direction of a major administrative function of a large health-related organization

CORE COMPETENCIES AND SKILLS

- Excellent written and oral communication skills
- Experience in implementing large programs, especially in operationalizing new programs in Medicaid-funded home- and community-based settings
- Exemplary interpersonal skills that allow the individual to work both independently and as part of a team across multiple agencies to assure robust program implementation
- Comprehensive understanding of the scope of long-term care in the state and the laws, rules, policies, and regulations governing long-term care and home- and community-based services; established relationships with state long-term care community-based service providers and stakeholder organizations

■ Experience managing Medicaid long-term community-based programs
■ Strong management and supervisory experience in policy-making organizations; ability to handle multiple, competing priorities

COMPENSATION

The compensation for a state health program director ranges between $98,000 and $125,000 per year. The salary is dependent on the number of years in service and merit increases.

EMPLOYMENT OUTLOOK

It is expected that the demand for state health program directors will grow at an average pace over the next 5 years. These are management level positions for which there is a regular amount of turnover, as people move into positions with greater amounts of salary and responsibility.

FOR FURTHER INFORMATION

■ Public Health Jobs (publichealthjobs.org)
■ American Public Health Association (www.apha.org)

NAME: EVAN BROOKSBY

Title: Director of Policy Analysis and
Special Projects
Organization: Healthcare Association of
New York State (HANYS)

1. Briefly describe your job responsibilities.

I currently oversee statewide policy initiatives with particular focus on the Delivery System Redesign Initiative Payment (DSRIP) program. I facilitate an executive leadership committee as well as performance improvement group. We advocate with state and regulatory bodies on behalf of hospitals and healthcare systems.

2. What would you consider to be a "typical" day for you?

My day is typically spent in meetings with state officials, other internal experts, and various members of the healthcare system, from providers to administrators and their assistants. Because our membership as an advocacy organization is statewide, I do spend about 20% of my time on the road traveling around the state building networks and relationships.

3. What education or training do you have? Is it typical for your job?

I have a bachelor's degree in finance, and a Master of Business Administration (MBA) in healthcare administration. Those are probably consistent with what one might find in this industry; however, I took a nontraditional route, and have about 15 years of other industry experience between my undergraduate and graduate degrees.

4. What is the most challenging part of your job?

The pace of change is faster than most organizations are accustomed to. The change the healthcare industry is going through is very rapid, and it is challenging and exciting to be on the cutting edge of the transformation in healthcare.

Continued

NAME: EVAN BROOKSBY Continued

5. What do you consider to be the best part of your job?

The people I meet, and knowing that the work I am doing has the potential to improve the lives of those not only in my community, but across the state, and potentially beyond.

6. What path did you take to get to the job you are in today?

I took a very nontraditional route. After I graduated with my finance degree, I began working in retail. I then became self-employed and worked for myself and began graduate studies in healthcare management while working in retail. Once I finished my MBA, I took an entry-level internship and worked at a large academic medical center. From there, I moved quickly to a large physician practice, and back to the hospital side, which led to my current position at the Healthcare Association of New York State.

7. What advice do you have for someone who is interested in a job such as yours?

Never stop learning, and hold yourself to high standards of integrity and performance. Be good, work hard, and have fun.

86 LOCAL HEALTH DEPARTMENT CONSULTANT

JOB DESCRIPTION

The local health department consultant represents the Public Health Division (PHD) by providing support and direct assistance to local health departments to develop and maintain the infrastructure needed to provide foundational public health services in a transforming public health system. Work will focus on assisting local health departments in increasing efficiencies and quality, so that improved health outcomes are achieved in their communities, while assuring compliance with state and federal requirements for public health. Some of this work occurs through the triennial reviews of local health departments with which this position coordinates, but also through real-time, ad hoc, and ongoing technical assistance opportunities. This position provides leadership in determining the technical assistance needs of local health departments and addresses those needs with public health department work teams. The position interprets public health program and local health department needs to both parties, as well as other partners.

EDUCATION AND EXPERIENCE

- A bachelor's degree in public health, business or public administration, behavioral or social sciences, finance, political science, or any degree demonstrating the capacity for the knowledge and skills
- Four years professional-level evaluative, analytical, and planning work related to public health

CORE COMPETENCIES AND SKILLS

- Experience interpreting public health laws, rules, and regulations, and applying them to specific local public health practice situations
- Knowledge and experience working with governmental public health system
- Knowledge of public health modernization and how to apply foundational capabilities and programs to local and state public health practice
- Demonstrated use of systems thinking to strategically support evolving public health systems and practices
- Demonstrated ability to understand and articulate potential/actual impacts of program decisions/activities on overall public health system
- Demonstrated ability to establish rapport with diverse staff, stakeholders and partners, including, but not limited to, executive level leadership, policymakers, program managers, and frontline staff

- Demonstrated ability to use Microsoft Office products to develop high-quality work products and to organize day-to-day work
- Experience working in state, local, and/or tribal public health settings to manage, coordinate, and/or deliver public health services
- Demonstrated consulting skills regarding identification and implementation of technical assistance projects
- Project management skills to coordinate cross-divisional efforts to improve policies, procedures, and processes that benefit the public health system

COMPENSATION

The compensation for local health department consultants ranges between $57,000 and $84,000 per year. The salary is dependent on the number of years in service and merit increases.

EMPLOYMENT OUTLOOK

It is expected that the demand for local health department consultants will grow at an average pace over the next 5 years. These are technical assistance level positions for which there is a regular amount of turnover, as people move into positions with greater amounts of salary and responsibility.

FOR FURTHER INFORMATION

- Public Health Jobs (publichealthjobs.org)
- American Public Health Association (www.apha.org)

87

PUBLIC HEALTH ANALYST

JOB DESCRIPTION

The public health analyst provides policy support for bilateral and multilateral activities that relate to the full range of international organizational programs. The analyst works with senior staff and others to collect and analyze information to prepare issue papers, memoranda, analyses, briefing documents, and program proposals; provides administrative and technical assistance to senior management on issues that impact the United States and international regions; manages work plans, forums, and meetings; establishes and maintains effective working relationships with internal and external stakeholders; conducts studies, writes policy analyses, issue papers, briefing books, and performs other analytical work; keeps abreast of relevant political, economic, and social health issues in the assigned area of responsibility.

EDUCATION AND EXPERIENCE

This position requires at least 1 year of specialized experience equivalent to at least the GS-09 level of federal service. Examples of specialized experience include analyzing, evaluating, and advising on global health programs and policy within the Asia region; and assisting in evaluating the methods, processes, and techniques of international public health programs and/or initiatives, objectives, responsibilities, and issues. Public health analysts typically require a Master of Public Health (MPH) or Master of Health Administration (MHA) degree with course work directly related to the work of the position to be filled.

CORE COMPETENCIES AND SKILLS

- Outstanding interpersonal skills including the ability to effectively communicate with persons throughout the organization
- Excellent verbal and written communication skills
- Demonstrated experience in overall management duties with planning, organizing, directing, and evaluating international support services
- Experience in evaluating and adjusting organizational structure to ensure most effective and efficient delivery of healthcare and healthcare programs
- Significant experience in leading quality improvement teams
- Experience in facilitating the prioritization of multinational health needs and identification and initiation of responsible solutions
- Knowledge of planning, coordination, and execution of business functions, resource allocation, and production

- Ability to influence, motivate, and challenge others; adapt leadership styles to a variety of situations
- Demonstrated ability to make sound, well-informed, and objective decisions; to perceive the impact and implications of decisions; to commit to action, even in uncertain situations, to accomplish organizational goals; to cause change
- Demonstrated understanding and practice of ethical and legal issues associated with health administration
- Outstanding quantitative skills

COMPENSATION

The average compensation for a public health analyst ranges between $51,000 and $95,000 depending on the person's rating as per the General Schedule (GS) and number of years in service.

EMPLOYMENT OUTLOOK

The demand for federal public health analysts is dependent on several factors including whether a federal hiring freeze is in place at the time of application. Assuming that the federal government is hiring, positions of this type are highly valued given the complexity of public health activities.

FOR FURTHER INFORMATION

- USA Jobs (www.usajobs.gov)

CHAPTER 18
CAREERS IN HEALTHCARE REGULATORY AGENCIES

88

ASSISTANT DIRECTOR, PRODUCT DEVELOPMENT

JOB DESCRIPTION

The assistant director of product development directs the development and enhancement of recognition, accreditation, or certification product(s) from initial concepts through product launch and maintenance. This involves leading development teams in their work from initial concepts through to final specifications. The assistant director works cross-functionally with other departments and teams on product creation and implementation.

EDUCATION AND EXPERIENCE

The assistant director of product development requires a master's degree, or combination of education and experience that demonstrates the necessary requirements of the position. An advanced degree in health services field is preferred, with 6 or more years' experience in relevant health policy development, project management industry, or related field.

CORE COMPETENCIES AND SKILLS

- Ability to direct one or more project teams and coordinate with other departments to build and update products within specified time frames
- Ability to work with department leadership to ensure proper resource allocation
- Ability to define feasibility of new product ideas and develop comprehensive business plans to guide development
- Ability to establish project scope, product specifications, detailed work plans including roles and responsibilities for team members; coordinate all activities on project; manage project budgets/forecasts; identify and resolve risks to projects
- Ability to model, draft, and refine standards and evaluation products
- Ability to facilitate department and cross-departmental meetings to keep leadership and team members apprised of progress and proactively resolve issues
- Ability to present new product ideas to advisory groups to obtain feedback and refine ideas; contribute to leadership team discussion on product ideas
- Ability to select and train team members
- Ability to assign projects for maximum effectiveness; build team spirit, morale, and interest in projects

- Ability to conduct performance planning and reviews
- Ability to assist departmental leadership with forecasting and maintenance of annual departmental budgets

COMPENSATION

Assistant directors of product development typically earn $75,000 to $110,000 per year depending on their level of experience. These are middle management jobs that carry with them a significant level of responsibility.

EMPLOYMENT OUTLOOK

The employment outlook for assistant directors of product development with regulatory bodies like the National Committee for Quality Assurance (NCQA) is generally good. Given that these are middle management jobs, there is a regular level of turnover as persons are promoted to positions with higher levels of responsibility.

FOR FURTHER INFORMATION

- National Center for Quality Assurance (www.ncqa.org)

ASSOCIATE DIRECTOR, BUSINESS DEVELOPMENT

JOB DESCRIPTION

This position reports to the executive director of hospital business development, and is responsible for delivering on accreditation/certification new application volume and revenue targets specific to the respective geographic territory. In addition, the associate director will work collaboratively with the executive director and other associate director colleagues to develop new business associated with multiterritory hospital corporations. The associate director, at the request of the executive director, will also support key account management activities related to large health system customers that incorporate a hospital component. Finally, the associate director, at the request of the executive director, will communicate and collaborate with other components of The Joint Commission to ensure consistent and coordinated management of the hospital customers in their territory.

EDUCATION AND EXPERIENCE

The associate director of business development typically possesses a master's degree in business administration or health administration. Experience in healthcare management is preferred, with a proven track record in sales, business development, and/or customer relations/account management.

CORE COMPETENCIES AND SKILLS

- Outstanding interpersonal skills including the ability to effectively communicate with current and potential customers, along with persons throughout the organization
- Excellent oral and written communication skills necessary to produce proposals, reports, and presentations
- Strong public speaking skills
- Ability to actively contribute to the successful achievement of strategic business unit (SBU) performance objectives by achieving or exceeding territory sales targets and effectively collaborating with colleagues across the SBU, the division, and the enterprise
- Exceptional skill in handling difficult situations and managing difficult conversations
- Strong data analysis, evaluation, and problem-solving skills
- Ability to organize and respond to complex information
- Well-organized with strong project management skills and able to troubleshoot

■ Ability to lead and/or participate in program advancement teams and other internal work groups as assigned

COMPENSATION

Persons at the associate director level typically earn $100,000 to $150,000 per year depending on their level of experience. These are middle management jobs that carry with them a significant level of responsibility.

EMPLOYMENT OUTLOOK

The employment outlook for associate directors with regulatory bodies like The Joint Commission is generally good. Given that these are middle management jobs, there is a regular level of turnover, as persons are promoted to positions with higher levels of responsibility.

FOR FURTHER INFORMATION

■ Joint Commission for the Accreditation of Healthcare Organizations (www .jointcommission.org)

 NAME: LEON HARRIS

Title: Operations Project Manager—
Patient-Centered Medical Home
(PCMH)
Organization: National Committee on
Quality Assurance (NCQA)

1. Briefly describe your job responsibilities.

- Supervise daily operation of recognition programs assignments; review and analyze survey materials supplied by applicants; evaluate supplied data for performance against program metrics and standards, and recommend scoring to oversight committee; ensure integrity of data entered into data collection tools.
- Oversee the prevalidation program for prospective electronic medical records (EMR) vendors to obtain autocredit for the PCMH Recognition Program with 11 vendors getting autocredit and generating over $80,000 in revenues.
- Conduct customer support activities to potential clinical practices to encourage their participation in appropriate recognition programs; give timely responses to customer inquiries; contribute to program improvements by developing materials and training programs.
- Serve as external liaison to public and private partners; provide support, clarification, and troubleshooting to sponsor—health plans and government—applicants and others working with recognition programs; ensure consistent responses.
- Conduct monthly webinars for customers on the PCMH Recognition Program standards and answer questions related to the program.
- Facilitate 2014 PCMH Recognition Standards educational workshops with external stakeholders.

2. What would you consider to be a "typical" day for you?

A typical day would consist of reviewing documentations from our practice sites that are interested in becoming recognized in our PCMH program. Also, providing assistance via telephone or e-mail to customers who may have questions regarding interpretation of our standards and or processes.

Continued

NAME: LEON HARRIS Continued

3. What education or training do you have? Is it typical for your job?

The George Washington University, Washington, DC 2010
School of Public Health and Health Services
Master of Health Services Administration: Management and Leadership

The George Washington University, Washington, DC 2011
School of Public Health and Health Services
Health Information Technology Certificate

Winston-Salem State University, Winston-Salem, NC 2003
Bachelor of Science in Biology and Chemistry
Patient-Centered Medical Home Certified Content Expert 2014

Yes, my educational training has been very helpful in my current role. My BS allowed me to hone my analytical skills. My MHSA degree gave me the foundation to understand the healthcare delivery system, how a high-functioning organization should operate, understating the significance of quality improvement in healthcare, and how to be an effective leader. My certification in HIT gave me a foundation to understand the role technology will play in providing good healthcare and the role our government plays in creating policies around data reporting and value-based care.

4. What is the most challenging part of your job?

The most challenging part of my job would be that I always try to provide good customer service to both internal and external stakeholders. No matter how I may feel that day, my customers should always get the best customer service possible.

5. What do you consider to be the best part of your job?

Knowing that I am a catalyst in improving the quality of healthcare in the United States; working for an organization whose mission and values are aligned with your personal values is the best feeling in the world.

6. What path did you take to get to the job you are in today?

I applied for a senior analyst position at NCQA at a career fair that was held at the George Washington University.

Continued

NAME: LEON HARRIS Continued

7. What advice do you have for someone who is interested in a job such as yours?

The best pieces of advice I can provide are:

- Be a master of your craft. Understanding the U.S. healthcare delivery system is very important.
- Improve your public speaking skills.
- Keep up to date on new policies that could affect how healthcare is delivered.
- Read materials related to the healthcare system and other industries.

JOB DESCRIPTION

The director, surveyor management and development provides oversight for surveyor management and performance, and develops approaches to learning and education of international surveyors that enhances surveyor performance and promotes the mission of The Joint Commission. The director leads the team to plan, organize, and manage all international surveyor field staff educational activities, both in-person and online, that support ongoing professional development for new as well as experienced surveyors, including full-time, part-time, intermittent staff, and independent contractors.

EDUCATION AND EXPERIENCE

The director of survey management and development typically possess a clinical degree in nursing, behavioral health, or other clinical area, coupled with at least 5 years of work experience in healthcare delivery. A master's degree is preferred in clinical, administrative healthcare management; or other advanced degree in business administration, organization and talent, or another relevant field is preferred.

CORE COMPETENCIES AND SKILLS

- Outstanding interpersonal skills including the ability to effectively communicate with current and potential customers, along with persons throughout the organization
- Excellent verbal and written communication skills
- Outstanding critical thinking skills along with teamwork skills
- Exceptional skill in handling difficult situations and managing difficult conversations
- Strong data analysis, evaluation, and problem-solving skills
- Experience in operational leadership and interpersonal skills to interact effectively with individuals at various levels, disciplines, and cultures, both inside and outside of the organization, sometimes in sensitive situations
- Well-organized with strong project management skills and able to troubleshoot
- Ability to travel intermittently, quarterly, to observe and mentor surveyors and other field staff, and to conduct training programs or participate in selected conference activities, as requested.

COMPENSATION

Persons at the director level typically earn $158,000 to $210,000 per year depending on their level of experience. These are senior management jobs that carry with them a significant level of responsibility.

EMPLOYMENT OUTLOOK

The employment outlook for directors with regulatory bodies like The Joint Commission suggests that persons in these roles tend to stay in place for an extended period. There is comparatively little turnover in these jobs.

FOR FURTHER INFORMATION

■ Joint Commission for the Accreditation of Healthcare Organizations (www .jointcommission.org)

JOB DESCRIPTION

Under the direction of the director of marketing operations, this position is responsible for executing enterprise marketing programs, including webinars, events, e-mails, and lead nurture. This position partners with other marketing teams to execute successful marketing programs to acquire and nurture leads and yield transactional purchases for products and services throughout the enterprise.

EDUCATION AND EXPERIENCE

The marketing operations specialist typically possesses a bachelor's degree in business administration or health administration, with an emphasis in marketing. Three to five years of general marketing experience are required. Experience in a demand generation/downstream marketing role is preferred.

CORE COMPETENCIES AND SKILLS

- Experience managing marketing programs in Marketo, including integration with Webinar platforms and e-mail creation
- Proficiency with customer relationship management (CRM) systems and data integrity; experience with salesforce campaigns and reporting preferred
- Knowledge of digital marketing channels—e-mail, search, digital content, web, and social media
- Demonstrated strong problem-solving and analytical skills
- Effective verbal and written communication skills, including the ability to give persuasive presentations to prospects and customers
- Strong PowerPoint and Excel skills, as well as proficiency with the entire MS Office suite
- Excellent planning, organizational, and scheduling skills; ability to work independently with limited direction
- Strong interpersonal skills
- Ability to implement marketing programs that span digital channels—e-mail, search, digital content, web, and social media
- Ability to communicate directly with clients and prospects via e-mail, phone, webinars, and in person on enterprise products and services
- Ability to collaborate with internal stakeholders on marketing programs
- Ability to participate in other initiatives to support the efforts of the marketing operations team

COMPENSATION

A marketing operations specialist typically earns $60,000 to $85,000 per year depending on his or her level of experience. These are entry-level jobs that reward those whose skills match the needs of the organization.

EMPLOYMENT OUTLOOK

The employment outlook for marketing operations specialists with regulatory bodies like The Joint Commission is generally good. Given that these are entry-level jobs, there is a regular level of turnover as persons are promoted to positions with higher levels of responsibility.

FOR FURTHER INFORMATION

■ Joint Commission for the Accreditation of Healthcare Organizations (www .jointcommission.org)

92

JOB DESCRIPTION

The job of the surveyor is to conduct site surveys of healthcare organizations throughout the United States on behalf of nongovernmental regulatory bodies. The surveyor applies systems analysis skills and inductive reasoning skills to determine the healthcare organization's degree of compliance with applicable standards and functionality of care delivery systems. The surveyor engages healthcare organizational staff in interactive dialogues on standards-based issues in healthcare to assess compliance and to identify opportunities for improving compliance, quality, and safety. The surveyor prepares management reports that clearly link individual standards deficiencies with potential systems vulnerabilities and related organizational risk points. Finally, the surveyor effectively communicates this information to healthcare organizational leadership in a constructive and collegial style.

EDUCATION AND EXPERIENCE

Surveyors typically possess a clinical degree in nursing, behavioral health, or other clinical area coupled with at least 5 years of work experience in healthcare delivery. Management experience in healthcare delivery is highly recommended.

CORE COMPETENCIES AND SKILLS

- Outstanding interpersonal skills including the ability to effectively communicate with current and potential customers, along with persons throughout the organization
- Excellent verbal and written communication skills
- Outstanding critical thinking skills along with teamwork skills
- Demonstrated skills in managing difficult and potentially confrontational situations
- Strong data analysis, evaluation, and problem-solving skills
- Ability to use standard computer office software

COMPENSATION

Surveyors typically earn $75,000 to $100,000 per year depending on their level of experience.

EMPLOYMENT OUTLOOK

The employment outlook for surveyors with nongovernmental regulatory organizations is stable. Organizations like The Joint Commission have a continuing need for new and replacement surveyors.

FOR FURTHER INFORMATION

■ Joint Commission for the Accreditation of Healthcare Organizations (www .jointcommission.org)

CHAPTER 19
CAREERS IN EXECUTIVE SEARCH FIRMS

RESEARCH ASSOCIATE

JOB DESCRIPTION

Executive search firms conduct senior personnel searches for a variety of organizations including hospitals and health systems. The research associate's primary role is to support candidate identification, database and business development for associates and partners in firms, both local and nationwide. In addition, the research associate will assist associates and partners in generating names of potential candidates using the phone, print materials, and online information resources. As a vital member of the search team, the research associate assists the associates in designing search strategies, develops company target lists, and works to identify potential business opportunities.

EDUCATION AND EXPERIENCE

The research associate requires a minimum of a bachelor's degree in health or business administration. Research associates typically possess experience in a recruiting or research function within an executive search firm.

CORE COMPETENCIES AND SKILLS

- Outstanding interpersonal skills including the ability to effectively communicate with current and potential customers, along with persons throughout their organization
- Excellent verbal and written communication skills
- Outstanding customer service skills
- Ability to pay attention to detail and the ability to successfully follow through with assignments
- Ability to work effectively in a team-oriented environment and provide healthcare industry–specific information to all members of the firm working in the healthcare sector
- Skill in conducting ongoing information audits to determine relevance of the information that is generated
- Ability to build and maintain strong client relationships
- Exceptional learning skills, ability to quickly develop industry, company, and functional expertise
- Excellent multitasking and time management skills
- Demonstrated ability to use standard computer software programs including Microsoft Office applications such as Word, Excel, Access, and PowerPoint

COMPENSATION

Research associates generally earn a base salary of $55,000 to $75,000. This salary will vary depending on the size and geographic location of the executive search firm.

EMPLOYMENT OUTLOOK

The employment outlook for research associates in executive search firms is good. This is an entry-level position in this industry, and talented and skilled research associates are frequently promoted to search associates. There remains a high level of demand for the services of executive search firms as healthcare organizations seek to fill vacant senior-level management positions.

FOR FURTHER INFORMATION

■ Association of Executive Search and Leadership Consultants (www.aesc .org/eweb/StartPage.aspx)

94

JOB DESCRIPTION

Executive search firms conduct senior personnel searches for a variety of organizations including hospitals and health systems. The associate's primary role is to manage the initial candidate identification and development process. In addition, the associate will assist consultants and shareholders in generating, managing, and/or executing search assignments including potential candidate development, screening and presentation to clients, and cultivating and/or maintaining client and candidate relationships. As a vital member of the search team, the associate has the ability to network with professionals and assist them in achieving their career objectives in organizations committed to improving the quality of life, to assess a candidate's skills against a client's needs, and to collaborate with colleagues across the firm.

EDUCATION AND EXPERIENCE

The associate requires a minimum of a bachelor's degree, with preference given to those with a Master of Health Administration degree. Senior associates typically possess 5 or more years of experience in healthcare executive search, with preference given to those with direct healthcare experience.

CORE COMPETENCIES AND SKILLS

- Outstanding interpersonal skills including the ability to effectively communicate with current and potential customers, along with persons throughout their organization
- Excellent verbal and written communication skills
- Ability to participate in and/or lead the search process including, but not limited to, working with clients and search committees, sourcing, interviewing, conducting references, negotiating, and closing assignments
- An understanding of the full search process
- Ability to proactively network and seek out candidates in an expeditious and cost-effective manner
- Ability to participate in candidate development, and, when appropriate, manage candidates through the search process, including candidate interviews, candidate presentations, and referencing
- Ability to build and maintain strong client relationships
- Ability to develop effective and compelling presentations to market the role and client company to prospective candidates; communicate position profile to potential candidates

- Relationship management, strategy development, problem-solving, and change-management skills
- Demonstrated ability to use standard computer software programs including Microsoft Office applications such as Word, Excel, Access and PowerPoint

COMPENSATION

Associates generally earn a base salary of $48,000 to $68,000. In many cases, bonus compensation in the form of cash is made available to associates who successfully place candidates with firms. Senior associates can earn upwards of $175,000.

EMPLOYMENT OUTLOOK

The employment outlook for associates in executive search firms is good. There is a high level of turnover in executive-level healthcare positions, and many hospitals and health systems turn to executive search firms to help identify candidates for these jobs. There is a limited number of large, national firms, and competition for the best associates is fierce.

FOR FURTHER INFORMATION

- The Association of Executive Search and Leadership Consultants (www .aesc.org/eweb/StartPage.aspx)

PROJECT COORDINATOR

JOB DESCRIPTION

The project coordinator is responsible for a variety of duties including managing travel schedules, creating PowerPoint presentations, and providing project support on financial projects. Persons in this role provide critical support to local and regional recruiting staff and to senior executives. They are responsible for making sure that the many details of the search process are successfully implemented.

EDUCATION AND EXPERIENCE

A bachelor's degree in business or health administration is the minimum educational preparation for a project coordinator. Additionally, 3 to 5 years' experience supporting executive-level staff is desirable.

CORE COMPETENCIES AND SKILLS

- Ability to manage the executives' calendars, arrange all aspects of international travel, and prepare detailed travel itineraries
- Ability to create engaging PowerPoint presentations, update Excel spreadsheets, and prepare corporate reports
- Ability to assist the financial department with tracking budgets, invoices, and departmental expenses
- Ability to oversee workflow, monitor department to-do lists, and attend weekly departmental meetings
- Ability to assist with the coordination of conference calls, webcasts, and shareholder meetings
- Ability to support the auditing process by distributing testing materials and reviewing documentation
- Superior organizational and time-management skills, with an emphasis on schedule and travel planning
- High-level of proficiency in Microsoft Office, with an emphasis on PowerPoint
- Ability to work effectively as part of a team and have a friendly and cooperative attitude
- Trustworthy nature—not only can your employer count on you to complete tasks on time, but people trust you with extremely confidential information

COMPENSATION

The annual salary for project coordinators is in the range of $33,000 to $74,000. This figure is dependent on the size and geographic location of the search firm. Frequently, year-end bonuses are made available to project coordinators.

EMPLOYMENT OUTLOOK

This is an entry-level position within executive search firms creating many opportunities for employment. Project coordinators who demonstrate proficiency in their jobs are frequently internally promoted into search associate roles.

FOR FURTHER INFORMATION

■ Association of Executive Search and Leadership Consultants (www.aesc. org/eweb/StartPage.aspx)

RECRUITING MANAGER

JOB DESCRIPTION

A recruiting manager designs, implements, and evaluates innovative strategies in recruiting, sourcing, hiring, onboarding, and branding. The successful candidate is a hands-on talent acquisition expert who will play a key role in driving recruiting and onboarding efficiencies that support executive search firm operations.

EDUCATION AND EXPERIENCE

A bachelor's degree is required; a Master of Business Administration, Human Resources Management, or related area is preferred. A minimum of 5 years of professional level human resources experience is required. Preference is given to those with campus and internship program management experience.

CORE COMPETENCIES AND SKILLS

- Ability to take on full ownership of recruitment department, reporting directly to the chief executive officer (CEO)
- Ability to develop recruiting strategies that continually feed the candidate pipeline, in a high-volume recruitment environment
- Ability to develop a sourcing approach that reflects both the uniqueness of the business and culture
- Ability to build processes and procedures that deliver a high level of satisfaction from both candidates and hiring managers
- Ability to provide training recommendations for hiring managers throughout the business to improve their interviewing skills and hiring decisions
- Ability to develop and manage effective quality service standards, procedures, and tools to ensure the recruiting function is operating at the highest level
- Ability to drive and translate metrics and budget reporting to ensure quality and efficiency
- Ability to manage staff of recruiters and engage in day-to-day recruiting efforts, as needed
- Ability to keep abreast of industry trends
- Ability to ensure return of investment on tactical recruitment activities (i.e., career fairs, advertising, agencies, etc.)
- Prior experience maximizing an applicant tracking system (iCIMS knowledge preferred)
- Creativity and proactive approach to solving problems

- Ability to be strong collaborator across all operational divisions
- Excellent verbal and written communication skills
- Excellent time/project management skills
- Strong organizational, managerial, and multitasking skills, along with the ability to handle sensitive and confidential information

COMPENSATION

The salary for recruiting managers at executive search firms ranges between $55,000 and $140,000 per year. This salary is a function of the size of the firm and the number of clients managed by the firm.

EMPLOYMENT OUTLOOK

The employment outlook for recruiting managers is higher than average. There is a high level of competition between firms for outstanding professionals in this area.

FOR FURTHER INFORMATION

- Visit local universities offering the Master of Health Administration (MHA) degree or equivalent. A list of these university-based programs can be found at the Association of University Programs in Health Administration (www.aupha.org)
- American College of Healthcare Executives (www.ache.org)
- Association of Executive Search and Leadership Consultants (https://www.aesc.org/)

JOB DESCRIPTION

The vice president of talent acquisition will develop, implement, and lead key strategies for executive, professional, and clinical recruiting, employment brand and positioning, candidate sourcing, recruitment technologies, and building talent pipelines for the firm's network. This involves partnering with C-suite executives, senior leaders in the human resources department, operations, and clinical areas to understand business needs, and align and manage recruitment efforts to support short- and long-term organizational objectives. This position will partner with internal resources to guide the development and implementation of employment branding to help ensure the firm is an employer of choice that can attract and retain a qualified, diverse workforce. The vice president will manage the budgets, tools, systems, services, search partners, vendors, and processes that support recruiting and onboarding efforts. This position will lead a team of talent acquisition professionals who are responsible for creatively sourcing, evaluating, and securing top talent for the organization and maintaining an external pipeline of diverse talent.

EDUCATION AND EXPERIENCE

A bachelor's degree in business or a related field, or equivalent experience is required; a master's degree is preferred. Ten or more years of experience leading talent acquisition strategies in a corporate or executive search environment is required. Expertise in full-cycle talent acquisition processes in a healthcare environment is preferred.

CORE COMPETENCIES AND SKILLS

- Ability to sell open assignments to prospective travelers
- Ability to place travelers on open assignments of various lengths throughout the United States
- Ability to negotiate salary, housing, travel, bonuses and benefits package to maximize gross profit margin
- Ability to provide customer service to travelers such as benefit, location, and facility information
- Ability to provide complete follow-through on all placements through regular communication with traveler
- Ability to establish relationships with pool of traveling employees in order to further individual and division growth

- Ability to keep and maintain active base of travelers on assignment via frequent verbal and written contact
- Ability to document all contacts in employee database
- Ability to track competitive activity to ensure that the company is offering fair and competitive packages
- Ability to recruit travelers from all sources including competitors via phone, Internet, or other sources
- Ability to build a loyal traveler base to ensure increase in number of placements
- Ability to administer all paperwork pertinent for each traveler such as Physical, PPD, W-4, I-9 and other necessary paperwork required by company and facility
- Ability to work to identify key positions in order to recruit the most viable candidates
- Ability to constantly communicate with travelers regarding concerns, questions, and so forth; provide appropriate resources or necessary information
- Ability to meet daily/weekly metrics required by management

COMPENSATION

The salary range for vice president of talent acquisition is between $120,000 and $275,000 per year. Additional compensation can be provided through year-end bonuses and other incentive programs.

EMPLOYMENT OUTLOOK

The employment outlook for vice presidents of talent acquisition in executive search firms is good. There is a moderate level of turnover in executive-level healthcare positions, given that incumbents are being recruited to move to larger and higher profile firms. There is a limited number of large, national firms. and competition for the best in talent acquisition is fierce.

FOR FURTHER INFORMATION

- Association of Executive Search and Leadership Consultants (www.aesc .org/eweb/StartPage.aspx)

JOB DESCRIPTION

The administrator manages all aspects of the day-to-day operations of the program. This involves ensuring regulatory compliance, actively overseeing quality assurance performance improvements. Additionally, the administrator collaborates with all corporate departments and outside consultants, ensures all regulatory requirements are met, and acts as the representative of the program to state/county agencies, community partners, and consumer groups.

EDUCATION AND EXPERIENCE

A bachelor's degree, preferably in business, health administration, social services, or public health is required along with 4 years of experience in an administrative management position in a healthcare setting. Preferred education includes a master's degree in social services, psychology, public health, business or health administration.

CORE COMPETENCIES AND SKILLS

- Knowledgeable about budgeting, human resources, and applicable program regulations
- Good communication, team building, and problem-solving skills
- Familiarity with psychiatric conditions and recovery principles
- Good customer relations skills
- Skilled at identifying and removing barriers to change
- Ability to plan, organize, direct, and control the program; be responsible for the administrative functioning of the program
- Ability to act as the privacy contact for the program, maintaining all required records, logs, and systems in compliance with Health Insurance Portability and Accountability Act (HIPAA) regulations
- Ability to implement all program policies and procedures through the appropriate assignment of duties to the administrative staff
- Ability to manage all strategic planning activities of the program, with the primary goal of ensuring ongoing effectiveness of the program
- Ability to develop and maintain a productive work relationship with state and local agency representatives; actively participate in meeting customer needs and adapt to changing customer and community needs at all times; act as liaison between the program and state/county customers and community partners

- Ability to establish staffing requirements for all departments; direct the recruitment, selection, and, when necessary, disciplinary action within the program
- Ability to manage the program within allocated budgetary parameters and collaborate in the development of the fiscal budget
- Ability to supervise all department managers, and maintain supervisory authority over personnel assigned to the departments
- Ability to direct recruitment, employee selection, and, when necessary, disciplinary action within the program
- Ability to ensure that the program is in compliance with all applicable laws and regulations and keep informed about changes in regulations
- Manpower planning skills; employee training and development
- Knowledge of regulations and court orders governing care, custody, treatment, programming and environment of consumers/residents in regional psychiatric hospitals and developmental centers
- Understanding of community mental health services and psychiatric rehabilitation concepts and the recovery philosophy

COMPENSATION

Inpatient behavioral health program administrators can expect to earn between $78,000 and $144,000 per year. Salaries are a function of the size of the organization and number of years' experience in the field.

EMPLOYMENT OUTLOOK

There is a slow but steady increase in the number of inpatient mental health services. While the majority of mental health care is provided in an outpatient setting, many hospitals and proprietary organizations are operating inpatient facilities.

FOR FURTHER INFORMATION

- Mental Health America (www.mentalhealthamerica.net)
- National Council for Behavioral Health (www.thenationalcouncil.org)

NAME: MARI K. STOUT

Title: Chief of Quality Improvement and Compliance

Organization: Adapt (a nonprofit organization that operates a community mental health program, substance abuse treatment programs, and a federally qualified health center)

1. Briefly describe your job responsibilities.

■ Establish and oversee the elements of an effective corporate compliance program to prevent, detect, and correct illegal, unethical, or improper conduct
  ○ Develop, maintain, and revise policies and procedures
  ○ Collaborate with other departments to investigate and evaluate compliance issues/concerns within the organization
  ○ Respond to alleged violations of regulations, policies, or code of conduct
  ○ Identify potential areas of compliance risk, develop and implement corrective action plans, and provide guidance/training on how to prevent/detect similar situations in the future
  ○ Monitor and report results of compliance efforts to the chief executive officer (CEO) and board of directors
  ○ Ensure proper reporting of violations to enforcement agencies, as appropriate
■ Collaborate across the organization in the development and successful completion of the quality improvement plan
  ○ Develop, maintain, and revise policies and procedures
  ○ Identify, implement, and analyze quality data and tools to control and improve processes and reduce variation
  ○ Work across the organization to build understanding and support for continuous improvement
  ○ Collaborate with leadership and staff to facilitate quality/performance improvement initiatives, implement evidence-based care models, and assist systems/teams in becoming more patient centered
■ Directly report to CEO; dotted line reporting to the board of directors

2. What would you consider to be a "typical" day for you?

■ Stop by a department to say "hi" (You'll get to meet new faces, help people know you're approachable, and have the chance to

Continued

respond to questions without a follow-up email. Plus, getting eyes on things can go a long way in spotting potential risks before they occur.)

■ Review the new payer contract and provide recommendations to CEO for quality performance criteria/metrics and compliance requirements
■ Meet with department program director on the updated monthly performance metric results and develop priorities/action plans
■ Research and respond to the HIPAA/42 CFR part 2 disclosure question from Medical Records team (If answer is still unclear, e-mail attorney for further guidance.)
■ Discuss the results of access improvement strategies at the FQHC's monthly quality committee meeting, chaired by the medical director
■ Investigate a suspected privacy violation
■ Review recent patient experience surveys and develop quarterly summary for senior management; send patients' open-ended comments to program directors
■ Send training plan revisions to clinical director for the upcoming all-staff training on trauma-informed care
■ Review results and priorities from our organization's self-assessment on Culturally Linguistically Appropriate Service (CLAS) principles; call human resources (HR) director to discuss when/how we can roll out the updated staff performance evaluation template with additional CLAS elements

3. What education or training do you have? Is it typical for your job?

Bachelors of Science degrees in accounting and healthcare administration
Master of Health Services Administration (MHSA)

4. What is the most challenging part of your job?

My default setting is one of positivity and keeping the focus on incremental improvement. While we strive for delivering world-class, evidence-based care to every patient every day, there are some days when it feels like the majority of my time is spent managing mistakes or underperformance. We are providing much-needed services in a rapidly changing environment and to patients who have complex needs and situations. It

Continued

can be a challenge to keep perspective, prioritize, and pace myself while managing the growth and complexity of the role.

5. What do you consider to be the best part of your job?

My motivation and energy soars when a team pulls together to problem solve and achieve success that will result in better care for patients. Then it's made even better when comments from patients or other quality data support the changes that the team implemented.

6. What path did you take to get to the job you are in today?

Straight from grad school, I went to work for a large, physician-owned and operated clinical system in a much larger area than I'd ever lived. It was a great organization for observing transformational leadership and getting the chance to work on many types of projects/service lines. It helped me find where my strengths were and what I found the most fun. I gravitated toward and found success in project management, strategic planning, process improvement/Lean, and interim management. Then I met my husband and we saw our life folding out in a different area. I was also curious to see what things would be like on the payer side of things. Leveraging my gained experience in process improvement, I accepted a quality improvement/provider engagement position with a Medicare Advantage health plan. I developed annual quality work plans, developed reporting tools, and did outreach with network providers to help assist with quality improvement and achievement of shared quality targets. It was incredibly valuable to learn how a payer approaches quality improvement and utilizes massive amounts of data. Common success factors between my positions in the clinical system and the health plan were an ability to quickly build relationships, collaborate with providers, and effectively use data to drive process improvement. It wasn't too long and I missed being on the provider side of things; having a closer connection to the care being provided to patients, the teams providing that care, and influence on the systems that are involved.

7. What advice do you have for someone who is interested in a job such as yours?

■ Get very familiar with process improvement methodology/tools and be comfortable facilitating teams on an improvement project.

Continued

NAME: MARI K. STOUT Continued

- Interact/engage with providers. Show that you too care about patients and you're interested in helping the system work well (i.e., make the right thing, the easy thing).
- Volunteer to assist with quality improvement/compliance projects at your organization; review the work plans your organization has for quality improvement and compliance; suggest ways you can help those efforts.
- Don't be afraid to try a new position or care setting that's out of your comfort zone. I didn't have experience working with substance abuse treatment programs or mental health when I started this position. You can learn.
- Consider internships! You're welcome to contact me and see if we have openings. maris@adapt-or.org

99

MENTAL HEALTH ADMINISTRATOR—STATE CORRECTIONAL INSTITUTION

JOB DESCRIPTION

A mental health administrator (MHA) works under general direction and requires extensive knowledge of manpower planning, general management principles and techniques, and mental health and mental retardation technology. The position coordinates institutional behavioral healthcare services to include contract services and monitoring, training, and operational issues. The position can be responsible for developing and implementing components of the institution's quality assurance/improvement program; assigning responsibility for a designated area of service delivery including coordination of a particular programmatic area; supervising assigned staff, processes, and approving timesheets and leave forms for assigned staff.

EDUCATION AND EXPERIENCE

The minimum education required for this position is a bachelor's degree in mental health or social work. Additional training in business or health administration is highly desirable. A minimum of 1 year of work experience in correctional health management is required, with additional work in the field a desired part of the applicant's background.

CORE COMPETENCIES AND SKILLS

- Outstanding interpersonal skills including the ability to effectively communicate with persons throughout the organization
- Excellent verbal and written communication skills
- Demonstrated experience in overall management duties with planning, organizing, directing, and evaluating clinical and environmental support services
- Ability to define problems, collect data, establish facts, and draw valid conclusions
- Ability to cooperate with coworkers on group projects
- Ability to handle sensitive contacts with community groups, the public, and representatives of governmental agencies
- Ability to prepare and/or review and edit individual consumer/resident rehabilitation plans and/or prepare meaningful, concise, and accurate reports
- Knowledge of general management; supervisory principles/techniques
- Ability to influence, motivate, and challenge others; adapt leadership styles to a variety of situations

- Demonstrated ability to make sound, well-informed, and objective decisions; perceive the impact and implications of decisions; commit to action, even in uncertain situations, to accomplish organizational goals; cause change
- Manpower-planning skills; employee training and development
- Knowledge of regulations and court orders governing care, custody, treatment, programming, and environment of consumers/residents in regional psychiatric hospitals and developmental centers
- Ability to utilize standard computer-related applications

COMPENSATION
Mental health administrators in state correctional institutions can expect to earn between $50,000 and $72,000 per year. Persons in this role are state employees and are paid according to the published pay schedule for the particular state.

EMPLOYMENT OUTLOOK
Correctional health jobs are growing much faster than average. Federal, state, and local governments are experiencing a growth in correctional institutions. Inmates in these institutions are required by law to have a comprehensive set of medical and mental health services.

FOR FURTHER INFORMATION
- American Public Health Association (www.apha.org)

100

OUTPATIENT BEHAVIORAL HEALTH ADMINISTRATOR

JOB DESCRIPTION

The administrator manages all aspects of the day-to-day operations of the program. This involves ensuring regulatory compliance, actively overseeing quality assurance performance improvements. Additionally, the administrator collaborates with all corporate departments and outside consultants; ensures all regulatory requirements are met; acts as the representative of the program to state/county agencies, community partners, and consumer groups.

EDUCATION AND EXPERIENCE

A master's degree, preferably in business, health administration, social services, or public health is required along with 4 years of experience in an administrative management position in a healthcare setting. A successful track record working with, and sensitivity to, multicultural populations and issues in urban settings are highly desirable.

CORE COMPETENCIES AND SKILLS

- Knowledge about budgeting, human resources, and applicable program regulations
- Good communication, team building, and problem-solving skills
- Familiarity with psychiatric conditions and recovery principles
- Good customer relations skills
- Skilled at identifying and removing barriers to change
- Ability to plan, organize, direct, and control the program; responsible for the administrative functioning of the program
- Ability to act as the privacy contact for the program, maintaining all required records, logs, and systems in compliance with Health Insurance Portability and Accountability Act (HIPAA) regulations
- Ability to implement all program policies and procedures through the appropriate assignment of duties to the administrative staff
- Ability to manage all strategic planning activities of the program with the primary goal of ensuring ongoing effectiveness of the program
- Ability to develop and maintain a productive work relationship with state and local agency representatives; actively participate in meeting customer needs and adapting to changing customer and community needs at all times; act as liaison between the program and state/county customers and community partners

■ Ability to establish staffing requirements for all departments; direct the recruitment, selection, and, when necessary, disciplinary action within the program

■ Ability to manage the program within allocated budgetary parameters and collaborate in the development of the fiscal budget

■ Ability to supervise all department managers and maintain supervisory authority over personnel assigned to the departments

■ Ability to direct recruitment, employee selection, and, when necessary, disciplinary action within the program

■ Ability to ensure that the program is in compliance with all applicable laws and regulations and keep informed about changes in regulations

■ Manpower-planning skills; employee training and development

■ Knowledge of regulations and court orders governing care, custody, treatment, programming, and environment of consumers/residents in regional psychiatric hospitals and developmental centers

■ Understanding of community mental health services and psychiatric rehabilitation concepts and the recovery philosophy

COMPENSATION

Outpatient behavioral health program administrators can expect to earn between $95,000 and $130,000 per year. Salaries are a function of the size of the organization and number of years' experience in the field.

EMPLOYMENT OUTLOOK

There is a steady increase in the number of outpatient mental health services. Most mental health services are delivered in the outpatient setting. There are many free-standing organizations made up of many different types of mental health providers.

FOR FURTHER INFORMATION

■ Mental Health America (www.mentalhealthamerica.net)

■ National Council for Behavioral Health (www.thenationalcouncil.org)

101

JOB DESCRIPTION

The primary care practice supervisor manages all administrative and operational aspects of the on-site primary care services. This includes, but is not limited to, managing medical equipment ordering and supply; managing patient scheduling and flow; billing; credentialing; training, quality assurance, and compliance associated with primary care; budgeting, financial review, purchasing, accounts payable, payroll administration, financial tracking and reporting, and managing and completing assigned projects.

EDUCATION AND EXPERIENCE

A bachelors' degree in health or business administration is required; a nursing degree/certification is preferred. An associate degree may be accepted in lieu of experience along with 2 years of experience in an administrative management position in a healthcare setting.

CORE COMPETENCIES AND SKILLS

- Proficiency in Microsoft Office products
- Ability to handle sensitive patient information with confidentiality
- Comfort and skill in working with those with severe mental illness
- Good customer relations skills
- Strong organizational and leadership skills
- Ability to manage daily operations of the practice including establishing controls, purchasing, receiving, and overseeing ordering of medical supplies while maintaining a professional workplace
- Ability to schedule and coordinate patient appointments to optimize client satisfaction and facility efficiency
- Ability to record and update patient personal and financial information
- Ability to verify patient insurance
- Responsibility and accountability for billing and collection activities
- Ability to resolve billing and insurance claims issues
- Ability to maintain total confidentiality of member health and financial data
- Ability to supervise and direct the work of all employees assigned to the clinic
- Ability to schedule staff, ensure adequate coverage, and control labor expense
- Ability to recruit, select, and train nonclinical staff

- Ability to identify, recommend, and implement practice needs: staffing, services, equipment, and facilities
- Ability to practice marketing with patients, referring practices, local businesses, and industry
- Ability to assist with the preparation of the annual budget
- Ability to manage practice within budgetary guidelines
- Ability to determine economic aspects of equipment, facility, and new service decisions
- Ability to collaborate with other on-site managers to coordinate responsibilities of facilities and premises management
- Ability to communicate well with behavioral health staff on-site and to efforts to provide quality coordinated care

COMPENSATION

Outpatient behavioral health primary care practice supervisors can expect to earn between $55,000 and $80,000 per year. Salaries are a function of the size of the organization and number of years' experience in the field.

EMPLOYMENT OUTLOOK

Behavioral health primary care practice supervisors are entry-level management jobs for persons with an interest in management within outpatient behavioral health settings. There is a constant level of turnover in these roles as persons leave to take higher-paying positions in larger and more complex organizations.

FOR FURTHER INFORMATION

- Mental Health America (www.mentalhealthamerica.net)
- National Council for Behavioral Health (www.thenationalcouncil.org)

PART III

LEADERSHIP AND HEALTHCARE MANAGEMENT

PART III

LEADERSHIP AND HEALTHCARE MANAGEMENT

CHAPTER 21
LEADERSHIP COMPETENCIES FOR
AN UNCERTAIN FUTURE

An important truism in healthcare today is that change is the only constant. Indeed, it seems as if the entire world is changing at warp speed. The external and internal environment seems to be populated with a whole new set of rules, regulations, devices, diseases, and demands. Consider the following set of terms added to the healthcare landscape: MACRA, population health management, accountable care, retail medicine, value-based purchasing, bronze/silver/gold/platinum plans, Zika, personalized medicine, consumerism, big data, and augmented reality. To quote the late Dr. Ken Cohn, "the tectonic plates (of healthcare) are shifting."

Whether by incremental movement or in large, unexpected jolts, the environmental forces confronting healthcare leaders today are creating conditions that pose significant challenges to even the most experienced executives. But healthcare is not alone. Most sectors of the economy in the United States are facing similar rapid changes in their environments. Technology, consumer demand, globalism, supply chain, and workforce challenges are forcing nearly every industry to rethink their business model and make rapid adjustments to their operations. Those who fail to do so become obsolete and soon disappear from sight. Those who adapt, live to fight another day.

CASE IN POINT

Let us consider the case of healthcare delivery to examine how the industry has responded to the environmental forces affecting organizations. While there has been consolidation in the industry, healthcare delivery in the United States is still concentrated in hospitals and independent practitioners (recognizing that many physicians are moving into group practices that are affiliated with hospitals) that are paid by some variation of traditional fee-for-service reimbursement.

Physicians are still trained using a template that was first put forth in 1910 within the Flexner Report. Nurse education continues to be fragmented between associate degrees, bachelor degrees, and master's degrees. And despite the presence of policies, procedures, rules, regulations, and overwhelming good intentions, estimates are that 400,000 people die in U.S. hospitals every year owing to medical errors, and between 10 and 20 times that number are harmed, but do not die, as a result of unintended errors.

Meanwhile, information technology that makes up the backbone of almost every other industry sector has been slow to adoption in healthcare. Many physicians continue to use paper-based medical records. Organizations that have brought in electronic health record (EHR) systems find that patient records do not always "talk" with the EHR from a different vendor. The key point here is that healthcare delivery in both the outpatient and inpatient settings continues to operate in ways that were effective 30 years ago.

CALL FOR NEW COMPETENCIES

For those of you who are either considering entering an undergraduate or graduate healthcare management program (or if you are already in one), look at the competencies that are part of the program. Not long ago, education was measured on the student's attainment of specific learning objectives—that is, what do you know? More recently, education (and specifically professional programs like healthcare management) is measured on the student's attainment of specific competencies— that is, what can you do?

Look at the competencies of your healthcare management program. They should be available on the program's website. The Association of University Programs in Health Administration (AUPHA)-certified undergraduate and Commission on Accreditation of Healthcare Management Education (CAHME)-accredited graduate programs are required to be structured around a published set of competencies. You will likely see things in the areas of finance, economics, information technology, strategy, verbal and written communication, law and regulation, and many others. The fact is that there is nothing wrong with all these competencies. All of them are required by effective healthcare management practitioners. The competencies that form the heart of most every healthcare management educational program are fine for the world that exists today, and probably into the near-term future. Our concern is that once the student graduates and is out in the workplace, the competencies obtained in school may be of diminishing value, particularly as the person rises in rank and responsibility.

If healthcare management is going to survive and thrive in the years to come, leaders need to quickly adopt a new set of competencies and personal practices. In addition to the competencies that make up the core of typical healthcare management programs, we propose a series of additional competencies that should be part of the education of every effective healthcare leader. These competencies are drawn from several sources including conversations with senior healthcare executives, our review of the relevant management literature, our collective experience in undergraduate and graduate healthcare management education, and our assessment of the strong and weak signals in the healthcare environment.

#1. Improve Your Emotional Intelligence

For too long, we assumed that intelligence as measured by IQ was the critical measure of leadership and organizational success. If we filled the management ranks with the smartest and most insightful among us, all would be well. As we know, though, that is not the case. Indeed, with so many intelligent members of the workforce, why is healthcare in a mess?

Our observation is that in healthcare, emotional intelligence (EQ) is probably more important than IQ. In *Emotional Intelligence*, Daniel Goleman notes that there are five key elements to EQ: knowing one's emotions, managing emotions, motivating oneself, recognizing emotions in others, and handling relationships. Given the centrality of human interactions at all levels in healthcare, all five of these skills are vital for healthcare leaders. The good news is that rather than IQ, which is relatively fixed, it is possible to improve on each of the five elements of EQ.

#2: Think Big Picture in Terms of Systems

Healthcare organizations are, by their nature, complex organizational forms with multiple layers of management. Too often, within a single organization, health-care operates as multiple silos, with each member of that silo isolated from others outside his or her domain. As expected, members of a group/department/division typically work to optimize their world without consideration for how others might be affected. Experts refer to this as "suboptimization."

While not inherently bad, suboptimization tends to detract from the function of the whole system. The challenge for highly effective healthcare leaders is to create organizations where the walls of the hardened silos are transformed into semipermeable membranes that allow for the free flow of information and best practices out of one part of the organization into another. Collaboration and coop-eration between and among departments is the key to highly effective systems.

#3. Improve Your Conversation Skills

Human relationships are based in large part on the quality of conversations we have with one another. Assuming that none of us are truly telepathic, conversa-tions require three elements: a sender, a message, and a recipient. But conversa-tions go beyond a simple sharing of information, and generally suggest that the sender and receiver are genuinely interested in one another and the quality of the message being delivered. Conversations imply a back and forth in which both par-ties are interested in the welfare of the other.

Healthcare organizations are made up of a whole series of conversations. Some are short, some are long. Some are highly complex, some are relatively sim-ple. Some are easy to engage in, some are extraordinarily difficult. It is incumbent on healthcare leaders to have conversations that matter. This includes a number of important attributes, including carefully listening to others, clear and unambigu-ous language, checking for understanding, and assuring that commitments made are carried out.

#4. Embrace Change Management

For most of us in healthcare, change is hard—and often met with resistance, hos-tility, and downright anger. If we accept the premise that the only constant in healthcare is change, then how do we help others and ourselves deal effectively with change along with our own emotional reaction when confronted with change that is imposed on us by some outside group or agency?

Effective healthcare leaders need to start by accepting the fact that when encountering change, everyone is giving up something, no matter how large or small. There is an emotional response that is automatically triggered and varies depending on the scope and intensity of the change at hand. It is not enough to tell staff to "simply get over it and get back to work." Although there are multiple change models in the business literature, healthcare workers must be given a compelling reason for the change, a clear sense of hope, and optimism for the outcome of change—and then given the time to make whatever is changing part of the new normal.

While change is constant, the human response to change is also constant. Healthcare leaders need to lead change with the understanding that change management is an ongoing and continuous process.

#5. Adapt to Chaos and Complexity

No doubt, some days our organizations seem to be a chaotic and complex mess that is completely out of control. This observation actually aligns with how the universe works. Chaos and complexity are the norm. Organizations try to manage chaotic and complex behavior by imposing rules and regulations or policies and procedures. But how well are those working for you?

There is a compelling body of scientific and organizational literature that suggests that overcontrolling a complex system (like a healthcare organization) has little chance of lasting success. An alternative is to present a few simple rules that apply throughout the organization, and then consistently put them into operation. While full control might not be possible, healthcare leaders who adopt this perspective can get all staff moving in the same direction and working with a common purpose.

NEXT STEPS

It is worth noting that none of these competencies fall into what we refer to as the typical healthcare buckets, such as finance, IT, legal, and so forth. Many would characterize these competencies as soft skills, which, by their name, are typically not considered as important as those things that we consider hard skills. From our perspective, we would prefer to think of the competencies mentioned as "essential skills," which must be part of the tool kit of every healthcare leader who wants to make a real difference in his or her organization.

The challenge for all of us is how do we learn about these competencies? What is more, how do we continually improve in our daily practice? The consistent execution of the competencies will make a profound difference in the performance of healthcare organizations now and into the future. We invite you to explore how to develop your talent in each of these competencies and then put them into place in your professional and personal lives.

INDEX

education and experience, 330
employment outlook, 331
job description, 330

Telehealth Program Manager, 83–84
The Joint Commission, 117
Title VII of the Civil Rights Act, 117

U.S. Department of Labor, 106
U.S. Department of Labor Bureau of
Labor Statistics, 21
U.S. Public Health Service (USPHS)
Commissioned Corps, 22

veterans administration (VA)
health systems, 218–219
program analyst, 220–221
vice president of talent acquisition
compensation, 346
core competencies and skills, 345–346
education and experience, 345
employment outlook, 346
job description, 345
volunteer services coordinator
compensation, 140
core competencies and skills, 140
education and experience, 140
employment outlook, 141
job description, 140